# PERSONAL SELLING

## AN INTRODUCTION

**WILEY/HAMILTON SERIES IN MARKETING**
**DAVID A. AAKER, ADVISORY EDITOR**

# PERSONAL SELLING

## AN INTRODUCTION

**ROBIN PETERSON**

New Mexico State University, Las Cruces

**JOHN WILEY & SONS**

Santa Barbara   New York   Chichester   Brisbane   Toronto

A WILEY/HAMILTON PUBLICATION

LIBRARY OF CONGRESS CATALOGING IN PUBLICATION DATA

Peterson, Robin.
  Personal selling.

  (Wiley/Hamilton series in marketing)
  "A Wiley/Hamilton publication."
  Includes bibliographies.
  1. Selling. 2. Marketing. I. Title.
HF5438.25.P48          658.85          77-10979
ISBN 0-471-01743-4

Printed in the United States of America

10  9  8  7  6  5  4  3  2  1

TO TIM AND KIM
MOST EXCELLENT SELLERS

# About The Author

Robin T. Peterson is professor and head of the Department of Marketing and General Business at New Mexico State University at Las Cruces. He has also taught at St. Cloud State University in Minnesota, Idaho State University in Pocatello, and Southeast Missouri State College in Cape Girardeau. In addition, Professor Peterson was a Fulbright lecturer at the University of Nis, Yugoslavia, in 1973.

A native of Wyoming, Dr. Peterson earned his Ph.D. in Marketing at the University of Washington, in Seattle. He is an active member of the American Marketing Association, Sales and Marketing Executives, International, The Southwestern Marketing Association, the Academy of Marketing Science, Beta Gamma Sigma, and Alpha Kappa Psi.

Many of the concepts contained in the book are a result of research and consulting conducted by the author. He has served as a consultant in personal selling in numerous states and in Yugoslavia. In addition, Dr. Peterson has held two personal selling positions. He is the author of *Marketing: A Contemporary Introduction* (Wiley/Hamilton, 1977) and *Business Forecasting* with Charles W. Gross (Houghton Mifflin, 1976).

# Contents

## Chapter 6 Planning the Sales Presentation   106

## Chapter 7 The Communication Process   133

**Chapter 14 Ethics, Social Responsibility, and Governmental Regulation of Personal Selling   333**

**Glossary   353**

# Preface

Personal selling is a field with great career opportunities, but whether you are contemplating going into personal selling or some other field, you will find the material in this introductory book useful in many occupations and day-to-day activities.

I have written the book from the viewpoint of a person who wants to know, "How can I be an effective sales representative?" Thus, it is concerned with "how to sell" and how to sell in both business and nonbusiness organizations. I have tried also to show how personal selling fits in with the total marketing mix and its relation to sales management. In addition, throughout the text I have come back repeatedly to two important aspects: how to improve the effectiveness of personal selling, and how to sell in an ethical and socially responsible way.

The book is tightly integrated with early chapters developing overall conceptualization of the selling process and later chapters discussing the details. All chapters have seven common elements to simplify learning:

1. Chapter highlights are listed at the beginning of every chapter;

2. A *summary* is provided at the end of each chapter;

3. A set of *discussion questions*, designed to promote learning of chapter materials;

4. *Practical exercises*, to involve actively the student in the learning process;

5. A *selling project*, also involves the reader—research shows such involvement is a far superior way of learning than to simply read text material and take notes;

6. A *case problem*, which allows students to analyze a hypothetical selling situation and apply what they have learned in the text (and in the practical exercises and selling project);

7. A set of *suggested readings,* for further study.

The material in the text has been developed over many years. Much of it is based on my own experience as a salesman. A great deal of it has been tested in the classroom and my students tell me they find it useful and interesting—indeed, some of my students who are already experienced sales representatives have said they found it invaluable in improving their performance.

I am deeply indebted to two people whose keen insights, resourcefulness, and patience greatly improved the manuscript: David Aaker, Wiley/Hamilton Advisory Editor, University of California, Berkeley, and Roger Holloway, Wiley/Hamilton Marketing Editor. I also wish to thank the following marketing educators for their helpful comments on the various drafts of the manuscript: Dr. M. D. "Mike" Rice, Santa Barbara City College, Dr. John E. Swan, University of Arkansas; Mr. Jagdish "Jack" R. Kapoor, College of DuPage.

Robin Peterson

# PART I

## Preliminaries to Personal Selling

This first part of the text, which consists of three chapters, provides the building blocks for an understanding of personal selling philosophies and techniques. Chapter 1, the introduction, describes what personal selling is and what parties benefit as a result of the process. It demonstrates that selling is part of the overall marketing effort. Chapter 2 indicates how personal selling operates in carrying out the marketing strategy of an organization. The third chapter deals with the sales job—the nature of sales work and those who do this work.

# 1

# Introduction to Personal Selling

*After reading this chapter you should be able to demonstrate a knowledge of:*

- *the meaning of the term "personal selling"*
- *the importance of selling to the economy*
- *the importance of selling to the company*
- *the importance of selling to the individual—you—in carrying out personal activities*
- *the usefulness of personal selling to nonbusiness organizations*
- *career opportunities in personal selling*

Everyone is familiar with some aspects of personal selling. A typical student, for instance, might be involved in all of the following personal selling experiences during a particular year:

- buying a camera from a saleswoman at a department store
- attending a cookware (such as Tupperware) "party plan" social engagement and purchasing dishware at a party

- contributing $10 after listening to the appeals of a local United Fund representative

- joining a local political party, after listening to the arguments of a party leader

Many personal selling activities, however, are not as visible to the typical student. Some examples are as follows:

- An IBM computer sales representative convinces a large manufacturer to lease a computer.

- A United Airlines representative calls upon the president of an insurance company and attempts to convince the latter to hold an upcoming business meeting in a resort served by the airline.

- A representative of the Clark Equipment Company persuades the owner of a supermarket to install Clark display shelves in the store.

- A salesman for the Rousch Industrial Cleaning Company persuades a hospital administrator to sign a contract that would make the cleaning company responsible for the hospital janitorial work.

This book is intended to familiarize you with many of these less visible selling positions. In this first chapter we define the field and cover its importance to the economy, the company, and the individual. We also describe the usefulness of personal selling to nonbusiness organizations and set forth career opportunities.

**Personal Selling Defined**

The traditional and somewhat outmoded term for personal selling is "salesmanship," which has been defined as:

> The art of successfully persuading prospects or customers to buy products or services from which they can derive suitable benefits, thereby increasing their total satisfactions. It is the opposite of con-man-ship.[1]

**Personal Selling as an Art**

Personal selling is very much an art rather than a science. Those who believe they can memorize a list of personal selling principles and as a result become successful sales representatives are very much mistaken. Some of the principles may work for some, different ones for others. The successful people are frequently those creative individuals who can combine existing

[1]Irving J. Shapiro, *Marketing Terms: Definitions, Explanations, and/or Aspects* (New York: S-M-C Publishing Co., 1973), p. 147.

knowledge in unique ways to develop techniques and philosophies that are new and different.

**Persuasion**

The traditional definition of personal selling emphasizes *persuasion*. This term refers to the process of convincing others that they should change their attitudes, opinions, or behavior. Examples of persuasion are in abundance. Gandhi was successful in persuading the citizens of India of the advantages of passive resistance. Winston Churchill persuaded the citizens of Britain that they should retain the will to fight during World War II. In a sense, these two individuals were salesmen. They practiced some of the techniques which succeeding chapters describe.

In business, persuasion by sales representatives is commonplace. Consider the case of the luggage division of the Samsonite Corporation. It used to be that many retailers placed Samsonite luggage in low traffic areas of their stores, and so many customers were not exposed to these products. Then in 1975 Samsonite sales representatives were successful in persuading numerous retailers to relocate luggage in high-traffic areas of the stores, by convincing the retailers such a move would be profitable.[2]

**Benefits to Customers**

A modern conceptualization of personal selling emphasizes benefits rather than persuasion. Selling exists because it provides benefits to various parties, especially customers of business and nonbusiness organizations. As Figure 1-1 indicates, salespersons first attempt to identify the customer's needs and then direct the entire sales effort toward satisfying these needs. This is done by presenting products and services to help fulfill the needs identified. The outcome of this process, then, is the provision of benefits to the customers.

**Figure 1-1. Provision of customer benefits through personal selling.**

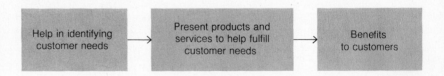

Salespersons who are effective are a source of benefits to their customers. They identify customers' needs and then shape

---

[2]"Samsonite's Marketing Band," *Sales and Marketing Management* 115, no. 10 (8 December 1975): 12.

their products and services in a manner that fulfills these needs. Thus, Bell Telephone Company sales representatives find prospective customers, determine if relief from time pressures is a genuine need, and show possible customers how they can manage their time effectively through the use of Bell equipment and services. Allis Chalmers farm equipment salespersons locate dealer-customers who are experiencing substantial complaints from consumers and help the dealers in handling these complaints. The salesperson can be a valuable source of information to customers, as when FMC sales representatives inform manufacturers of technological innovations in environmental-protection equipment that allows the manufacturers to meet federal regulations. In short, sales representatives endeavor to help resolve customer problems. They are problem solvers, rather than problem causers.

**Day-to-Day Applications**

Personal selling practices are applicable to the daily life of all of us. That is, most of us practice personal selling in our day-to-day activities.

In applying for a job, for instance, recent college graduates attempt to sell themselves to employers. New employees may try to sell their ideas to co-workers. Motorists driving illegally may try to sell the police officer into not writing a ticket. Parents attempt to sell their children into doing their homework. In reality, some form of personal selling takes places in almost every case when two or more people are in contact with one another. Even top executives for Pan American World Airways utilize personal selling principles in lobbying for new routes and subsidies from the federal government.[3] Mr. Richard C. Christian, president of Marsteller, Inc., indicates that "All successful advertising managers I ever knew are salesmen."[4]

**Importance of Selling to the Economy**

Selling is vital to the economy since it provides (1) the delivery of satisfaction to consumers, and (2) employment in business and nonbusiness organizations.

**The Delivery of Satisfaction to Consumers**

Personal selling results in furnishing consumers with that which they desire. This function provides time, place, and possession satisfaction to members of this group. Without these three kinds of satisfaction, physical goods and services are of

---

[3]"Behind Pan Am's Campaign for Subsidies," *Business Week*, no. 2346 (31 August 1974): 66–68.

[4]Richard C. Christian, "The Management Connection," *Industrial Marketing*, November 1972, p. 44.

little value to consumers. Samuel Slater recognized this when he brought the benefits of the English textile industry to America in 1790.[5] Soon after arriving in the United States, Slater found it necessary to engage two sales and marketing experts (William Almy and Smith Brown) so that his textile mills could effectively serve consumers and thus operate at a profit. Without such salespersons nineteenth-century consumers would not have enjoyed the fruits of Slater's labor.

Personal selling creates *time* satisfaction by ensuring that goods and services are available when they are needed. Sales personnel of the Pillsbury Corporation, food products manufacturer, call upon supermarkets and smaller grocery outlets and take orders for food products. The orders specify exactly when the goods are to be shipped. Accordingly, food market operators obtain their orders when the merchandise is needed. Members of the Pillsbury field force call upon their customers often enough to ensure that the customers' ordering needs are fulfilled. In turn, the retailers serve their ultimate consumer customers with goods when they are needed.

*Place* satisfaction is the value that goods and services have when they are in the places where consumers want them. SunKist oranges grown in California are of no value to consumers in Ohio until the items are transported to Ohio. Sales personnel who call on Ohio grocery outlets and make arrangements for shipments of California oranges are therefore creating place satisfaction. Without such sales people, the grocery managers would have to make their own arrangements for orange shipments.

*Possession* satisfaction is the value that goods or services have by being in the hands of those who want them. Sales personnel arrange for the transfer of ownership of a product (such as oranges) from the supplier (SunKist) to the buyer (grocery outlet manager).

Employment     Sales people help generate employment. Unless firms can sell what they produce, their revenues will be inadequate and they will go out of business, resulting in unemployment for their employees. Even nonbusiness organizations, if their goods or services are not sold, are likely to be disbanded. Hospitals, museums, government agencies, charitable organizations, and other nonbusiness institutions have disappeared because they

---

[5]N. S. B. Gras and Henrietta M. Larson, *Casebook in American Business History* (New York: Appleton-Century-Crofts, 1939), pp. 211–12.

were not "sold" to their consumers. Sales people, then, can be extremely valuable in convincing consumers they should purchase goods and services. By discovering prospective customers' needs and determining how their organizations can satisfy them, sales people produce satisfaction for the customer and revenue for the institution. There are, of course, other ways (such as advertising and publicity) of bringing in revenue other than by personal selling, but selling plays the most vital role.

Figure 1-2 shows how personal selling helps provide employment. Sales representatives help identify consumer needs and show products and services, thus providing customers with various benefits, in exchange for revenues. In turn, the revenues provide means of furnishing employees with wages, salaries, and other forms of compensation. In exchange for the compensation, employees create customer benefits (goods and services).

**Figure 1-2. Creation of employment through personal selling.**

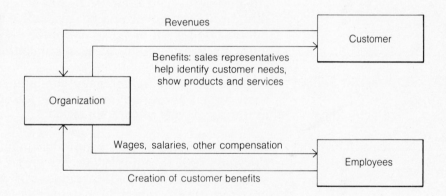

## The Importance of Selling to Companies

Personal selling is an important function for most business firms. Sales people are one of the major sources of sales revenues. In the words of Judson B. Branch, chairman of the board of Allstate Enterprises (a group of financial companies that includes Allstate Insurance), "Nothing happens until a sale is made."[6] An executive for a major bank has the following to say about account managers (those who deal with business and nonbusiness organizations, rather than with ultimate consumers): "We're trying to convince them that if they are not selling, if they are not analyzing the customer's needs and rec-

---

[6]John S. Wright, "Leaders in Marketing: Judson B. Branch," *Journal of Marketing* 37, no. 3 (July 1973): 72.

ommending services, they are at the professional level of dime store clerks.[7]

As we said, the selling process provides revenues, which are essential if the enterprise is to continue in existence. The financial success of companies such as Armstrong Cork, Procter and Gamble, and International Business Machines—all of which have outstanding sales forces—attests to the potential contributions of personal selling to the firm.

## The Importance of Selling to Nonbusiness Organizations

Most students take the view that personal selling is a *business* function. Although certainly most professional sales people are employed by business, selling is also a valuable tool to non-business organizations.

The United Fund, for instance, relies on thousands of "sales representatives" to generate contributions. Politicians employ personal selling insights to raise contributions and win votes, as do churches to build membership and obtain funds. Hospital administrators use personal selling to appeal for funding from their governing boards, police to develop a favorable public image. All of these nonprofit organizations benefit by knowing the principles of personal selling.

## Careers in Selling

An overview of careers in the personal selling field will show there are numerous advantages and job opportunities available and many levels of compensation.

### Numbers of Positions

Personal selling affords numerous job opportunities. During the years 1969 through 1975 sales workers constituted approximately 7 percent of the total persons at work.[8] The trend of job opportunities in this field is definitely upward. Consequently, the future should hold even more vacancies than are available at present.

There are, of course, substantial differences in the number of job opportunities in various types of selling positions. Although there are positions that offer only moderate pay and little opportunity for advancement, there are also numerous high paying personal selling positions available. A visit to the campus placement office or a glance at help-wanted ads will reveal many attractive positions.

---

[7]"Bankers Expand Their Markets by Adopting P & G Pizzazz," *Marketing Communications* 299, no. 6 (June 1971): 21.

[8]Joseph M. Finerty, ed., *Employment and Earnings* (Washington, D.C.: 1972, 1973, 1974, 1975, 1976).

Chapter 1 Introduction to Personal Selling

**Compensation**

Financial compensation is an area where personal selling is very attractive, relative to other fields. In 1975, median starting salaries for sellers of consumer goods (those used by ultimate consumers) was $10,700. The median starting salary for sellers of industrial goods (those purchased by business and non-business organizations and not resold to ultimate consumers) was $11,184.[9] Figure 1-3 sets forth median salary levels for sellers of consumer and industrial products with various degrees of experience in 1975. The range is from a sales trainee of consumer products at $10,700 to a sales supervisor of industrial products at $26,090. In the sales management field, compensation levels often are even higher than these. Thus, in 1975 the total compensation (including salaries, fees, incentives, and cash bonuses) of the vice-president of sales, the Russ Togs Company, was $240,015.[10]

**Figure 1-3. Median salaries (1975) for various types of sales positions.**

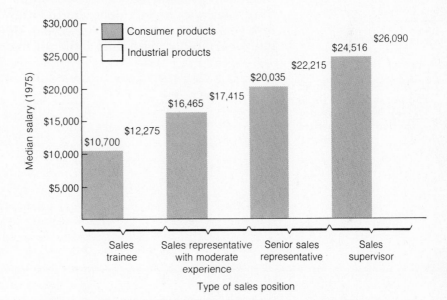

Source: "Compensation," *Sales and Marketing Management* 116, no. 2 (9 February 1976): 62.

Sales compensation levels are subject to increase when they are merited. Most organizations pay some form of commission, bonus, or other incentive to those who exceed sales or

---

[9]"Compensation," *Sales and Marketing Management* 116, no. 2 (9 February 1976): 62.
[10]"Compensation," *Sales Management* 115, no. 6 (6 October 1975): 51.

other quotas. This means that those members of the field force who have some combination of enthusiasm, desire to advance, and knowledge receive rewards for their efforts. This situation is unlike that associated with some dead-end jobs where productive personnel receive salaries identical to those of their poorly motivated or unknowledgable co-workers.

Some personal selling positions offer rates of pay for entry-level employees that are less than those for other occupational areas, such as in accounting and in engineering. Figure 1-4 illustrates a possible differential for a hypothetical organization. As time passes, the typical salesperson's compensation often tends to grow faster than does the compensation of those in the other fields. At the end of a time period of perhaps five years, the salesperson may be earning more than those in other occupations. This pattern appears in Figure 1-4. In the figure, the salesperson surpasses the accountant midway through the third year and the engineer shortly after the beginning of the fifth year. By the end of the tenth year, the salesperson is earning considerably more than either of the other two.

**Figure 1-4. Annual compensation for three employees, 10-year period (hypothetical organization).**

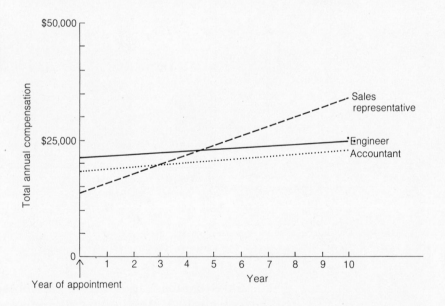

Independence The field of personal selling provides considerable independence, in the case of most jobs. Typical representatives have substantial freedom in determining selling methods, daily schedules, and in other aspects of work. After closing a sale, the representative may decide to spend the remainder of the day on a tennis court. Or he or she may choose to go after another sale. In the case of many positions, the choice is open to the individual.

Variety

In the life of most salespersons, each day is unique. Variety is common. There are new prospective customers to call upon, new products or services to demonstrate, and new selling techniques to try. In dealing with people, there are few absolute certainties from one time period to another. The prospective customer who liked Product A last month may prefer Product B this month. New prospects may have moved into the territory. The typical sales position is for those who do not wish to spend their working careers in monotonous activities such as shuffling papers at a desk.

Working with People

Personal selling jobs involve working with people. Sales people have close interactions not only with prospects but also with sales managers and marketing, production, finance, engineering, personnel, and other employees of the organization. They are also in close contact with people outside the organization such as advertising, government, transportation, and finance personnel. Accordingly, those who enjoy working with people are likely to be attracted to personal selling.

Developing Interpersonal Abilities

Typical sales representatives spend considerable amounts of time working with others. In the course of these activities, they learn how to work with, persuade, and get along with others. This ability carries over to daily activities. The effective sales representative can apply his or her knowledge to daily non-professional interactions with others. Representatives are "experts" at meeting people, getting to know them well, helping them with problems, and forming friendships.

Advancement to Higher Level Positions

Personal selling is an excellent avenue of promotion into management. Many institutions draw large proportions of their managerial staff from the field organization. Thomas S. Carroll, for instance, who is executive vice-president and member of the board of directors for Lever Brothers, was once a salesman with the company.[11]

---

[11]Gene F. Sehafer, "Leaders in Marketing," *Journal of Marketing* 29, no. 1 (January 1965): 73.

In the process of selling, people learn the interpersonal skills required to get along with, persuade, and work with others. This ability is vital in managerial positions. Further, sales representatives learn a great deal about the organization, its products and services, customers, competitors, and other facts in the course of their work. This well-rounded knowledge is needed for managerial responsibilities.

A common career advancement path for sales people is from sales representative to district sales manager, to regional sales manager, to sales manager, to marketing manager, to company president. Not all sales representatives advance into management, of course. Nevertheless, the opportunity is present.

**Personal Satisfaction**

Overall, sales representatives perform a vital role in maintaining and expanding the well-being of the economy, their organizations, and customers. They help provide time, place, and possession satisfactions and help solve problems experienced by customers. Sales people, in short, perform very important duties and can receive considerable personal satisfaction.

When a sale is made, expecially a big one, that is another source of satisfaction. There is reason for a feeling of pride and sometimes an occasion for celebration. Closing a sale can be a source of excitement and satisfaction that is not present in many other positions. Purchasing agents, for instance, do not normally celebrate when they make a good buy. Few production managers are elated when they have reduced production costs by 1 percent. Accountants do not feel undue excitement when they have discovered a new way of charging off depreciation. Conversely, many salespersons' spouses have enjoyed a festive dinner at an expensive restaurant as the result of the closing of an important sale.

**Preview of the Rest of the Book**

Chapter 2 outlines the meaning of the term "marketing strategy" and indicates how personal selling fits into that strategy. Chapter 3 covers the nature of selling jobs. The fourth chapter focuses upon information that sales personnel need.

Chapters 5 through 12 are concerned with the actual personal selling process. Individual chapters deal with (1) finding prospects, (2) planning the sales presentation, (3) communicating, (4) making the presentation, (5) handling objections, (6) closing, (7) understanding consumer behavior, and (8) working with customers after the sale has been made.

Chapter 13 focuses on sales management, the directing of personal selling activities. The final chapter covers ethics, social responsibility, and government regulation of personal selling.

**Summary**

Traditionally, personal selling has been conceived as the art of persuading prospective customers to buy products and services from which they can derive benefits. This process is an art, rather than a science. It involves helping customers identify needs and presenting products and services to help fulfill the needs. Personal selling is useful to nonbusiness organizations and to individuals in their day-to-day activities. Successful sales people provide benefits to and receive benefits from customers.

Selling is vital to the economy. This activity aids in delivering a standard of living by providing time, place, and possession satisfactions. Further, selling helps create employment.

The benefits of personal selling are not limited to the economy. This function provides needed services to business and nonbusiness organizations. These institutions are dependent upon the need-satisfying activities of salespersons for the achievement of their objectives.

The sales area offers numerous job opportunities. Among the advantages of such careers are (1) high levels of monetary compensation, (2) independence, (3) variety, (4) working with people, (5) opportunity to develop interpersonal abilities, (6) opportunity to advance, and (7) personal satisfaction.

**Discussion Questions**

1. What is personal selling? What is the primary objective of this activity?

2. Set forth some of the instances where you are involved in "selling" yourself or your ideas to others.

3. Describe the ways in which selling is of value to the economy.

4. Why is personal selling valuable to business and nonbusiness organizations?

5. What are the major advantages of a career in selling?

**Practical Exercises**

Visit a local retail store and observe a sales presentation. Was it effective or not? What suggestions would you make to the salesperson? What did you learn as a result of this exercise?

**Selling Project**

Think of a product or service that you would like to develop a personal selling program for. Future chapters will ask you to construct details of the selling program.

For instance, in Chapter 5 ("Finding Prospects"), you will be asked to indicate how you would seek out good prospective customers. The product or service can be actual or hypothetical.

**Case 1
The Eldridge
Refrigeration
Company**

The Eldridge Refrigeration Company is a medium-sized producer of industrial refrigeration units. The latter are used by meat packers, wholesale and retail grocers, chemical producers, and other firms to keep their raw materials and finished products at low temperatures. Eldridge is located in a large Pennsylvania city.

Sales representatives who work for Eldridge cover the northeastern portion of the United States. Each representative calls upon an average of fifteen prospects per week. Since the firm employs only twenty-three sales people, each one is involved in a considerable amount of travel. On the average, the representatives are out of their city of residence four days a week.

Eldridge sales personnel receive a salary of $550 per month; an expense account that covers travel, lodging, and food; a company car; and a commission of 6 percent of all sales generated. During the last year, the average dollar earnings for the sales staff was $22,500.

The products of this firm are of very high quality. In fact, many customers refuse to buy equipment produced by Eldridge's competitors. The high product quality is reflected in prices, which are above the industry average. This manufacturer spends about the same amount in advertising as do the competitors.

The Eldridge sales staff are highly trained. New sales personnel are recruited from the ranks of college graduates, primarily from schools of business administration. The newcomers go through a five-month technical course in the mechanics of refrigeration and the characteristics of Eldridge products. Then they are subjected to a one-month course of studies in personal selling. Finally, they experience six weeks of on-the-job training. This consists of working with an experienced salesperson as the latter goes through his or her daily tasks.

Over the past few years, the sales manager, Raleigh Cunningham, has been involved in hiring approximately four new sales representatives per year. Cunningham is not pleased with the quality of the applicants, however. In his opinion, these individuals are not as well qualified as were past applicants. He feels that the recruiters are not doing a good job of selling talented recruits on the advantages of a selling career. Cunningham is going to develop an outline of the advantages of such careers. The outline will be sent to recruiters to guide them in attracting top-level applicants.

What would you include in the outline?

**Suggested Readings**

Belasco, James A. "The Salesman's Role Revisited," *Journal of Marketing* 30, no. 2 (April 1966): 6–11.

"Packard Bell Incentives Fly High," *Industrial Marketing* 57, no. 11 (November 1972): 16, 18, 19.

"Sell, Sell, Sell," *Wall Street Journal,* 14 September 1971, p. 1.

Still, Richard R., and Edward W. Cundiff. *Sales Management: Decisions Policies and Cases.* Englewood Cliffs, N.J.: Prentice-Hall, 1976, pp. 15–17.

"The New Supersalesman: Wired for Success," *Business Week,* no. 2258 (6 January 1973): 44–49.

# 2

# Personal Selling and Marketing Strategy

*After reading this chapter you should be able to demonstrate a knowledge of:*

- *the meaning of the term* marketing
- *What is meant by* marketing strategy
- *how personal selling fits into the marketing strategy*

*The average student is exposed to a large number of marketing activities in an average week. He or she might:*

- read a magazine advertisement for a "Water Pik Deluxe Shower Massage"
- see a Volkswagen television commercial
- listen to a sales presentation made by a clothing store sales representative
- see A & P employees unloading groceries from a truck into the storage area of a supermarket
- note that a pharmacist is writing prices on packages of over-the-counter drug products
- see that a local bank is now offering a new service—banking by mail

In this chapter we will explore the concepts of marketing and marketing strategy, and the role of personal selling in the marketing strategy.

The chapter illustrates the relationships outlined in Figure 2-1. As the figure indicates, the marketing strategy involves specifying "target consumers"—those the organization attempts to satisfy—and designing plans for the products it will offer. In addition, the organization must determine the distribution (place) network to use in moving products to consumers, the promotion (communication with consumers) processes, and the prices to be charged consumers and middlemen.

**Figure 2-1. Personal selling and marketing strategy.**

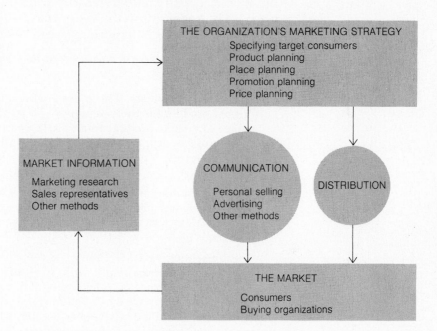

THE ORGANIZATION'S MARKETING STRATEGY
Specifying target consumers
Product planning
Place planning
Promotion planning
Price planning

MARKET INFORMATION
Marketing research
Sales representatives
Other methods

COMMUNICATION
Personal selling
Advertising
Other methods

DISTRIBUTION

THE MARKET
Consumers
Buying organizations

Two processes—communication and distribution—convey benefits from the organization to the market (consumers of the product or service) and buying organizations (middlemen). In the case of communication, methods such as advertising and personal selling are used to transmit ideas and concepts to the market. Distribution involves the physical dissemination of goods and services to the market, as when railroads move fresh vegetables from Oregon to Michigan or when wholesalers transmit automotive parts to variety stores.

Marketing strategy formulators are in need of information about the market, so that they can devise and refine effective strategies. Marketing research—the planned and systematic acquisition of marketing information through research projects —is one means of acquiring such information. Other means are through the written and oral reports of sales representatives. In short, sales representatives have both the important roles of communication and information provision.

## What Marketing Is
### Traditional Definition

In 1960 an American Marketing Association committee defined marketing as "the performance of business activities that direct the flow of goods and services from producer to consumer or user."[1] The key terms in this definition are "activities," "flow of goods and services," "producer," and "consumer."

**Activities.** Marketing is a process made up of four activities or functions:[2]

1. *Product activities.* These are concerned with developing the "right" product for the consumers the marketer is attempting to serve. The right product might be a Sperry Rand antihijacking device (to detect handguns in airports), Allstate insurance, Vantage cigarettes, Monroe calculators, or Diamond matches.

2. *Place activities.* These make the product available when and where consumers want it. Examples are when the St. Regis Company transports paper from Minnesota to Nebraska and when General Motors ships new Chevrolets from production plants to dealers.

3. *Promotion activities.* Promotion refers to those attempts by the marketer to communicate with consumers. It includes advertising, personal selling, sales promotion, publicity, and public relations. Examples are when Hilton Hotel advertisements describe the excellence of the hotel's services and when a stockbroker convinces a customer to purchase common stock of the Toledo Edison Company.

4. *Pricing activities.* Pricing involves determining the amounts of money that will be charged for goods and services. Examples are when Braniff Airlines sets rates from Chicago to Dallas, when Bank of America executives determine rates for deposit boxes, and

---

[1]Committee on Definitions, *Marketing Definitions: A Glossary of Marketing Terms* (Chicago: American Marketing Association, 1960), p. 15.

[2]E. Jerome McCarthy, *Basic Marketing: A Managerial Approach* (Homewood, Ill.: Richard D. Irwin, 1975), pp. 75–80.

when executives of the Clark Shoe Company decide on the prices of a new line of men's casual shoes.

Taken together, these four activities make up the marketing process. In turn, the activities direct the flow of goods and services.

**Flow of Goods and Services.**   As indicated in Figure 2-2, marketing activities direct the flow of goods and services from producer to consumer. Producers of goods and services have in their possession four resources: money, land, machinery, and personnel. If combined in the proper manner, these resources are capable of producing goods and services that consumers desire. Marketing is necessary to ensure that the resources produce satisfaction by delivering the goods and services to consumers.

**Figure 2-2. Marketing directs the flow of goods and services from producer to consumer.**

Effectively conducted marketing begins with determining the satisfactions that consumers desire. The marketer then designs a product and formulates a price to be charged for that product. In conjunction with these activities, the marketer decides how to distribute the product to consumers and how to promote it.

Consider a manufacturer with the money, land, machinery, and personnel needed to produce clothing. The firm is effective in directing the flow of goods and services to the consumer. Further, the enterprise has conducted research and has determined that consumers have a large demand for heavy woolen sweaters, four-button coats, and conservatively styled sports coats. The executives of the firm realize that they must create products and services that some consumers will feel to be superior to those of competitors and thus will buy. The executives are aware that developing a plan for the product line is the most critical element of a company's marketing planning activity.[3]

---

[3]See Yoram Wind and Henry J. Claycamp, "Planning Product Line Strategy: A Matrix Approach," *Journal of Marketing* 40, no. 1 (January 1976): 2.

This concern is involved in place activities. Management realizes that products are of little value to consumers unless they are at the right place at the right time. Company managers must therefore see to it that the products are transported to the retail locations where consumers want them. The managers must also make arrangements for periodic storage and order processing.

Promotion efforts are a necessity for this enterprise. Consumers are in need of communications from the concern—they require knowledge as to what goods are available and what the characteristics of the goods are. This information can be gained from reading advertisements, talking to salespersons, seeing clothing on display, and other means. Without such communication, the flow of goods will not take place.

Consumers purchase company products only if they believe the price to be "correct." Therefore, company management must determine the price levels that will produce an acceptable flow of goods yet yield an adequate return to the firm. If consumers believe that the price is too high, in relation to those of competitors, they will not buy company products. Conversely, if they see prices as too low (signifying "cheap" or "shoddy" merchandise) the flow will also not take place.

**The Marketing Concept.** A philosophy that coincides with the traditional definition of marketing is the *marketing concept*.[4] This concept holds that production, marketing, finance, and other personnel should all strive together in a coordinated manner to satisfy the consumer at a profit. The philosophy is based upon two fundamental notions:[5]

1. the consumer is the focal point for all business activity;

2. profit, rather than sales volume, is the criterion for evaluating marketing activities.

The activities of Chrysler Corporation executives in the mid-1970s illustrate they failed to apply the marketing concept.[6] During this time automotive engineers were very powerful in determining the major courses of action undertaken by the firm. In fact, engineering considerations dictated the kind of

---

[4]McCarthy, *Basic Marketing*, 24–33.

[5]Hiram C. Barksdale and Bill Darden, "Marketers' Attitudes Toward the Marketing Concept," *Journal of Marketing* 35, no. 4 (October 1971): 29–30.

[6]Peter Vanderwicken, "What's Really Wrong at Chrysler," *Fortune* 91, no. 5 (May 1975): 77.

automobiles that the company produced. Thus, instead of producing for the consumer, Chrysler was producing for the Chrysler engineers. This philosophy only resulted in declining profits and share of market for the enterprise.

The General Electric Company, on the other hand, has adopted the marketing concept. Included in the specific actions undertaken by this firm are: (1) placing considerable emphasis upon marketing planning; (2) positioning marketing executives at top levels of management; and (3) orienting all company operations toward satisfying consumers at a profit. This firm is recognized as one of the pioneers in developing and utilizing the marketing concept.

More Modern
Definition of
Marketing

Current definitions of marketing recognize that organizations deal with and must satisfy the needs of numerous parties, in addition to ultimate consumers. Marketers are faced with the need to satisfy groups such as (1) the public at large, (2) organized labor, (3) governmental units, (4) stockholders, and (5) minority groups.

Modern conceptualizations of marketing recognize that the key to this concept is *exchange*.[7] Exchange takes place when one party gives up something of value in return for something else that another party gives up. Organizations have exchanges with numerous parties besides ultimate consumers. Some, for instance, spend funds on public service advertising (using themes such as "fasten your seat belts"). If the public perceives the advertising as having value, it may support the organization through patronage, favorable word-of-mouth publicity, and other means. Organizations may also engage in exchanges with minority groups by, for instance, locating unprofitable retail units in ghetto areas, for which in return they may obtain favorable treatment by ghetto residents and government officials. Figure 2-3 illustrates the exchange process.

The concept of marketing as exchange has strong implications for marketers. It means that organizations must provide satisfactions to numerous parties, rather than the target consumer alone. Some marketers phrase this need in terms of "social responsibilities." The latter are obligations of the organization to its various important outside parties, including consumers, governmental units, the public at large, and others.

---

[7]Richard P. Bagozzi, "Marketing as Exchange," *Journal of Marketing* 39, no. 4 (October 1975): 32–39.

**Figure 2-3. Exchanges between the marketer and other units. The lines with arrows denote provisions of something of value to other parties.**

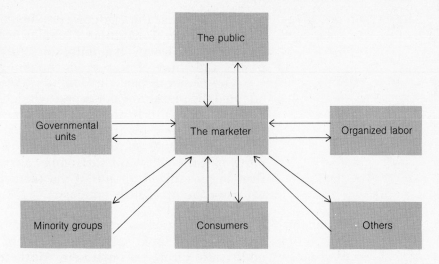

## Marketing by Nonbusiness Organizations

Businesses are not the only units that are engaged in marketing. Nonbusiness organizations are also involved in exchanges with consumers and other parties. Sometimes this involvement is evident in the organization chart—the Boy Scouts of America, for instance, has a director of marketing.

The Christian Children's Fund is also involved in marketing. This nonbusiness organization arranges for sponsors in the United States to "adopt" deprived children in the U.S. and other countries. The adopters pay a monthly fee for the children's support and are encouraged to write them and send them periodic gifts. The "products" of this organization are the services that it offers.

The CCF assesses prices, in much the same manner as do business firms. Adopters are billed on a monthly basis and pay a fee that provides for the basic costs of sustaining the child. These fees have been increased at various times in the past, to allow for increases in costs.

This organization employs promotion as a means of communicating with current and potential adopters. The CCF carries advertisements in several consumer magazines. In addition, it maintains communications with adopters through periodic letters that report on the status of the organization and prospects for the future.

Since the Christian Children's Fund sells services, physical distribution is not a problem area. Questions of where to locate retail stores or whether or not to utilize wholesalers do not arise.

This institution is involved in transactions with numerous

parties, in addition to the "consumer" (adopter) group. These include employees, United States government officials, foreign government officials, and religious organizations. The success of the CCF is dependent upon its ability to handle these transactions effectively.

In effect, then, nonbusiness organizations can benefit from marketing theory, concepts, and research to the same degree as their business counterparts. Failure to conduct effective marketing programs can be equally damaging to both.

## Marketing Strategy

The marketing strategy is the unique way in which an organization presents itself to consumers. More specifically, marketing strategy formulation consists of:[8]

1. specifying a "target consumer";

2. designing a "marketing mix" to satisfy the target consumer.

### Specifying a Target Consumer

Marketers experience difficulty when they try to satisfy everyone. Such a posture is likely to be so compromising as to render it ineffective. Various examples attest to this principle.

In 1976 the W. T. Grant Company, a variety store chain, was ordered by a federal bankruptcy judge to liquidate.[9] The chain had not been able to develop a strong image in any particular class of consumers. Shoppers did not know what Grants "stood for" and as a result did not bother to shop in the outlets. Was it a store for young or old? blue collar or white collar consumers? urban or rural residents? By trying to satisfy everyone, the enterprise was not successful in satisfying anyone.

The Hilton Hotel chain is an organization that has prospered by orienting its marketing efforts toward consumers in upper income levels.[10] Visitors are likely to get this impression shortly after arriving in a Hilton outlet. The facilities are lavish and the service extensive. Consumers with high incomes and associated life styles are likely to feel at home in these surroundings, and perceive other guests as "my kind of people."

A number of marketers in the 1970s specified young single people as target consumers. Some characteristics of this group are that it is large, expanding in size, is affluent, and is free of

---

[8]Harry A. Lipson and John R. Darling, *Marketing Fundamentals: Text and Cases* (New York: John Wiley & Sons, 1974), pp. 332–38.

[9]"Dividing What's Left of Grants," *Business Week*, no. 2421 (7 March 1976): 21.

[10]"New York's Selective Hotel Boom," *Business Week*, no. 2418 (9 February 1976): 29.

family responsibilities. Some of the products that are in high demand for the young singles are motorcycles, travel, entertainment, recreation, casual clothing, and personal improvement courses.[11]

**Designing a Marketing Mix to Satisfy the Target Consumer**

The second step in formulating marketing strategy is to design a marketing mix oriented toward the unique characteristics and desires of the target consumer. In turn, the marketing mix is some combination of:

1. product activities;
2. place activities;
3. promotion activities;
4. pricing activities.

**Product Activities.**   Products or services are vehicles for providing the benefits that target consumers desire. These activities include designing physical products and services and determining brand names, packaging, and labels.

In reality, consumers do not desire actual products. What they really want are the benefits the products bring. Hence, effective marketing requires that the marketer determine what benefits are desired, then provide them through products and services.

The Morning Treat Coffee Company found that some consumers like the idea of preparing hot beverages in immersible bags (like tea bags). This led the company to drop its lines of instant and freeze-dried coffee and to produce "coffee bags." The firm identified a consumer desire and then set out to produce a product that would provide the appropriate benefit.[12]

**Place Activities.**   A good marketing strategy makes the product available when and where target consumers want it. Most consumers, for instance, buy razor blades in supermarkets, variety stores, and drug stores. Hence, Gillette Twinjector Blades are to be found in these outlets. Since most consumers buy automobiles in the city they live in or nearby, Detroit automobile producers have to arrange for the timely shipment of their prod-

---

[11]"Burgeoning Singles Group Can Be Marketer Boon: Esty," *Advertising Age* 47, no. 9 (1 March 1976): 61.

[12]"Morning Treat Adds Markets Following Test of Coffee Bags," *Advertising Age* 47, no. 10 (8 March 1976): 4.

ucts to communities both large and small all over the United States.

Some concerns are very effective in achieving advantages over rivals through physical distribution activities. Retail druggists, for instance, need to have very rapid delivery of some of their medicines and drugs, and the pharmaceutical firm that can provide such quick delivery can gain a stronger position over its competitors—one that is difficult to override by low prices or heavy promotion.

Other strategies relate to the channels of distribution. If a manufacturer can induce retailers to promote its brands aggressively and to grant them considerable display space, the brands are likely to develop substantial sales volumes. The Harlequin Book Company has been successful to this end. With a program of well-designed advertising and personal selling the firm has convinced numerous book distributors and retailers to stock Harlequin's paperback books, give them considerable shelf space, and amply advertise them. As a result, Harlequin sales are flourishing.

**Promotion Activities.** The various promotion activities are advertising, personal selling, sales promotion, publicity, and public relations. Let us describe each of these.

*Advertising.* Advertising, according to one authority, is "mass communication involving an identified sponsor, the advertiser, who normally pays a media organization, such as a television network, to run an advertisement that has usually been created by an advertising agency."[13] Advertising is a form of mass communication, which means it is aimed at large groups. Thus, advertisements for Taster's Choice freeze-dried coffee are intended for large rather than small groups of consumers. Advertising always has an identified sponsor. In the campaign JOIN THE GIRL SCOUTS—BECOME A LEADER, the sponsor is the Girl Scouts of America. The advertising media that are available include newspapers, magazines, radio, television, and billboards. Marketers frequently use advertising agencies, since they are specialists in creating and implementing advertising campaigns.

*Personal Selling.* Personal selling is interpersonal communication through individual representatives with target con-

---

[13]David A. Aaker and John G. Myers, *Advertising Management* (Englewood Cliffs, N.J.: Prentice-Hall, 1975), p. 3.

sumers. Whereas advertising attempts to reach large numbers of such individuals at a low cost per person, personal selling involves attempting to contact only one (or sometimes a small group) of persons at one time. Because of the interpersonal nature of this promotion method, the sales representative can tailor the message to the unique characteristics of the individual consumer.

The marketing strategies behind some products require substantial personal selling. For instance, the Honeywell Corporation, which among other things produces large, expensive control systems for buildings (such as for heating, cooling, ventilating, security, and fire safety) relies on heavy personal selling. Since the systems involve a major purchase, by the client, sales people are needed to present product benefits, discover the needs of prospective customers, determine how the control systems can best fulfill these needs, and answer the questions raised by the prospective customer. Advertising could not accomplish such tasks.

*Sales promotion.* Sales promotion supplements advertising and personal selling. Examples of sales promotion are displays, trading stamps, premiums, contests, and demonstrators in stores. Many of these schemes are nonrecurring; they are not carried on continuously. One user of sales promotion, Armour, arranges for its sausages to receive extensive display space; sometimes they are also served by demonstrators in stores. Reader's Digest sponsors contests, in order to induce subscriptions in the magazine. The Nestle Company features periodic "cents-off offers" for its Taster's Choice freeze-dried coffee. All these efforts reinforce and supplement the advertising and personal selling activities the organizations utilize.

*Publicity.* Publicity is free news or other information about the marketer and its products or services. It is nonpaid communication to groups of consumers. News releases are important elements of publicity. Publicity can be positive or negative, since the marketer is not in control over what appears in the news media. The Lockheed Corporation received considerable negative publicity in the 1970s owing to illegal political campaign contributions on the part of corporate officers. Actually, for most organizations, publicity plays a relatively minor role in the promotion program.

*Public relations.* Public relations refers to the communications of organizations with their various outside groups, including the public at large, stockholders, employees, journalists, public-interest groups, and government agencies. The manufacturers of the Concorde engaged in an extensive public relations campaign in 1976, to try to convince the American public and governmental agencies that the airliner was not unduly noisy, dangerous to the atmosphere, or consumptive of fuel. Again, like publicity, public relations is not a paramount part of the promotion programs for most institutions.

**Pricing Activities.**   Pricing activities lead to the determination of the amounts of money to be assessed target consumers, retailers, and wholesalers. Organizations establish a base price that consumers are expected to pay. From that base price are subtracted various discounts and allowances granted because buyers have foregone some benefits or are performing functions for marketers. Thus, discounts and allowances are granted for such actions as paying bills on time, buying goods in large quantities, and (in the case of wholesalers and retailers) advertising a manufacturer's brand.

Some organizations use price as a very active element in the marketing strategy. The National Car Rental Company lists prices lower than some of its larger competitors. The Radio Shack Company advertises citizens band radios at prices substantially below those of major rivals.

Coordination of the Marketing Mix

An effective marketing mix is coordinated. Product, place, promotion, and pricing activities all work together in appealing to target consumers. Figure 2-4 depicts such a coordinated mix. The focus of each marketing activity is the target consumer, and the various activities are bound together to try to provide the benefits desired by the target consumers.

To attain this kind of coordination, timing is needed. Most packaged goods companies, for instance, are careful to make sure that new products are available on retail shelves when they are announced in advertisements. Consumers are antagonized when they cannot buy a new product they see announced.

Another consideration in coordination is that marketing activities must emphasize the same things. It would not make sense, for instance, for fork-lift trucks to be promoted by sales representatives for being high in quality (and in price), while advertisements indicated they were bargains.

The Marketing Environment

Marketing strategy is not formulated in a vacuum. Rather, management is faced with the need to recognize the environ-

**Figure 2-4. A coordinated marketing mix.**

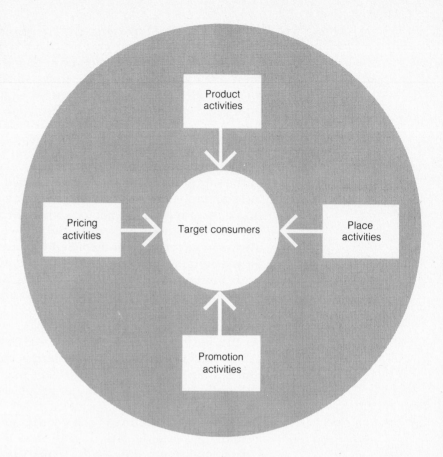

ment that will affect the success of the strategy. The relevant environments are as follows:[14]

1. the economic environment;

2. the societal environment;

3. the competitive environment;

4. the legal environment.

As Figure 2-5 indicates, these four forces influence the effectiveness of strategy in satisfying the desires of target consumers.

---

[14]Louis E. Boone and David L. Kurtz, *Contemporary Marketing* (Hinsdale, Ill.: The Dryden Press, 1977), p. 26.

**Figure 2-5. Marketing strategy and relevant environments.**

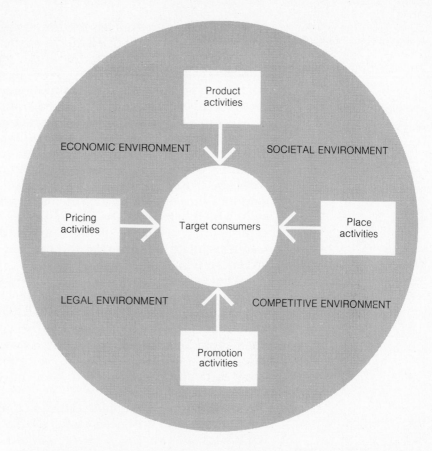

**The Economic Environment.** As the economy experiences upturns, downturns, and stable periods, different strategic decisions are in order. Generally, periods of expanding employment, Gross National Product, and national income present the greatest marketing opportunity. During such times, marketers are most likely to introduce new products and expand their operations. Conversely, periods of economic stagnation often produce product deletions and cutting back of expansion plans.[15]

**The Competitive Environment.** One of the more important determinants of the success of a marketing strategy is the com-

---

[15]See Eugene J. Kelley and L. Rusty Scheewe, "Buyer Behavior in a Stagflation/ Shortages Economy," *Journal of Marketing* 39, no. 2 (April 1975): 44–50.

petitive environment. This environment affects the choice of target consumers and of elements of the marketing mix.

Oftentimes marketers find that particular target consumers are being pursued by rivals in an effective manner. Under such circumstances, the management may be well advised to choose different target consumers.

Assume a firm is considering going into the cereal production and marketing business. A team of marketing researchers analyzes the market and discovers that it is pretty much dominated by General Mills, Kellogg, Post, and General Foods. It would be most difficult for a small, new company to attempt to convince the consumers who are buying from these big firms to switch their patronage. Indeed, if the new enterprise captured a significant percentage of the market, the larger companies might retaliate by lowering their prices and increasing their advertising budgets.

The new company could try to escape this dilemma by considering markets not being served by the large competitors. For instance, it might find the armed services, with their millions of people, a better choice of target consumers. If the company could acquire the Navy, say, as a customer, substantial sales could result. In this case, the presence of competition could force the new firm to look for markets it might not otherwise consider.

Competition influences the choice of the elements of the marketing mix. Most successful marketers seek to establish what has been called *differential advantage* over rivals.[16] That is, they try to provide unique benefits through a marketing mix that consumers perceive as being superior to the mixes of rivals. The Adoph Coors Brewing Company, for instance, emphasizes product quality; Anheuser-Busch emphasizes advertising in the marketing mix. Both companies pave the way for local brewers to feature low prices in their mixes.

**The Societal Environment.**   Being part of society, marketing institutions are subject to the constraints society imposes. Generally, the influence of society is reflected through groups. These range from large cultural aggregates to small groups.

Cultures are large groupings of individuals—the American culture, the Mexican culture, the Japanese culture, for instance. Each culture has certain values, standards, and taboos.

---

[16]Wroe Alderson, *Dynamic Marketing Behavior: A Functionalist Theory of Marketing* (Homewood, Ill.: Richard D. Irwin, 1965), chap. 8.

Marketers must conform to the cultures in which they operate. For example, in the United States, two important cultural values are independence and the right of a person to control his or her destiny. Organizations that attempt to subvert these values (as by telling sales personnel how to conduct themselves when they are on their own time) are likely to be met with resistance.

International marketers must be especially aware of cultural effects, since foreign cultures may differ in many ways. For example, one American firm, the Simmons Company, experienced difficulty selling mattresses in Japan because for centuries Japanese have slept on floor pallets and so the idea of sleeping on mattresses seemed strange.[17]

**The Legal Environment.**   Many aspects of marketing are regulated, and in chapter 14 we will discuss governmental regulation of personal selling. Here let us briefly describe five of the more important prohibitions of governing bodies in the United States that affect marketing. They are:

1. actions creating monopolies or restricting competition;
2. price fixing among competitors;
3. marketing unsafe or ineffective products;
4. misleading advertising and personal selling;
5. actions driving competitors out of business by unfair means.

Marketers ought to be constantly aware of the status of and changes in government regulations. Failure to do so may result in enforced changes in marketing strategy, costly lawsuits, and loss of public confidence. The legal environment may have even more far-reaching effects in the future as more and more government regulations of marketing activities materialize.[18]

## The Role of Personal Selling in Marketing

Personal selling is only one element in marketing strategy. There are others, and management must determine the role of each element in reaching organization goals.

### Promotion

Personal selling is a form of promotion. Management should take steps to ensure that the role of promotion has been specified

---

[17]Ronald D. Michman, "Culture as a Marketing Tool," *Marquette Business Review* 19, no. 4 (Winter 1975): 179–80.

[18]Lynn J. Loudenback and John W. Goebel, "Marketing in the Age of Strict Liability," *Journal of Marketing* 38, no. 1 (January 1974): 62–63.

and that steps to coordinate promotion with other elements of the marketing strategy have been taken.

For a large producer of clothing products, promotion has four functions. These are to:

1. help build and maintain a favorable image in the minds of target consumers and other groups;

2. inform consumers of the existence of new company products;

3. remind consumers of the existence of old company products and of the company at large;

4. convince noncustomers that company products and services are superior to those of rivals.

These functions are all compatible with the product, place, and pricing functions of the enterprise. To be sure they receive adequate attention, management places those in charge of promotion functions at a high level in the marketing department, as illustrated in Figure 2-6. Placing promotion personnel directly under the vice-president in charge of marketing makes it possible for this person to take steps designed to coordinate promotion with other activities. The vice-president determines the role of promotion at large and also the role of individual promotion methods, including personal selling.

**Figure 2-6. Marketing organization of clothing manufacturing company.**

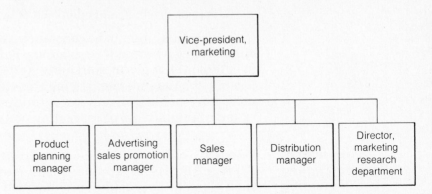

Personal Selling

Personal selling can perform some of the promotion tasks more effectively than can other promotion methods. It is a person-to-person communication process, as illustrated in the top part of Figure 2-7. This is in contrast to other forms of promotion, especially advertising, which focus upon groups of consumers (as illustrated in the bottom part of Figure 2-7).

**Figure 2-7. Patterns of communication through personal selling and other promotion methods.**

Sales representative   ●————————————→● Target consumer

Person-to-person communication through personal selling

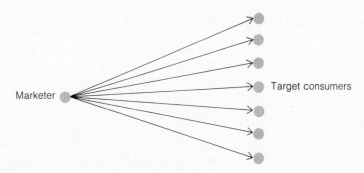

Target consumers

Communication to groups through advertising and other promotion methods

Since personal selling is person-to-person, it can tailor the promotion message to the characteristics and needs of individual prospective customers. The sales representative acts as a problem solver for each target consumer called upon, rather than as a disseminator of mass information. He or she can present a basic message, observe the effect of the message on the target consumer, then adjust the presentation in light of the observed effect.

Overall, personal selling is a very intense promotion method. Consumers can easily ignore, dismiss, or forget advertising and other promotion exposures. They find it more difficult to ignore, dismiss, or forget personal selling presentations, however. As a result, management should use personal selling where individualized and intense communication with target consumers is desired.

Personal selling has another role. Sales representatives can actually take orders and transmit them to order processing personnel. Except for mail order advertisements, no other promotion method can do this.

Finally, personal selling provides for the completion of various nonselling activities. Many sales representatives furnish written and oral reports of their activities that generate feedback information that is needed by management. As we indicated earlier, this information may lead to the refinement of past and the development of new marketing strategies. Further, salespersons are involved in such tasks as evaluating consumer needs, installing and maintaining new products, training the personnel employed by customers, and making efforts to win goodwill among customers. Where these are among the desired promotion tasks, personal selling can play an important role.

At the clothing manufacturing company we referred to earlier, personal selling is relied upon to help carry out all four of the promotion functions. Advertising plays a heavy role in maintaining and building the company image and in reminding customers of the existence of old products and of the company at large, however. Personal selling is dominant in informing consumers of the existence of new company products and in convincing noncustomers that its products and services are superior to those of rivals. Management has found that personal selling is uniquely effective in fulfilling these functions. Further, sales representatives are occupied in taking orders and in various nonselling functions, including providing information to management on such matters as the activities of competitors and the reaction of customers to new offerings.

In determining the role of personal selling, then, management should first specify the desired promotion and associated functions of the organization. Then a decision can be made as to what functions are best performed by sales representatives and what functions by other personnel. All of the various functions are oriented toward the target consumer and are coordinated with the others.

**Summary**    The traditional definition of marketing is the performance of business activities that direct the flow of goods and services from producer to consumer. Among the activities involved in marketing are those relating to product, place, promotion, and pricing. If all of the company activities are coordinated and are oriented to satisfying consumers at a profit, the marketing concept is in effect.

A more current definition of marketing recognizes that marketers deal with numerous groups in addition to target consumers. Marketers are involved in exchange (mutual giving up of things of value) with a variety of groups. Modern definitions of marketing also recognize that both business and nonbusiness organizations engage in this activity.

A marketing strategy is the unique way in which an organization presents itself to target consumers. Strategy formulators specify a target consumer and then design a marketing mix to satisfy the target consumer.

An effective marketing mix is coordinated. One element of coordination is that activities should be timed so that they occur in proper sequence. Another is that the marketing activities ought to emphasize the same things.

Strategy formulators are faced with the need to consider the marketing environment. The most important environments are:

1. economic—the behavior of the economy;

2. competitive—the characteristics and behavior of rivals;

3. societal—the influence of society, as reflected through groups;

4. legal—regulatory activities.

The precise role of personal selling in the marketing strategy varies from one organization to another. Generally, all promotion activities should be coordinated with the marketing strategy. In turn, personal selling should be coordinated with other promotion activities. Personal selling has the features of being person-to-person, having the ability to alter messages while they are in process, having feedback of information features, and being an intense promotion technique. Further, sales representatives can take orders and engage in various non-selling activities.

**Discussion Questions**

1. What is the relationship of personal selling to marketing strategy?

2. What activities are included in marketing?

3. Define marketing using the (a) traditional and (b) more modern definitions.

4. Describe the marketing concept. What are the implications of this concept to marketing managers?

5. "Nonbusiness organizations are heavily involved in marketing." Discuss.

6. What is marketing strategy? What are the two components of marketing strategy?

7. Explain why the marketing mix should be coordinated.

8. Describe each of the following marketing environments: (a) economic; (b) competitive; (c) societal; (d) legal.

9. What organization structure lends itself to coordinating the elements of the marketing mix?

10. "Personal selling can perform some of the promotion tasks more effectively than can other promotion methods." Explain.

**Practical Exercises**

1. Examine several magazine advertisements sponsored by a large organization.

a. Do the advertisements give you any insights as to the target consumer the organization is pursuing? Explain.

b. Do they give you any insights as to the marketing mix the organization is using? Explain.

c. In your opinion, is the organization effective in carrying out its marketing strategy? Explain.

2. Think of a product or service that you have recently purchased. In what ways might the marketing environment influence the marketing of this product?

**Selling Project**

Regarding the product that you have selected:

a. Define the target consumer.

b. Outline the highlights of the marketing mix you would employ.

c. With what individuals and organizations would you have exchanges?

d. Explain how the marketing environment would influence your strategy.

e. What role would personal selling play in the marketing mix?

**Case 2**
**The Stiles Mattress Company**

The Stiles Mattress Company is a producer and retailer of mattresses and related items. This organization has fifteen units, each located in a city in the southeastern portion of the United States. During the last year, total Stiles sales were $4,210,000.

Each Stiles unit has production, retail, and storage facilities. The production areas are located in the backs of the buildings. Here mattress components are received, unloaded, and assembled into finished products. In turn, finished mattresses are placed on display, delivered to customers, or put into storage.

In the retail area of Stiles units, goods are displayed and sold. The product line includes mattresses, bedsprings, beds, bedroom furniture, and miscellaneous small furniture items such as footstools, table lamps, and clocks. Stiles manufactures only the mattresses. The firm purchases all of the other items from producers or wholesalers.

This company sells its own mattress brand and a brand of a large national company (the Art Company). Stiles mattresses bring in approximately three-fourths of the total revenues. Art mattresses produce roughly 10 percent of sales. The remaining 15 percent is from the sale of items other than mattresses.

The Stiles firm produces what its management considers to be a very high quality mattress. Further, production and other costs are such that the price of a Stiles mattress is approximately 20 percent less than the price of an Art product of similar quality. Despite this fact, many consumers prefer Art. The Stiles management believes this is due to the reputation and company image of the large firm.

In each city with a Stiles unit, 10 percent of that unit's sales is spent on advertising. The bulk of this money goes into newspapers; smaller amounts are spent for radio. The ads stress Stiles mattresses and related items and usually make reference to the fact that the store carries the famed Art brand.

A typical Stiles unit has eight employees. Four of these work in the retail section, although they are frequently used to help production personnel and to make deliveries to local customers. A unit manager, who spends approximately two-thirds of his time on retail matters, is in charge. He recruits, selects, trains, and supervises the efforts of the sales force. Stiles salespersons receive incomes in the $10,000–$18,000 range. They are paid on the basis of salary plus commission basis, and their training is primarily on-the-job in nature.

Top management of the organization believes that Stiles tends to attract blue collar families age twenty-one to thirty. Accordingly, management has designated such individuals as target consumers. Advertisements and personal selling messages are constructed so as to appeal to these families.

From time to time the marketing management group at Stiles has considered dropping the Art line. This is because the margin of profit per mattress sold is approximately twice as large for the former as for the latter. Management is reluctant to drop the line, however, since it is felt that many customers come into Stiles stores and buy Art mattresses, but would never buy Stiles products. Further, management feels that carrying Art offerings enhances the image of Stiles.

The Stiles management has considered upgrading the quality of the sales force. Perhaps more college graduates should be hired. It may be that formalized training programs should be instituted. Increases in compensation might produce more effective sales performance. Answers to these issues have not been forthcoming to date, however.

Evaluate the marketing efforts of the Stiles company.

**Suggested Readings**

Bagozzi, Richard P. "Marketing as an Organized Behavioral System of Exchange," *Journal of Marketing* 38, no. 4 (October 1974): 77–81.

Bagozzi, Richard P. "Marketing as Exchange," *Journal of Marketing* 39, no. 4 (October 1975): 32–39.

Boone, Louis E., and David L. Kurtz. *Contemporary Marketing.* Hinsdale, Ill.: The Dryden Press, 1977, chs. 1, 2, 4.

Kotler, Philip. "A Generic Concept of Marketing," *Journal of Marketing* 36, no. 2 (April 1972): 46–54.

Kotler, Philip. *Marketing For Nonprofit Organizations.* Englewood Cliffs, N.J.: Prentice-Hall, 1975, chs. 1, 2, 3, 4.

McCarthy, E. Jerome. *Basic Marketing.* Homewood, Ill.: Richard D. Irwin, 1975, chs. 1 and 2.

Stanton, William J. *Fundamentals of Marketing.* New York: McGraw-Hill Book Company, 1975, chs. 1 and 2.

Schwartz, David. *Marketing Today: A Basic Approach.* New York: Harcourt Brace Jovanovich, 1977, chs. 1, 2, 3, 4.

# 3

## The Sales Job

*After reading this chapter you should be able to demonstrate a knowledge of:*

- *what various types of sales representatives do*
- *the characteristics needed by sales representatives for various kinds of positions*
- *how sales representatives can manage their time effectively*

- The representatives of a chemical producer call upon the refiners of petroleum products. These salespersons carry chemicals used in the process of refining crude oil. Each representative calls upon twenty or fewer customers. Thus, the representatives know their customers well and are treated more as professional colleagues than as salespersons representing another company.

- An insurance company employs representatives to sell its life insurance to ultimate consumers. The salespersons do much of their selling during evenings and sometimes on weekends. They are trained to analyze insurance and other financial needs of individuals and families. Much of the sales-persons' incomes are a result of renewals on existing policies. The average income of a representative who has been with the company for ten years is $40,000.

- A computer manufacturer utilizes representatives to sell computers to various business and nonbusiness organizations. Some salespersons are specialists in selling to educational institutions. The representatives work with company technical experts as part of a team. They have extensive background in the information needs of college, community college, vocational school, high school, and elementary school administrators and educators.

- The armed services employ recruiters to sell their branches of the service to young potential recruits. These representatives have been associated with the armed services long enough so that they can provide recruits with an informed view of opportunities in the service. Some recruiters specialize in attempting to acquire officer candidates from the ranks of forthcoming college graduates.

This chapter describes the nature of various kinds of sales jobs and the qualifications needed to fill the jobs. The chapter also provides guidelines on a problem common to most sales jobs—namely, how representatives can get the most from their time.

## Five Different Types of Sales Jobs

There are tremendous numbers and varieties of selling positions, both in business and nonbusiness organizations, and each has certain duties and responsibilities and requires particular characteristics on the part of the salespersons. Let us describe the duties, responsibilities, and characteristics typical of five kinds of positions:

1. selling to retail stores;
2. missionary selling;
3. industrial goods selling;
4. selling to ultimate consumers;
5. real estate selling.

## Selling to Retail Stores

Numerous sales personnel are involved in selling to retailers. The latter are firms that purchase consumer goods and sell them to ultimate consumers. Consumer goods are defined as

| | |
|---|---|
| Consumer and Industrial Goods | goods bought for personal or household satisfactions.[1] Examples are chewing gum, sports clothing, personal use automobiles, and coins for coin collections. Industrial goods and services, on the other hand, are purchased by members of organizations to help satisfy needs of the organizations. Examples are typewriters used in offices, machines that bore holes in sheets of steel, coal used to fuel steam turbines, and advertising services. |
| The Nature of Selling to Retail Stores | Representatives who sell to retailers usually are heavily involved in making regularly scheduled calls upon assigned customers in a territory. A great amount of time is spent in order taking rather than order getting. Order taking consists of making routine calls on customers, checking their needs, taking their orders, and perhaps providing various nonselling activities. Order getting, on the other hand, involves calling upon prospects who are not customers and converting them into customers. Typically, order getters receive higher compensation than do order takers. Most selling positions involve both of these activities, although positions vary according to the extent to which they emphasize one or the other. |

The activities of a representative who sells clothing to department and variety stores are somewhat typical of those who sell to retailers. A customary work day for her is as follows:

9:00— Reports to the office for a 30-minute training conference conducted for representatives who sell in the local district.

9:30— Briefly reviews the planned sales calls for the day in the office.

10:05— Calls upon a local department store buyer. The call results in an order for a new pantsuit line and for several lines already carried.

11:04— Calls upon a buyer for a ladies clothing department in a variety store. The representative points out that inventories of several products are low and should be replaced. The buyer promises to place an order soon.

11:55— Has lunch with another buyer.

---

[1]Irving J. Shapiro, *Marketing Terms: Definitions, Explanations, and/or Aspects* (New York: S-M-C Publishing Co., 1973), p. 38.

1:35— Calls upon a department store buyer. The representative helps the buyer rearrange several store displays.

2:20— Goes back to the office to pick up a copy of an advertisement that will soon appear in the local newspaper.

2:55— Calls upon a variety store buyer. The representative shows the advertisement to the buyer and notes that he might want to tie some of his store's personal selling appeals to it.

3:45— Calls upon a department store buyer. The representative takes the buyer to a nearby restaurant for coffee. Basically, this is a routine friendly social visit.

4:35— Calls upon another department store buyer. The representative tries to convince the buyer to carry several new coat lines but is unsuccessful.

5:05— Takes 10 minutes to fill out several reports, which all company salespersons must complete at the end of the day.

5:15— Goes home.

Some representatives who sell to retailers carry a large number of products and brands. Representatives who sell grocery products to supermarkets and other grocery outlets, for instance, sometimes carry more than 10,000 different items. Those who sell large numbers of offerings cannot easily engage in aggressive promotion of any one item. Some salespersons are involved primarily in asking prospective customers what needs they have and showing them what the organization offers by turning to the appropriate pages in catalogs. Positions such as this are largely order-taking jobs.

Many of those who sell to retailers are not as aggressive as those who are involved in other selling roles. Rather, these individuals are friendly, honest, and dependable persons who call upon a group of customers whom they know personally. Sales calls are somewhat routine, low key, and relatively free of tension. The sales representative is viewed as an advisor and often a friend, rather than as an "outsider." The rather routine nature of these positions dictates the use of compensation plans that feature salaries rather than commissions.

Chapter 3  The Sales Job

**Missionary Selling**     Some manufacturers who sell to retailers make use of missionary sales representatives. Although the manufacturers also employ order takers to carry on routine selling activities, they depend on their missionary salespersons not to take orders but to build goodwill for the organization and interest in the product line. These individuals are especially useful when the order-taking representatives carry a wide line and cannot devote sufficient attention to individual products, or when they do not have the time or expertise needed to accomplish missionary tasks.

Numerous missionary activities are designed to aid the prospective customer. The representatives of a hardware manufacturer, for instance, do the following things for retailer customers:

- arrange displays and other point-of-purchase promotion materials;
- help retailers in designing and conducting training programs for their employees;
- help retailers plan advertising campaigns and design individual advertisements;
- act as consultants in fields such as inventory control, pricing, design of store facilities, and credit;
- show the results of research studies to retailers, and even conduct research for retailers from time to time.

Effective missionary representatives are highly skilled individuals. Their work is nonroutine and often challenging. Those organizations that utilize missionary personnel need to ensure that those they hire are highly qualified, since an inept or unmotivated missionary sales representative is not an asset to the organization, and indeed may be a tremendous liability.

**Industrial Goods Selling**     Another type of sales job is handling industrial goods—those that buyers purchase in order to satisfy the needs of the organization. Thus, industrial goods salespersons include those who are employed by the Xerox Corporation, Manufacturers Hanover Trust Bank, and United States Steel Corporation.

Individual Customers Are Important     In some industrial selling the dollar amount of individual transactions is high, individual customers account for large percentages of the marketers' revenues, and customers demand considerable service (often technical in nature). As a result, sales representatives must devote substantial time and energy to the needs of individual customers. Thus, sellers of products such as Honeywell computers and Crane water and waste treatment systems may spend months working with a single prospective customer before a sale results. The representatives must also devote significant amounts of time to working with customers after the sale to ensure that the product works as it should and that service requirements are being met.

Territorial Marketing Managers
Many sellers of industrial goods are heavily involved in planning and other nonselling activities. In fact, such representatives assume multiple functions to the extent that they are called "territorial sales managers" or "territorial marketing managers," rather than sales representatives. The following duties and responsibilities are some of those associated with sales positions for a leading manufacturer of building materials:

1. preparing a yearly management by objectives report on sales goals and sales plans for the coming business year;

2. managing a sales territory within the expense budget;

3. reviewing with district management progress toward achieving sales goals and territory objectives;

4. participating in the activities of industry trade associations and local business groups;

5. providing customers with technical information on company products.[2]

Typical Duties
Order getting is an important function among many sales representatives in the industrial goods category. Those who sell heavy-duty trucks to industrial buyers, for instance, spend a great deal of time in order getting. A typical workday for such a salesperson is as follows:

8:00— Briefly reviews the list of calls for the day.

8:30— Has a conference with the sales manager on what to do about a particularly difficult prospective customer.

---

[2]Lawrence M. Lamont and William G. Lundstrom, "Defining Industrial Sales Behavior: A Factor Analytic Study," *1974 Combined Proceedings, American Marketing Association* (Chicago: American Marketing Association, 1975), p. 496.

9:15— Calls upon what appears to be a good prospective customer. The representative, who has heard that this firm is in the market for heavy-duty trucks, makes a sales presentation and leaves some brochures explaining important facts about the company's products.

11:20— Calls upon a recent purchaser of several company trucks to see if the buyer is satisfied.

12:00— Has lunch at a service club. The representative feels that membership in the club helps to solidify relations with potential customers and others and aids in building goodwill.

1:30— Calls upon a prospective customer. The representative has been working with this firm for five weeks but has not yet convinced its management that they should purchase the company brand of trucks. After the call, the prospective customer asks the representative to come back again the following week.

2:47— Demonstrates a truck to a bakery executive who has asked for a demonstration. The salesperson takes the executive out for coffee and passes on some basic information about the company and its products.

4:30— Checks to make sure that delivery has been made on a recently placed order.

5:50— Goes home.

The representative did not make a single sale on this particular day. This is not unusual for sellers of expensive durable goods. The sales are infrequent, but when they do happen they are large.

Not all those who serve industrial accounts are order getters, of course. Order taking activities are necessary in the industrial goods sector, just as they are for consumer goods. Order taking is especially likely for sales representatives who have a wide product line and cannot devote a lot of attention to any one offering.

**Selling to Ultimate Consumers**

Another class of salespersons sell consumer goods and services to ultimate consumers. These include familiar representatives of such firms as the J. C. Penney Company, the Fuller Brush Company, and the Kirby Company (vacuum cleaner manufacturer). Some examples of this class of representatives are those who sell:

- clothing in specialty stores;
- insurance through offices and in customer homes;
- real estate through offices and in homes;
- securities through brokerage houses;
- automobiles in auto dealerships;
- branches of the armed services through recruiters;
- political candidates through house-to-house visits with prospective voters.

Manufacturers' Employees

Various manufacturers employ salespersons to reach the ultimate consumer, based upon the belief that employees of the manufacturer can do a better selling job than could retailers. The firms that employ this method of distribution include Avon, Electrolux, Fuller Brush, Tupperware, and Realsilk. The individuals who staff these positions are very much order getters and oftentimes earn high rates of pay. College students can sometimes make a lucrative living selling knives, encyclopedias, pots and pans, and similar items on a part-time basis while attending school.

Retailers' Employees

Many retail sales representatives have interesting and challenging jobs. A clothing saleswoman, for example, can act as fashion advisor to many of her customers. When customers contemplate a dress purchase, the saleswoman determines the general physical characteristics of the consumer (such as heavy or slim), the intended purpose of the dress (such as party or casual), the consumer's life style (such as swinger or working mother), and the price range the consumer is willing to pay. She then selects for the customer's inspection several dresses in what appears to be the right size, style, and color. Because this approach has proven to be successful, the saleswoman is highly regarded by customers and earns more in commissions than do the other store representatives.

There are positions in retail stores that are essentially order-taking in nature but also require numerous nonselling activities such as stocking shelves, putting prices on products, ringing up sales, wrapping merchandise, making deliveries, or helping to maintain the physical facilities of the store.

Some jobs of selling to the ultimate consumer require highly skilled personnel and pay very well. Examples are securities and insurance sales. Although popular opinion often holds that sales representatives selling directly to the consumer (especially those of the door-to-door variety) engage in a lot of unethical conduct, usually stockbrokers and insurance salespeople deal with customers in what parallels a doctor-patient or lawyer-client relationship, one that is both ethical and conducive to making sales. In 1975, for instance, a Dallas insurance agent refused to sell a new form of individual retirement annuity because "In good conscience, I would find it hard to recommend any of these plans to my customers."[3] Like many others, the agent was a problem solver for his customers, who relied upon him for help in fulfilling insurance needs.

## Real Estate Selling
### Nature of Real Estate Positions

A special type of selling is found in the real estate industry. Those who occupy such positions are actively involved in order getting and in creatively attempting to solve the problems of their prospective customers.

Some real estate salespersons serve ultimate consumers, who purchase homes for their own individual and family use. Others specialize in commercial, industrial, and farm properties. Some representatives (mostly in smaller agencies) serve both markets.

Many salespersons in this field enjoy large incomes, although it usually requires a period of apprenticeship and hard work, as evidenced by the following case.

### A Realtor's Case

Frederick Carlson is one of the most successful realtors in his state. In fact, his annual earnings exceed $100,000. He was not a born salesman, however. When he first began his career, he was employed as a salesman for a local realtor in his home town. He had studied real estate in college and had passed the required state examinations, and so had a good understanding of the technical aspects, but he was not a good salesman.

During his first year of employment his sales were very disappointing, to both him and his employer. In the middle of the second year, however, he found that he was learning how to sell—the result of a personal selling course he had taken at a

---

[3]"Belated Rules for the IRA Boom," *Business Week,* no. 2410 (8 December 1975): 26.

local college, training by his employer, and on-the-job experience. By the end of that year, he had learned how to be an effective salesman, and in the third year was the top sales representative in the office. Ultimately, Carlson's success led him to establish his own real estate business.

## Managing Time Effectively
### Importance of Managing Time

As the discussion of the five differing types of sales jobs shows, sales representatives are responsible for a variety of duties and responsibilities. Many of these are nonselling in nature, such as providing information for marketing managers, collecting bills from customers, and traveling. Because of the diverse activities undertaken by salespersons, they must have the ability to be flexible in adapting their behavior to many different types of tasks.[4] Thus, a sales representative may have to engage in intense negotiation with a customer, then spend two hours traveling, with no social contact, and finally spend an hour waiting to contact another customer.

Time is one of the sales representative's most valuable resources. It is imperative that you plan the use of time in order to make maximum use of it.[5] Much of this planning must be accomplished by the individual salesperson rather than by sales managers and other executives. In other words, self-planning is essential.

### A Procedure for Managing Time Effectively

Figure 3-1 outlines the steps involved in making efficient use of time. First, you should determine which activities should be performed during the time period under consideration. Then you should determine the priority of each activity and estimate how long each activity will take. Next you should compare the desired time with the actual time. The information gained in the preceding steps will provide feedback that will be useful in your future time planning.

**Determining the Activities To Be Performed.**  The first step is to determine what must be accomplished during the time period under consideration. Many sales representatives make one general plan for a longer time, such as for a week or month, and another more detailed daily plan.

---

[4]James A. Belasco, "The Salesman's Role Revisited," *Journal of Marketing* 30, no. 2 (April 1966): 8.

[5]For a useful discussion of how to manage time effectively, see "Time and Territorial Management," *Sales and Marketing Management* 117, no. 2 (July 1975): 33–40.

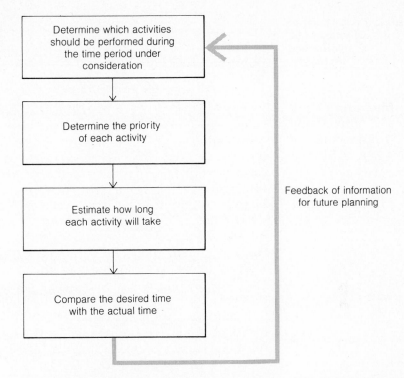

**Figure 3-1. Steps in making efficient use of time by salespersons.**

Determine which activities should be performed during the time period under consideration

Determine the priority of each activity

Estimate how long each activity will take

Compare the desired time with the actual time

Feedback of information for future planning

Ivan Vannelli is a successful seller of trucks to manufacturers, wholesalers, retailers, farmers, and nonbusiness organizations. Figure 3-2 presents a list of activities Ivan planned for a typical week. Every Sunday evening Ivan develops a list for the following week. In the process he reviews last week's list, goes over the reports he submitted to management, and thinks about what should be done to adequately serve his customers and reach his sales and other goals. In addition to this weekly plan, he prepares detailed daily plans.

**Determining the Priority of Each Activity.** After determining the activities to be performed you need to determine the order of importance of the activities. This means taking care of the most important activities first, then, if time permits, the less important activities.

One important decision is when to do the planning. Since planning is such a significant matter to sales representatives, they should engage in this activity when they are feeling at their best—during what one authority calls highly productive "alone time" (also called "internal prime time"). During this period

Figure 3-2. Ivan's list of activities to be performed next week.

1. Call upon the following potential new customers and introduce the company and product line to them:
   A. Prospect A.
   B. Prospect B.
   C. Prospect C.
   D. Prospect D.
   E. Prospect E.
   F. Prospect F.
   G. Prospect G.
   H. Prospect H.

2. Have daily conferences with the sales manager.

3. Callbacks to see if customers are satisfied:
   A. Customer I.
   B. Customer J.

4. Demonstrate company trucks to prospective customers:
   A. Prospect K.
   B. Prospect L.
   C. Prospect M.

5. Fill out daily written reports to management.

6. Call advertising department to find out why promised changes in local advertisements have not taken place.

7. Be available when company trucks are delivered to customer N.

8. Go over a list of possible new prospects that the sales manager has furnished.

9. Lunches with prospects O, P, and Q. The purpose of these is to build goodwill for the company, product line, and Ivan.

Figure 3-3. Ivan's list of
priorities of activities
to be performed
next week.

1. Have daily conferences with the sales manager --
   a required activity.

2. Fill out daily written reports to management --
   a required activity.

3. Be available when company trucks are
   delivered to customer N.

4. Call upon prospects A, B, and C. These are
   very good potential customers.

5. Demonstrate company trucks to prospects K and
   L. These are good potential prospects.

6. Call upon prospects C, D, E, and G. These
   are fairly good prospects.

7. Demonstrate company trucks to prospect M,
   who is a fairly good prospect.

8. Callbacks to see if customers I and J
   are satisfied.

9. Lunches with prospects O, P, and Q.

10. Call advertising department to find out why
    promised changes in local advertisements
    have not taken place.

11. Call upon prospect H -- not a high-priority
    prospect.

12. Do over a list of possible new prospects that
    the sales manager has furnished.

you should concentrate on planning high priority items and avoid distractions such as telephone calls.[6]

Figure 3-3 sets forth Ivan's activities for the next week, arranged in decreasing order of importance. In determining his priorities, Ivan imagines the consequences of *not* doing them, then decides upon the severity of the consequences. For instance, the consequences of failing to be available when company trucks are delivered to customer N are expected anger and resentment on the part of a valued customer. As a result, Ivan places this activity high on his priority list. The consequence of failing to call on prospective customer H is only possible irritation on the part of a target consumer with just a small fleet of trucks who in any case may soon be moving his business out of state. Hence, this activity is not high on Ivan's priority list.

For each week, Ivan translates the weekly plan into a daily plan. Figure 3-4 sets forth the daily plan for Monday, for instance. Ivan has arranged the schedule so that many high priority activities can be accomplished on that day. Other high priority activities that could not be carried out on Monday were allotted to following days.

**Estimate How Long Each Activity Will Take.**  When determining which activities to do which days, you should estimate how much time each activity will take. Otherwise, your plan may be unrealistic. Moreover, estimates of expected times will provide

**Figure 3-4. Ivan's list of activities to be performed during one day (Monday) next week.**

1. Have conference with the sales manager.

2. Fill out daily written reports to management.

3. Call upon prospects A and B.

4. Demonstrate company trucks to prospect K.

5. Call upon prospect C.

---

[6]Tom Carter, "Yes, You Do Have the Time," *Mainliner* 20, no. 2 (February 1976): 41.

Chapter 3 The Sales Job

benchmarks for comparisons of actual with expected times. Figure 3-5 shows Ivan's expected times for a particular Monday. These time estimates allow him to make a schedule for the entire day that ensures he allocates his time properly and conduct all the activities that should be undertaken.

| Activity | Estimated time consumed (hours) |
|---|---|
| 1. Have conference with sales manager. | .30 |
| 2. Fill out daily written reports to management. | .20 |
| 3. Call upon prospect A. | 1.50 |
| 4. Call upon prospect B. | |
| 5. Demonstrate trucks to prospect K. | |
| 6. Call upon prospect C. | 2.10 |
| Total hours | 8.55 |

**Compare the Desired Time with Actual Time.** An important step in the time-management process is to compare the desired or expected times with times actually required to perform the tasks. Such a comparison allows adjustments in the schedule necessitated by unanticipated delays or faster than expected performance and is useful in judging your efficiency.

Ivan had to make some adjustments in his schedule. The sales manager was ill on Monday and could not attend the meeting. As a result, Ivan used the time to call the advertising department to find out why the promised changes in local advertisements had not taken place. In addition, prospective customer B had to cancel his appointment because of unexpected breakdowns in his plant. Ivan used this time slot to go over the list of possible new prospective customers that the sales manager had furnished.

**Feedback of Information for Future Planning.** The comparisons of desired and actual times provide information that is useful in formulating future plans. For instance, Ivan found that he took 35 minutes to fill out the written reports. Believing this to be excessive, he resolved to be more diligent about report writing in the future. He also found that none of the calls upon prospective customers took as long as he had expected. This made him realize he could call upon customers more frequently than his original plans had called for.

**Use of the Time-Management Process.** The time-management process outlined above can be very useful to sales representatives, for three reasons: (1) They ensure that all high priority activities are undertaken. (2) They provide for the accomplishment of activities in the order of their importance (3) They improve the efficiency with which the activities are accomplished. As a sales representative you need not plan time management in exactly the same way Ivan did, of course, but the general procedure is still useful.

**Summary**

In this chapter we dealt with the nature of the sales job. Sales positions differ, depending upon a number of factors, one of the most important being whether the sales representative handles consumer or industrial goods.

Five different types of typical sales positions were described:

1. selling to retail stores;
2. missionary selling;
3. industrial goods selling;
4. selling to ultimate consumers;
5. real estate selling.

With the exception of missionary selling, each of these involves some mixture of order getting and order taking. The missionary salesperson does not take orders but attempts to generate goodwill for the organization and interest in the product line.

Effective management of time is very important for sales representatives. To make efficient use of time one must determine the activities to be performed, decide upon the priority of the activities, predict how long each will take, compare expected with actual times, and use the results of the comparisons in future planning.

Planning the use of time is essentially an individualized process. Each sales representative must accomplish this, rather than relying upon sales managers. Both extended (such as weekly or monthly) and daily plans are useful.

**Discussion Questions**

1. What are some of the features of positions involving the sale of consumer goods to retail stores?

2. Describe the responsibilities of missionary sales representatives.

3. What types of responsibilities exist for those who sell industrial goods?

4. "Most industrial goods sellers are order takers." Discuss.

5. Discuss the operations of representatives who sell to ultimate consumers.

6. How does real estate selling differ from selling consumer goods to retail stores?

7. Why is time such an important resource to sales representatives?

8. Outline the process for the effective use of time.

**Practical Exercises**

1. Observe the activities of a retail salesperson. Would you classify this individual as an order getter or an order taker? Is the salesperson effective in this role? Why? What did you learn as a result of this exercise?

2. Make a plan for the effective use of your time (a) next week, and (b) the first day of next week. What did you learn as a result of this exercise?

**Selling Project**

Which of the five selling positions described in this chapter comes closest to the selling job that would be needed for your product? What are the implications for the way in which the product should be sold?

**Case 3 Anchor Hotels, Incorporated**

Anchor Hotels, Incorporated (AHI) is a chain organization with hotels located in twenty-four sites in the United States. The firm has as its target consumers (1) individuals and families who travel for pleasure, (2) business travelers, and (3) groups holding conventions, conferences, and meetings. These categories make up 15, 35, and 50 percent, respectively, of the revenues of the chain.

AHI units are luxury units. They all are relatively new and have a modern design. Each one contains spacious and well-kept rooms, several restaurants and lounges, boutiques in the lobby, swimming pools, exercise rooms, and saunas. The AHI management believes its chain occupies a position in between Holiday Inns and Sheraton-type hotels. Accordingly, room and other prices are in between the prices of units in those chains. The hotels are mainly located downtown or near airports.

The company advertises its facilities in several different magazines: airline in-flight magazines, travel magazines, business magazines (such as *Forbes* and *Business Week*), and some trade magazines. The appeals featured in the advertisements are luxury, convenience to business and downtown areas, and high quality restaurants.

AHI maintains a staff of six salespersons charged with selling to groups holding conferences, conventions, and other meetings. The representatives call upon whatever officers of these groups are responsible for determining the meeting sites and hotels. Many of the prospects are discovered through inquiries to advertisements. Others originate through calls on the officers of associations known to have periodic meetings.

Essentially, the salespersons are order getters. All have college educations and extensive training in hotel management, personal selling, and the operation of meetings, conventions and conferences. They make appointments well in advance of their presentations, present a well-planned sales story that features the appeals mentioned in the advertisements, and attempt to fit the AHI facilities into the needs of the prospect organization. Of necessity, these salespersons engage in extensive travel. However, they receive high salaries, bonuses, and generous expense accounts.

The marketing manager of the chain, Mr. Andreas, has a proposal on his desk prepared by one of the sales representatives in which it is suggested AHI representatives sell advertising space in *Anchor Age*, a magazine which the chain produces and distributes to its guests. The *Age* contains facts about hotel facilities and services, cities where company hotels are located, and news that is of interest to travelers. In addition, the magazine carries advertising. At present, advertisements in the *Age* are sold by the managers of Anchor hotel units.

The saleswoman who proposes the advertising selling is Ms. Gruen. She has noted that many of the associations that hold meetings conduct advertising designed to attain ends such as building the association image and acquiring new members. Ms. Gruen reasons that company salespersons, who are already in touch with association officers, might as well sell advertising space to them while attempting to acquire their meeting business. The result would be that associations would obtain a good advertising medium, the salespersons would receive commissions, and AHI would receive additional advertising revenues.

Would you suggest that Mr. Andreas accept the proposal or turn it down?

**Suggested Readings**

Anderson, George. "Tell Him What You Told Him," *Marketing Times* 19, no. 1 (January/February, 1972): 10–14.

Cash, Harold C., and W. J. E. Crissy. "A Point of View for Salesmen," *The Psychology of Selling.* New York: Personal Development, 1957, pp. 10–30.

DeBoer, Lloyd M., and William H. Ward. "Integration of the Computer into Salesman Reporting, *Journal of Marketing* 35, no. 1 (January 1971): 41–47.

Hill, Richard M., Ralph S. Alexander, and James S. Cross. *Industrial Marketing.* Homewood, Ill.: Richard D. Irwin, 1975, pp. 458–66.

Rathmell, John M. *Managing the Marketing Function: Concepts, Analysis, and Applications.* New York: John Wiley & Sons, 1969.

"Retailing: Kurt Barnard Says: Don't Be a Salesman," *Sales Management* 109, no. 11 (27 November 1972): 25–26.

Stanton, William J., and Richard H. Buskirk. *Management of the Sales Force.* Homewood, Ill.: Richard D. Irwin, 1974, pp. 171–74.

# PART II

## The Selling Process

*The nine chapters in this part focus upon the actual process of personal selling. The accompanying figure outlines the components of the process. Chapter 4 covers the preapproach and other information needed by sales representatives—the facts they need about a prospect prior to carrying out the sales presentation. Chapters 5 through 10 deal with how to contact prospects, plan the sales presentation, handle the communications (an activity that is actually essential in all components of the selling process), conduct the sales presentation, and close the sale. Chapter 11 is concerned with consumer behavior, something you should be familiar with so you can see how benefits are provided to target consumers. Finally, Chapter 12 describes postselling activities, what you must do after the sale has been made.*

**Outline of elements involved in the selling process.**

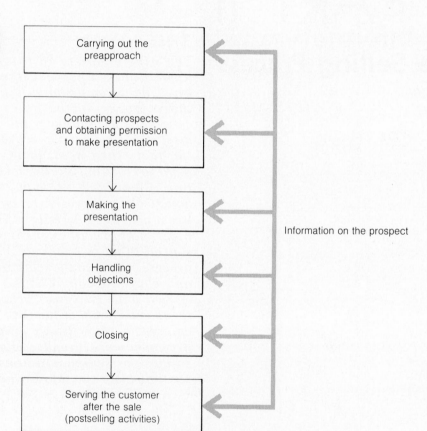

# 4

# Information Needed by the Sales Representative

*After reading this chapter you should be able to demonstrate a knowledge of:*

- *the information about target consumers that salespersons need*
- *the information about their organizations that salespersons need*
- *the information about the environment of the organization that sales representatives need*

As a sales representative you are not likely to be very effective unless you are informed so that you can conduct your activities in a preplanned, rational manner. In addition, knowledgeable salespersons can be very useful sources of insights to the people they call on. For instance:

- A seller of wholesale building materials tells lumber yard retailers about a new roofing material that a supplier has developed.

- A seller of prescription drugs describes several new antibiotics to doctors and pharmacists.

- An automobile sales representative points out the features of a prospective company automobile to an inquiring consumer.

- A Marine Corps recruiter points out the advantages of his branch of the service to a high school senior.

- A public health administrator explains to a group of state legislators how citizens will benefit if the state public health budget is increased.

- A door-to-door solicitor for the Heart Fund tells consumers what the funds collected are used for.

In these instances, sales representatives are means of conveying information to customers and prospective customers, and frequently they are more effective than alternative sources such as advertising, sales promotion, and publicity.

## The Need for Information

Every responsible employee of a business or nonbusiness organization attempts to gain information before attempting to carry out his or her responsibilities. Advertising managers need to know about target consumers, actions of competitors, and the main features of company products, before they can design ads. Engineers need to know how consumers will use a product and what company technology is available before they can make recommendations on the design of a new product. Attorneys need to know about the client's background and the exact nature of the case at hand so they can develop good arguments on the client's behalf.

And like these other professionals, sales representatives too must have relevant information. They must (1) acquire needed information, (2) sort out what is relevant from what is not, (3) develop plans based upon the information, (4) act upon the plans, and (5) change the plans based upon information that develops as they act on the plans.[1] Figure 4-1 outlines these acquisition and utilization activities.

## Categories of Information Needed

According to one authority, "Being knowledgeable means knowing your product, customer, competition, market, and all salable facts."[2] More specifically, the information that sales representatives require falls into three main categories:

---

[1]Future information needs are likely to exceed those in existence today. See R. E. Evans, "The Field Sales Manager of the Future," *1974 Combined Proceedings American Marketing Association* (Chicago: American Marketing Association, 1975), p. 520.

[2]"Marketing Briefs," *Marketing News* 8, no. 2 (15 July 1974): 2.

**Figure 4-1. Information acquisition and utilization.**

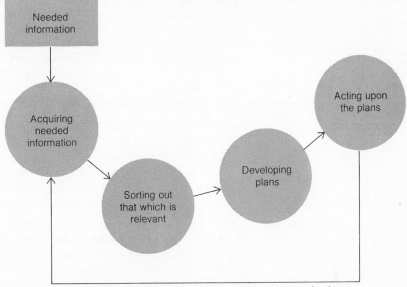

Subsequent information that may necessitate changes in plans

1. information about the target consumer;

2. information about the sales representative's organization;

3. information about the environment of the organization.

The rest of this chapter describes the details of these three types of information needs.

## Information About the Target Consumer

Chapter 2 discussed the importance of orienting the marketing strategy toward specific types of target consumers. If sales representatives are to play their role in the marketing strategy, they must focus their efforts upon the target consumer and deemphasize or ignore others. They must strive to determine the needs and desires of the target consumer and work toward fulfilling them. Otherwise, it is like being the owner of a new building who rented space to a computer company but when the latter moved in, it was found the building did not even have facilities to handle computers.[3] In this case, the needs of the consumer were certainly not given careful study by the marketer.

---

[3]H. A. Carroll, "AT&T Ads to Tell Builders to Preplan for Communication," *Industrial Marketing*, July 1972, p. 14.

In order to be well informed, sales representatives need four main types of information about consumers:

1. Who the target consumers are and what their characteristics are—as when a machine-tool salesman identifies industries whose production levels are nearing capacity and thus are good sales prospects.

2. What the needs of the target consumers are—as when a real estate sales representative identifies the needs of executives transferred into the city for a fast sale, and makes arrangements with local financial institutions for rapid financing.

3. What products are currently owned and used by target consumers—as when a computer sales representative finds out which clients have older computers that are no longer satisfying their needs.

4. Who the key decision makers are (if the target consumer is an organization)—as when the computer salesperson finds out who makes computer buying decisions in an organization.

The sales representative who has insights into these four topical areas is in a position to conduct sales presentations that are coordinated with the overall marketing efforts of the enterprise, that meet the specific needs of target consumers, and that are directed to the proper persons in the customers' organizations. When this information is collected for a particular customer and a particular sales call that is coming up, it is called *preapproach information*. The purpose of the preapproach information is to provide guidance for an upcoming sales presentation. In turn, the sales representative who is in possession of such information is ready to conduct a sales presentation that meets the specific needs of individual customers or prospective customers.

An Example of the
Use of Information
About the Target
Consumer

The alumni director of a midwestern university has defined his target consumers as alumni in upper-middle and upper income groups. These are the individuals to which the bulk of the fundraising effort is directed. Experience has suggested that the university is more successful in appealing to upper-middle and upper income individuals than it is to other alumni. Figure 4-2 bears this out. It sets forth the percentages of the total contributions to the alumni funds from individuals in various annual income groupings. The alumni director defines "low-income individuals" as those earning $9,999 a year or less, and this category accounts for only 5 percent of the contributions.

The bulk of the funds come from those earning between $10,000 and $29,999 a year. This is followed by those earning more than $30,000. The alumni director therefore focuses his fund raising activities on these two groups.

**Figure 4-2. Percentages of university alumni contributions from five annual-income groups.**

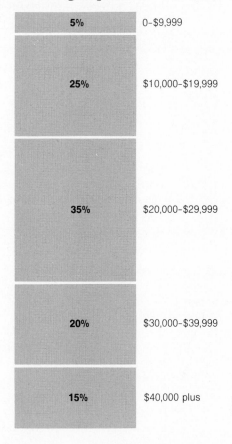

| | |
|---|---|
| 5% | 0–$9,999 |
| 25% | $10,000–$19,999 |
| 35% | $20,000–$29,999 |
| 20% | $30,000–$39,999 |
| 15% | $40,000 plus |

Information about target consumer desires and characteristics is vital, if the alumni director is to conduct an effective marketing plan. He is aware that income, age, and other characteristics have a bearing upon consumer desires, as a result of having seen a magazine article describing differences in desires between various occupational groups.[4] The article pointed out, for instance, that one firm had found that young

---

[4]"Getting the Story Straight at Oskosh B'Gosh," *Sales Management* 108, no. 13 (26 June 1972): 4.

white collar people liked bib overalls, but that young blue collar employees wouldn't be caught dead in them. After reading the article, the director sought to categorize alumni so as to distinguish contributors from noncontributors and point out differences in consumer desires. In the course of his research, he obtained information about target consumers through two sources:

- informal discussions with alumni; and
- a mail survey of alumni asking for (1) their characteristics (mainly age, income, occupation, and family size) and (2) what benefits they thought their university and alumni association should supply them.

The director's analysis indicated that annual income was the best means of distinguishing contributors from noncontributors. The research also enabled him to prepare a profile (Figure 4-3) of the desires of target consumers, which he could refer to when planning advertising campaigns and sales presentations.

**Figure 4-3. University alumni director's profile of target consumer desires.**

The primary reasons why target consumers make contributions are to satisfy desires for:

1. Feeling that one is doing what is expected of him or her.
2. Achieving an opinion that one is helping others who need help.
3. Status and prestige.
4. Feeling that one is doing what is morally right or "ethical."
5. Affiliation-maintaining contacts and friendships with the university and with other alumni.
6. Obtaining federal and state income-tax relief.

With the aid of the profile, the director has developed some very effective sales presentations. For instance, regarding the first desire listed in the figure (that a person is doing what is expected of him or her), he has on file impressive documentation of the contributions (total, mean, and individual) made by all alumni. When asking for contributions, the director refers to the file for useful information. In one case, preapproach information suggested that an alumnus felt that "doing what is expected of him" was an important need. This information was useful, as revealed in the following diologue:

> ALUMNUS: I'd like to make a contribution. How much do you feel is appropriate?

> DIRECTOR: According to our records, the mean annual contribution is $125. The highest one last year was $2,250.

> ALUMNUS: I'll donate $200. That's well above average.

The director uses the other five elements in the profile for purposes of developing points for sales presentations. By appealing to these desires, he has obtained substantial contributions for the university.

In the case of some potentially large contributors, the director makes use of information on "what products are currently owned and used by target consumers." He attempts to determine what nonprofit organizations are currently receiving target consumers' contributions. If he finds these contributions are made primarily to organizations other than the university, he appeals for a change in the pattern. For instance:

> ALUMNUS: I'm sorry, I can't make a contribution to your fund. I'm already giving $500 a year to the city self-improvement fund.

> DIRECTOR: That's an important fund, alright. However, would you consider devoting a portion of that amount to our alumni fund? We're in great need of donations.

> ALUMNUS: I'll set aside $100 for you.

Sometimes, information on "who are the key decision makers in the organization" is useful to the director. He has found that in the target consumer group some families are "male dominant," with the husband making most decisions relative to contributions, while other families are "female dominant" and still others are "democratic," with both husband and wife having a major say in contribution decision making. If the spouse of the alumnus or alumna is dominant or is involved in a "democratic" role structure, the director attempts to include the spouse in his sales presentation. His position is that if the spouse exerts a significant influence on contribution decisions, he or she should be exposed to the presentation when possible. The result is the director has managed to generate more contributions per alumnus than any other alumni director in his area.

## Information About the Sales Representatives Organization
### Reasons for Acquiring Information About the Organization

There are three major reasons why sales representatives should be knowledgeable about the organization they work for:

1. They need this information in order to bring customers the benefits they seek.

2. They need the information in order to be able to advance to higher level positions in their firms.

3. They need the information in order to effectively represent their organizations to the public.

**Bringing Customers the Benefits They Seek.** Customers deal with salespersons because they expect that the latter will provide them with benefits not currently received. The customers of the Emery Air Freight Company, for instance, want fast and reliable transportation of products, with minimal damage. In turn, representatives must be informed about company products, resources, policies and other fields, if they are to bring about these benefits.

Consider the experience of an office furniture salesman named John. The office manager of a large insurance company who was seeking to replace desks, chairs and filing cabinets currently in use had invited John and representatives of other office furniture firms to make presentations regarding their companies' offerings. John made a good presentation, but when asked if his company carried Danish modern furniture he replied "No." John had thought the company had dropped its Danish modern line, but actually the company was just not emphasizing the style in its advertising, although it still carried it. John's statement, then, resulted in the loss of a sale. If he had been informed, he might have obtained an order, since the company's offerings were just what the buyer wanted.

**Allowing Sales Representatives to Advance.** As salespersons acquire information about the organization, they attain the knowledge needed for promotion to higher level positions. Sales jobs are especially good avenues for promotion in most organizations, one reason being that sales representatives get considerable information about the concern.

**Representing the Organization to the Public.** For many outsiders, sales representatives don't just represent the organization; they *are* the organization. They may not know production, finance, engineering, advertising, and other personnel, but they know the sales people. To the buyer of fertilizers, for instance, the Olin Chemical Company sales representative is the organization. Unknowledgeable sales representatives, then, can give outsiders the impression of incompetence on the part of the entire organization. Thus, from the standpoint of public relations, sales personnel should be well informed.

<table>
<tr><td>What Specific<br>Information Is Needed</td><td>Sales personnel should be informed on the organization's products, marketing strategy, resources, other departments, and policies. Let us discuss each of these.</td></tr>
</table>

**Products.**   One important field in which sales representatives should have knowledge is the product or products they handle. Product knowledge is so important, in fact, that companies with technical products commonly devote more than half their sales training programs to product training.[5]

In particular, representatives need to know four aspects of their company's product:

1. production;

2. performance;

3. research; and

4. price.

*Production.*   Sales representatives who are aware of the components and methods of production of the product are in a good position to provide answers to questions raised by prospective customers. Sales personnel for a carpet manufacturing company attended training sessions at the company manufacturing facility shortly after they are hired, and much of the training focused on methods and procedures utilized in producing company products. In addition, after studying booklets on production methods, new sales representatives were required to pass a test. Thus, the representatives of this company received continual training on the elements of the company production processes, which put them in a position to provide detailed knowledge to prospective customers concerned with production facilities, methods and standards.

Production knowledge is especially important for complex products' those whose capability and performance are difficult to assess. Examples of such products are ready-mix concrete, clothing, and copying machines. Many target consumers have difficulty in judging the quality of such products, and must rely

---

[5]Richard R. Still and Edward W. Cundiff, *Sales Management: Decisions, Policies, and Cases* (Englewood Cliffs, N.J.: Prentice-Hall, 1969), p. 227.

on representatives for information. If the representatives have some insights on how the product is manufactured, they can speak intelligently about its quality.

*Performance.* Salespersons should know exactly what performance or benefits their product will bring to customers. A realtor, for instance, may use the chart pictured in Figure 4-4 to highlight some of the benefits that lessees of industrial park properties will enjoy. The realtor's "product" is really a group of benefits flowing to those who place their installations in the park. The chart highlighting the major benefits impresses many prospective customers. The following scenario illustrates the importance of product knowledge:

**Figure 4-4. Realtor's chart of benefits available for lessees in the industrial park.**

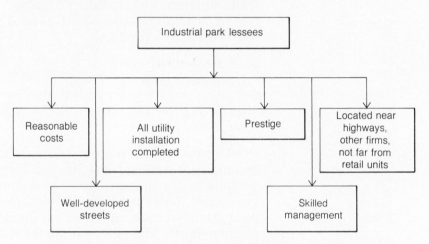

PROSPECT: I'm definitely going to locate one of our company warehouses in your city, but I can't see that your industrial park is better than the other sites I've looked at.

REALTOR: Look at the chart. It gives a systematic way of considering the benefits.

PROSPECT: The chart says prestige is a benefit. I'm not concerned about that.

REALTOR: Yes, but your sales representative will. I can give you the names of at least three lessees in the park who have evidence that their prestige location resulted in increased sales.

PROSPECT: I'd like to follow up on that. Can you give me their names?

The prospective customer did contact the three lessees, and after verifying the realtor's assertions took a lease in the park.

*Research.* Oftentimes knowledge about research conducted on the product is valuable to the sales representative. Buyers of technical products are concerned with company research on the performance, durability, cost of operation, and safety of the product. Some salespersons are aware that their organizations' offerings are subjected to grueling performance tests before they are placed on the market. They are thus in a position to provide prospective customers with the outcomes of the test to help build confidence in the performance characteristics.

Marketing research information is also useful. Buyers for supermarket chains, for example, sometimes demand research information to show that a proposed new product will sell in volume. Without the salesperson's knowledge of marketing research conducted for the product, a sale will not take place. Successful marketers, such as the Proctor & Gamble, do research on product salability and make research results available to salespersons.

While sales representatives need not be experts in marketing research, they should have an awareness of how the research was conducted and what the conclusions were. Buyers may be interested in such facets as:

- research objectives;
- who conducted the inquiry;
- when the study was made;
- what safeguards were made for valid and objective data collection; and
- what the results of the research were.

*Price.* The price of the product is a vital area of knowledge. Sales representatives should know the mechanics of computing prices, as well as the pricing objectives and strategies. It helps to be able to tell prospective customers "We'll guarantee the listed prices for six months; the cost assessed you will not go up during that time." Or, "Our prices consist of overhead and direct costs plus 10 percent of this figure."

Some salespersons have the authority to set or negotiate for prices. They can make concessions off the list price or can grant discounts and allowances in cases where, say, customers pay their bills within a specified time or buy in quantity. Sales people should be fully aware of the discount and allowance policies of their organizations so they can adjust prices as needed to win sales without violating organization policy.

**Marketing Strategy.** In chapter 2 we pointed out the importance of coordinating all elements of marketing, including personal selling, in satisfying target consumers at a profit. Sales people cannot be expected to fulfill their role in the marketing strategy unless they are well informed as to what that strategy is. They need to know (1) who the target consumers are, and (2) which ways the tools of the marketing mix are to be used to satisfy them.

Marilyn Probir is a sales representative for the Cerces Fabrics Company, which markets high quality prestige clothing. She is aware that management has defined target consumers as business and professional people with above average income. She knows that the firm's newspaper and magazine advertising attempt to build an image of quality and prestige. She also knows that Cerces clothes are high quality and are priced slightly higher than competing clothing lines. Finally, she knows the clothes are distributed through department stores, boutiques, and high fashion clothing outlets. With all this information she is able to go about her sales duties in a manner that contributes to the marketing strategy.

Oftentimes, retailers ask Marilyn for advice on how to sell Cerces products to ultimate consumers. "Emphasize the quality and prestige elements," she tells them. "Orient your advertising and personal selling to above-average income business and professional types, and keep your prices at commensurate levels. You'll sell a lot of Cerces clothes at a good profit." In other words, she advises retailers, her customers, to do their part in carrying out the marketing strategy.

Without all this knowledge, Marilyn's efforts might run counter to company advertising, product planning, pricing, distribution, and other efforts. She might, for instance, advise retailers to put low prices on Cerces clothes and promote them as durable offerings for blue collar families.

**Resources.** Organization resources consist of financial resources, personnel, and equipment.

*Financial Resources.* Some prospective customers are concerned with the financial position of their suppliers,[6] and are apt to ask representatives for evidence of the financial health of

---

[6]For useful background on this topic, see Robert Cavet, *The Anatomy of a Sale* (Grand Rapids, Mich.: Edward M. Miller & Associates, 19—). This is a 33-rpm record album.

their organizations. The salesperson should be in a position to provide well-informed replies to such requests.

*Personnel.*    Sales representatives should be aware of the backgrounds of key personnel in their organizations—top executives, sales division middle managers, and other prominent employees. If the organization is associated with some famous names (such as Joan Crawford for the PepsiCo Company), they can be mentioned or alluded to in the sales presentation.

*Equipment.*    Sales people should be knowledgeable about the production and distribution facilities of their organization. Some salespersons find that making frequent references to these equipment aspects is very impressive to prospective customers. Knowledge of equipment capabilities also enables them to make informed statements to customers; they can tell how rapidly customers can obtain deliveries, for instance, or why their products have performance features not provided by competing brands.

**Other Departments.**    Sales people should be familiar with other departments in their organization, not only because such knowledge promotes coordination between departments but also provides the sales representatives with insights useful in dealing with customers. Of special significance is knowledge of research departments. A salesperson should be aware of what is happening in research, since this information is often useful in sales activities. For instance, research conducted by one company found twenty-three alternative uses for concrete pipes, in addition to the usual drainage and water uses.[7] Such information is invaluable, since it helps sales personnel in selecting prospective customers to call on and in determining what product characteristics to feature in sales presentations.

**Policies.**    Policies are general rules of action that guide the day-to-day behavior of organization personnel. Sales representatives should be familiar with policies both because as employees of the organization, they are responsible for adhering to them and carrying them out and because customers may want to know organization policy on certain matters.

Every organization is replete with policies. Some a sales representative should be familiar with are: pricing, returns of defective goods, credit extensions, and delivery.

---

[7]"Secrets Salesmen Know," *Sales Management* 108, no. 12 (12 June 1972), p. 14.

*Pricing.*　Most customers are highly concerned with the pricing policies of the supplier. Some of the issues of concern are:

- Does the supplier frequently change prices? If yes, are customers notified beforehand?
- Are price discounts made for larger customers?
- Will the supplier lower prices if competitors lower theirs?
- Will the supplier raise prices in the face of inflationary trends in the prices of raw materials and labor?

*Returns.*　Prospective customers also are interested in the organization's policy regarding returns of defective orders. If inferior merchandise is received, the supplier is obligated to make some sort of adjustment. Sometimes questions as to what is "inferior" arise. The adjustment may take the form of replacement of returned goods, cash refund, credits on the supplier's books, or repair of inferior merchandise on the buyer's premises.

*Credit.*　Since many purchases are made on credit, prospective customers are likely to ask for information regarding the organization's financing arrangements. These may include:

- installment loans;
- open book (charge account) loans;
- credit card arrangements;
- postdating invoices (giving customers a period of time during which they have "free credit");
- helping customers raise funds on the money markets or with financial institutions.

*Delivery.*　Prospective customers often raise questions regarding delivery policies. They may be concerned with the length of time between when they place an order and when they actually receive the merchandise. They may also want to know what provisions exist for handling insurance, what carriers do the transporting, and how reliable the carriers are.

## Information About the Organizations Environment

No organization operates completely independently. Everyone is affected by environmental factors, the most important being:

1. competitors;
2. suppliers;
3. other customers;

4. employees;

5. government agencies; and

6. financial institutions.

These are shown in Figure 4-5, which also includes "Others" as a category—those particular entities that influence specific organizations but that are too numerous to describe here. Now let's examine the six principal environmental factors.

Figure 4-5.
Environmental entities
of which the
salesperson should be
informed.

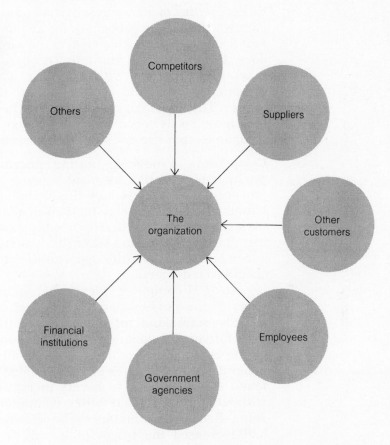

Competitors    Few organizations are without competitors, even those popularly considered monopolies.[8] Although only one railroad may

---

[8]Ralph S. Alexander and Thomas L. Berg, *Dynamic Management in Marketing* (Homewood, Ill.: Richard D. Irwin, 1965), pp. 330–31.

serve a community, that railroad may compete with cars, trucks, buses, airlines, boats, and pipelines. In virtually every case where organizations can fulfill consumer desires at a profit, competition materializes.

Sales people need to be informed of the marketing strategies and tactics of competitors. They must know about their target consumers, products, distribution activities, price activities, and promotion activities.

**Competitors' Target Consumers.** Competitors pose a direct threat to the sales representative and should be watched closely. A Pillsbury salesman, for instance, knows that a General Foods representative vies for the same retail customers he does. He should also know that General Foods has a strong marketing program, with extensive advertising, aggressive personal selling, and well-conceived sales-promotion techniques. The salesman should observe the marketing strategies of General Foods very closely but not watch so attentively other companies that are not such direct competition.

**Competitors' Products.** Getting information on competing products is essential, for a salesperson must be able to show prospective customers how the products differ. Because customers also purchase satisfactions in addition to physical products, the sales representative needs to know about the delivery, installation, repair, and other services competitors offer, in order to be able to identify opportunities for advantages to prospective customers.

An IBM computer saleswoman maintains an exhaustive study of the products and services of competing firms. She attends professional meetings, talks with competing sales representatives and their customers, and reads the literature competing companies produce. She does all this in order to gain insights on the offerings of IBM's major competitors. She has found she cannot make a very insightful sales presentation without knowing what other computer manufacturers are doing. Recently, for instance, she discovered that a major rival had increased the prices of leasing a particular computer model. This led her to rely more upon appeals regarding IBM's lease rates than she had in the past.

**Competitors' Distribution Activities.** A salesperson should know several characteristics of the channels of distrubition of competitors. If the representative is with a firm that sells direct, and knows important competitors sell through wholesalers, a good selling appeal may be that the firm provides better and more customized service.

Sales representatives should be alert for evidence that competitors are attempting to increase the number of middlemen in their channels of distribution. For instance, some time ago an Oneida Company silverware saleswoman noticed that a rival company was trying to increase the number of its retail outlets in her territory. She reacted by stepping up her efforts to retain and acquire retailers, and so was able to avoid losing much business from any of her large retail customers.

A good sales representative is aware of the physical distribution operations of competitors and knows the speed, reliability, and cost of delivery that the competitors promise. This knowledge may provide useful selling points, such as:

- "We can deliver within two days—no competitor can match that."

- "Our competitor sometimes delivers as much as twenty-four hours late. We never let that happen."

- "Our delivery costs are 10 cents per hundredweight less than those of competitor X."

**Competitors' Pricing Activities.** For some products a good selling point is "Our brand is less expensive than their brands." Sales representatives who handle such products must therefore be aware of the prices competitors charge. Even if one's own organization does not cut prices in response to reductions by others, rival price information is useful. One can meet price reductions in ways other than lowering prices, such as by making more sales calls, trying harder in each call to build brand loyalty, and promising faster deliveries or better service to existing customers.

**Competitors' Promotion Activities.** A good sales representative knows what the competition is doing in advertising, personal selling, and sales promotion, and so is able to react timely to promotion activities. Such knowledge can also suggest meaningful selling points, such as:

- Your store should carry our brand. If you watch the newspapers, you know we do more advertising than any other competitor.

- I can guarantee we'll provide more end-of-aisle display containers than any of our competitors will.

- We can service you much better than any other firm since we have twice as many sales reps in this area as any other supplier.

Suppliers
Suppliers furnish raw materials, processed goods, finished goods, power, funds, and other resources to the salesperson's organization. Knowing about suppliers can provide the representative with useful selling points, such as:

- The people who supply our coffee beans are family-owned businesses who take pride in the fact that they have been providing the best coffee beans for generations.

- This product carries our private brand. In reality, however, it is made by producer X (a large and well-known manufacturer).

- Some of our competitors put inexpensive domestic hops in their beers, but we don't. All our hops are imported.

- We can supply you with all the aluminum castings you need. Our relationships with suppliers are such that we can get all of the aluminum that we need. No competitor can say that.

- Our price is low, not because our quality is inferior but because we buy in quantity, and our suppliers give us quantity discounts.

Other Customers
In trying to sell to a particular target consumer, the sales representative may find it useful to employ information obtained from other current or prospective customers. For example:

- Several competing stores are carrying our brand. Perhaps you should consider doing likewise.

- I know you have doubts about dealing with us because our company is new in the area. But why don't you call Herman Lehman up in San Francisco? He's been a loyal customer for years and can tell you about the quality of our products and services.

- Your neighbor Mr. Strauss has an insurance policy with us. He suggested I call on you and show you the benefits that we can guarantee.

- Our tractors are very durable. I can give you the names and telephone numbers of several satisfied customers who have been using them for years.

Employees
Knowledge about the employees of the organization is an excellent source of appeals to customers. Since the purpose of the organization is to provide benefits to customers, each employee in some way contributes such benefits. Accordingly, some possible appeals are:

- We can probably offer you continuous service, since we haven't had a strike in decades. Our production workers are very loyal.

- Our servicemen have much better training than those of our competitor.

- Our products are of the highest quality since we employ skilled craftsmen rather than rely on an assembly line.

- If you buy from us you'll have our marketing research personnel at your disposal, who can conduct research showing where you should be putting your advertising dollars and what appeals to use in your advertising.

- Buying from our organization will affiliate you with some very talented people. Our advertising personnel, for instance, have won some of the top awards. Let me provide you with some examples.

## Government Agencies

Marketing activities are regulated by various federal, state, and local government agencies, and sales representatives need to be aware of the nature of the regulations or run the risk of legal fees, fines, even imprisonment, both for themselves and the organization. (Government regulation of personal selling is discussed in much more detail in chapter 14.)

## Financial Institutions

In some industries, knowledge of the offerings of financial institutions is a definite advantage. A seller of major equipment such as steam turbines must be well-versed on various types of financing and be able to bring expert advice to prospective customers who want to purchase equipment but who lack the knowledge required to carry out the financing.

Some sales transactions involve very large amounts of money. A buyer of a new plant or of large volumes of major equipment may be unable to make a purchase without selling capital stock or bonds. In these cases, sales representatives who possess knowledge about the equity (stock) and debt (bonds and notes) markets may have an edge over competitors who do not. The sales representatives need not be financial analysts to be competitive in this regard. If they can suggest means of financing—or bring in organization specialists who can provide expertise in financing—they can have the advantage.

Some organizations enjoy very good relations with financial institutions and are able to obtain capital relatively easy. This may be a selling point that the sales representative will choose to emphasize in talking with prospective customers, who may be so concerned with the solvency of their suppliers they will not want to enter into contracts with institutions they think might suffer financial hardship. Hence, evidence of good relations with financial institutions can be a definite selling point.

Others
Outside parties may be sources of information—people from advertising agencies, transportation, the media. The sales representative must determine which particular outside parties have inputs into his or her institution.

Summary
All employees of business and nonbusiness organizations need information, and sales representatives are no exception. Their work involves acquiring information, sorting out what is relevant, developing plans based upon the information, acting upon the plans, and changing plans based upon subsequent information.

Sales representatives require insights about target consumers. These insights are supplied by examining the ways in which management views target consumers. Specifically, the salesperson requires information on who are target consumers and what are their characteristics, the needs of target consumers, the products currently owned and used by target consumers, and who are the key decision makers.

Another type of information is about the organization for which the sales representative works. This information allows representatives to bring customers the benefits they seek, to effectively represent the organization to the public, and to advance in the organization.

The information about the organization the salesperson should have is of (1) organization products, (2) organization marketing strategy, (3) organization resources, (4) other departments, and (5) organization policies.

Sales representatives also require insights about the environment—competitors, suppliers, other customers, employees, government agencies, and financial institutions.

Discussion Questions

1. Describe the process of information acquisition and utilization that sales representatives undertake.

2. What information about target consumers should sales people seek?

3. Why should representatives acquire information about their organizations?

4. What should sales representatives know about the marketing strategy?

5. What should sales representatives know about organization resources?

6. What kind of information on products should sales representatives seek?

7. What kind of information regarding organization policies should sales representatives seek?

8. Indicate the facets of competitors that the sales representative should seek insights on.

9. How can the sales representative use information about organization employees?

10. Describe how information about financial institutions can be of value to sales representatives.

**Practical Exercises**

1. Go to a retail store and observe a sales person making a sales presentation. Did he or she appear to be adequately informed or supply additional information? What did you learn from this exercise?

2. Read a magazine advertisement for a product or service. Guess how the sponsor describes target consumers. How did you arrive at this conclusion? What did you learn from this exercise?

**Selling Project**

Indicate what information about the organization, the environment, and the target consumer you would need to prepare a personal selling program for your product.

**Case 4
The Cento
Manufacturing
Company**

This South Carolina firm sells a wide line of small electric motors to industry for use in such products as hair dryers, electric shavers, electric drills, and fans.

The financial position of the firm was stable for many years, but is showing some signs of weakening. In three years, sales have not grown as rapidly as have those of the industry at large. In two years profits have declined, primarily a result of large increases in the costs of materials and labor.

The Cento product line is very diverse. The company provides almost any kind of small electric motor that a manufacturer might need. Very astute buying and production methods have enabled this company to keep costs, and therefore prices, at levels lower than its main competitors. In recent years, however, costs have increased substantially.

This enterprise's sales force covers that part of the United States east of the Mississippi river. The force consists of 24 well trained representatives, who call upon manufacturers located in their respective territories.

Cento advertising is through trade magazines and a combination of company catalogs and brochures sent to prospective customers through the mail. The advertisements feature high product quality, low selling prices, and extensive technical expertise of company employees. Each advertisement presents considerable technical detail about the items in the product line. This is logical, according to the marketing manager, Mr. Spring, because most of those who do the buying of motors are technically trained and oriented.

The recent declines in sales and profits prompted Spring to ask the company marketing research director, Mr. Celeste, to undertake research designed to discover the reasons for the undesirable performance. Celeste found that competition in the industry had increased substantially over the past four years, that new rivals had entered the industry and old rivals were stepping up their efforts to be competitive. At the same time, Cento had done little to counteract these moves.

Spring decided that the best way to react to the competition was to improve the performance of the sales force. He felt that a good sales staff was the key to success in this industry. Spring therefore asked the sales manager, Mr. Abraham, to take steps that would lead to increased revenues per sales representative.

Abraham talked to members of the sales force and to some large customers on the telephone and in person. His objective was to discover means of improving the sales generating performance of the sales force. The outcome of the fact finding effort was the startling revelation that Cento sales representatives were not well-informed, in comparison with the representatives of competing companies. The essence of his finding is summed up by the statements of a long-standing customer:

> Your sales representatives simply do not know enough about what is going on at Cento and in the marketplace. Competing sales representatives are well informed regarding, the policies and activities of their firms and of competing firms. Yours do not appear to be so informed. This is reflected in their selling practices. They emphasize socializing—wining and dining—and friendships in their selling activities. This is fine, but such an approach does not take the place of providing informed advice as to what this and other companies have to offer.

> A case in point. Last week, I asked one of your representatives for information regarding the new "Long Life" product your advertisements have been featuring. The representative knew little about the performance of the product, how it was made, when it could be delivered, specific advantages of competing products, and a host of other points. He attempted to cover all of this up with invitations to take myself, my staff, and our spouses out for dinner. This approach just doesn't work.

Mr. Abraham has decided that he must institute a program to inform sales representatives. He is undecided, however, as to just what information should be provided.

1. Outline the essentials of what such a program should cover.

2. Indicate who in the organization is likely to be in a position to provide this information.

**Suggested Readings**   Buskirk, Richard H. *Principles of Marketing*. New York: Holt, Rinehart and Winston, 1975, ch. 27.

Comer, James M. "The Computer, Personal Selling, and Sales Management," *Journal of Marketing* 39, no. 3 (July 1975): 27–33.

Dunn, Albert H., Eugene M. Johnson, and David L. Kurtz. *Sales Management: Concepts, Practices, and Cases*. Morristown, N.J.: General Learning Press, 1974, chs. 3 and 10.

Hanan, Mark. *Life-Styled Marketing*. New York: American Management Association, 1972.

Hisrich, Robert D., and Michael P. Peters. "Selecting the Superior Segmentation Correlate," *Journal of Marketing* 38, no. 3 (July 1974): 60–63.

Levitt, Theodore. *Marketing for Business Growth*. New York: McGraw-Hill Book Company, 1974, ch. 7.

Lipson, Harry A., and John R. Darling. *Marketing Fundamentals: Text and Cases*. New York: John Wiley & Sons, 1974, pp. 64–82.

Reynolds, Fred P., and William R. Darden. "Intermarket Patronage: A Psychographic Study of Consumer Outshopping," *Journal of Marketing* 36, no. 4 (October 1972): 50–54.

Schwartz, David J. *Marketing Today: A Basic Approach*. New York: Harcourt Brace Jovanovich, 1977, ch. 2.

Stidsen, Bent, and Thomas F. Schutte. "Marketing as a Communication System: The Marketing Concept Revisited," *Journal of Marketing* 36, no. 4 (October 1972): 22–27.

Twedt, Dik Warren. "How Important to Marketing Strategy Is the Heavy User?" *Journal of Marketing* 28, no. 1 (January 1964): 71–72.

# 5

# Finding Prospects

*After reading this chapter you should be able to demonstrate a knowledge of:*

- *what is meant by the term* prospecting
- *the importance of prospecting to sales representatives*
- *the kinds of information sought in prospecting*
- *various prospecting methods*
- *the process of maintaining prospecting records*

A new sales representative who is not adequately skilled in prospecting may waste considerable periods of time calling on the wrong prospective customers. Consider the case of Al Jones, who decided to go into business for himself selling semiprecious stones, which he cut, polished, and mounted in rings. Al's first month of selling was not very successful, because the method of prospecting he used was not suited to his selling task. Here is what happened:

- One prospective customer contacted was a jewelry store owner. She revealed that she purchased only from well established suppliers, and would never consider buying from a newcomer. Still, Al called upon her several times, in a futile attempt to change her mind.

- Another prospective customer, a gift shop owner, already had a wide line of semiprecious stone jewelry and had no shelf space for more. He did not make a purchase, even after Al had called upon him four times.

- A third prospective customer, another jewelry store owner, did not carry and refused to even consider semiprecious stone jewelry. Al called upon this individual three times before deciding there was no point in making further visits.

- The fourth prospective customer, a variety store manager, could not buy from Al since all company purchasing was accomplished by professional buyers in the home office. If Al had acquired this information over the telephone, through the manager's secretary, he could have saved the time and effort of making even one call.

- The fifth prospective customer, a gift shop manager, was interested in the line but turned out to have such a poor credit rating that Al could not risk granting credit to the store. He could have obtained the credit rating from a credit bureau before making a call, thus saving considerable time and effort.

Al's first month in business was not very productive. One of the major reasons for this was that he failed to take advantage of various prospecting methods that would have enabled him to seek out the right potential customers to serve. In this chapter we will examine various alternate means of prospecting and point out their significance to sales representatives.

**What Prospecting Is**

In the mining field, prospecting means "to search for or explore (a region) for gold or other mineral deposits."[1] Mining prospectors do not ordinarily waste their time looking for minerals in sites that are likely to be barren of deposits. Rather, they utilize information, such as reports of seismologists and observation of the topography, in order to select out the more worthy sites for further exploration. In a sense, sales representatives become involved in much the same process. In personal selling prospecting means locating and selecting potential customers who:

1. have a need for the salesperson's product, and

2. are able to purchase.

---

[1] *The American Heritage Dictionary of the English Language* (New York: American Heritage Publishing Co., 1973), p. 1050.

Both of these elements are useful in qualifying "good prospects." A sales representative may find that, out of 100 possible prospective customers, only 60 have a need for the product. Out of these 60, perhaps only 50 are able to purchase and, as a result, are good prospects (see Figure 5-1).

**Figure 5-1. Specification of need and ability to purchase of 100 possible prospects.**

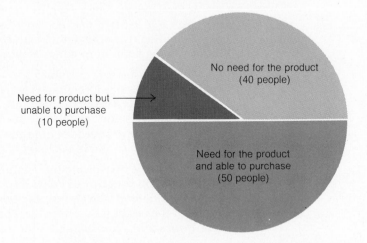

No need for the product
(40 people)

Need for product but unable to purchase
(10 people)

Need for the product and able to purchase
(50 people)

Representatives sometimes are able to determine whether individuals or organizations are good prospects without calling on them, instead examining written documents and having conversations with company and outside personnel. This is not always the case, however. Often the sales representative must make at least one call to determine if the individual or firm is a very good prospect who should be called upon frequently, a good prospect who deserves some attention, or a poor prospect who should be called upon infrequently or not at all.

Need for the Salespersons Product

Potential customers who have a need for the products and services offered by the sales representative are in a position to use the goods and services to satisfy their own objectives. Al Jones's first four calls were made upon firms that had no need for his semiprecious stones. With effective prospecting, Al could have detected this lack of need and eliminated the four firms from his prospect list.

The marketing concept means that all marketing personnel, including sales representatives, must strive for customer satisfaction. It is doubtful that satisfaction can be fulfilled when the buyers have no need for the salesperson's products. Customers might be induced to buy an unneeded product once,

Chapter 5 Finding Prospects

but find it was not useful to them and should not be purchased again—and this certainly will not help the sales representative with that buyer in the future. For instance, once a food wholesaler representative called upon the relatively inexperienced new owner-manager of a small rural grocery store. The representative was trying to get rid of an oversupply of canned peaches and so made a strong appeal to the store owner. Although the owner did not feel the peaches would sell well in his area, he finally yielded and bought several cases. Barely any of the peaches were sold during the following year, and the grocer's family literally had to eat his mistake. Needless to say, the representative was not welcome to call back at the store.

Ability to Purchase  The second requirement of a good prospect is ability to purchase. A need for the product may exist, but this is not sufficient if ability to pay is absent. This ability is measured by the prospect's assets relative to debts, revenue earning capability, borrowing ability, and authority to purchase. Al Jones's fifth prospect did not have the ability to purchase, as revealed by the credit rating. A sale to this customer might have resulted in a future bad debt for Al.

**Importance of**
**Prospecting**
Loss of Old Customers

It might appear that once a sales representative has been selling long enough to know his or her customers, prospecting can stop. This is not true. Prospecting is a continual process. While past customers often make up a large proportion of a sales representative's current prospects, old customers may also go out of business, change locations, switch their patronage to other suppliers, and make other moves that necessitate their replacement with new prospects. Most companies, according to one authority, "will continue to do business with the same suppliers until they are taken for granted or no longer receive the service or quality they are paying for."[2] As a result, the sales representative is well advised to continually develop and renovate the prospect list.

Variations in
Importance by Industry

The total amount of effort that sales representatives devote to prospecting varies from one industry to another. One study showed the following percentage of representatives' time spent on the prospecting function:[3]

---

[2]"Marketing Mix," *Industrial Marketing*, August 1972, p. 14.
[3]Marvin A. Jolson, "Standardizing the Personal Selling Process," *Marquette Business Review* 18, no. 1 (Spring 1974): 18.

| | |
|---|---|
| Department stores | 1% |
| Industrial packaging manufacturers | 3% |
| Distributors of gift items | 17% |
| Insurance companies | 31% |

The differences are readily explainable. Customers of department stores go to the store to shop or purchase, oftentimes in response to store ads, favorable comments of friends, or past experience. Here, salespersons often confine their prospecting efforts to sizing up browsers and picking the best prospects from this group. Industrial packaging manufacturers' salespersons call upon a group of potential customers that is relatively unchanging. Entry into and exit from the customers' industries is less extensive than in many other industries. Distributors of gift items face the opposite situation. Their prospect list must be revamped continually. Finally, insurance sales representatives must constantly seek out new prospects. Their compensation plans require that they continually seek out new prospects as well as serve old customers at the same time.

## Maintaining and Increasing Productivity

Prospecting is one of the major ways of making the efforts of the sales representative most productive. Prospecting not only helps eliminate or reduce the number of calls upon those who are not good possible customers. Prospecting is also a good source of information, which, as was stressed in the preceding chapter, the sales representative can use to develop programs that are likely to be effective in fulfilling customer needs. As we will show in later chapters, effective sales representatives are viewed by their customers as advisors, joint problem solvers, and sometimes as friends.

A realtor who employs information derived from prospecting to better serve target consumers looks for the following kinds of data:

- names of community residents who are looking or might be looking in the near future for properties;
- current address and telephone number;
- age, size, and other characteristics of current residence;
- type and location of residence desired.

With these facts the realtor is in a position to contact potential customers and often help them in locating a desired property. One month, for instance, he made the following contact, based upon prospecting-derived information:

REALTOR: Good morning, Mr. McCall. It has come to my attention, through a mutual friend, that you are looking for a lakeside home.

PROSPECT: Yes, we'd like to get on a lake. Both my wife and I like sailing and other water sports and enjoy the beauty of the water.

REALTOR: Yet, your present home is located at some distance from any body of water, I understand.

PROSPECT: You're right, and it's inconvenient. Does your realty list property that might satisfy our needs?

REALTOR: Definitely. Let me describe several and give you some photographs of them. We can visit those you like.

As this incident shows, prospects are likely to be impressed by a representative who is aware of their needs. They view such a representative as a source of help for problems and as a purposeful and resourceful individual. Prospects are therefore likely to be cooperative and receptive to the appeals of the sales representative.

Information derived from prospecting helps salespersons plan the details of the sales presentation. They can then tailor their presentations to the specific desires of the prospect, which is more effective than a canned presentation that may or may not be relevant to the prospect. The realtor knew what kind of property McCall wanted and was ready to show some specific properties that had the desired attributes. An uninformed representative would not be so prepared.

**Four Steps in Prospecting**

Figure 5-2 outlines four steps involved in prospecting. Salespersons (1) determine the types of information needed, (2) determine the prospecting methods to be employed, (3) gather the information, and (4) after using it place some of it in prospect records. These four steps are discussed below.

**Figure 5-2. Four steps involved in prospecting.**

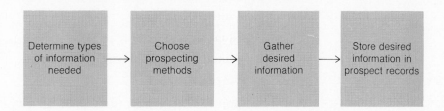

Determine types of information needed → Choose prospecting methods → Gather desired information → Store desired information in prospect records

**What Information to Seek in Prospecting**

Sales representatives seek prospecting information that will enable them to:

1. identify and locate potential customers;

2. design an effective sales presentation;

3. evaluate prospective customer need for the product;

4. evaluate prospective customer ability to purchase.

The specific information sought varies from one sales position to another. Representatives for a manufacturer of duplicating machines, for instance, are required to maintain a card file of prospects, as illustrated in Figure 5-3, which gives information on a hypothetical prospect, John Martin. The first three items (name, location, and telephone number) permit sales representatives to identify and locate potential customers. The next fourteen items are useful in designing effective sales presentations. The sales representatives can utilize some of these items to evaluate *need for the product:*

- type of business;
- type of target consumers;
- current duplicating problems;
- machines currently used;
- evaluation of machines;
- customer or noncustomer in the past;
- if noncustomer, likely reasons;
- friendliness, courtesy, and cooperation on past sales calls.

The following variables can be used to evaluate *ability to purchase:*

- type of business;
- approximate number of employees;
- type of target consumers;
- major competitors;
- machines currently used;
- likely current financial position;
- credit rating.

John Martin was identified as a very good potential customer. He possessed a product need and an ability to purchase. Further, the prospect file provided the information needed to design an effective sales presentation for him. He was clearly dissatisfied with the currently used brand of competing ma-

PROSPECT FILE

1. Name of prospect: *John Martin, Martin's Department Store*

2. Business location: *1104 S. 109th St., Minneapolis, Minn. 56401*

3. Telephone number: *612-816-2302*

4. Type of business: *Department store*

5. Job title of prospect: *President and General Manager*

6. Approximate number of employees: *35*

7. Product line: *Specializes in furniture and appliances*

8. Type of target consumers: *Upper income*

9. Major competitors: *Sears; Findel's Department Store*

10. Current duplicating problems: *Machines too slow, frequent breakdowns.*

11. Machines currently used: *Ajax SL-4800*

12. Evaluation of machines: *They aren't satisfactory.*

13. Likely current financial position: *Appears to be profitable*

14. Credit rating: *Excellent*

15. Customer or noncustomer in the past: *Non-customer*

16. If noncustomer, likely reasons: *Not sufficiently familiar with our line.*

17. Friendliness, courtesy, and cooperation on past sales calls: *Very amiable and cooperative.*

chines and purchased the firm's brand after being visited by a sales representative.

**Methods of Prospecting**

This section describes particular methods that can be used in the prospecting process: (1) examining written documents, (2) observation, (3) cold canvass, (4) the referral approach, (5) the introduction method, (6) follow-up of advertisements, (7) observing news stories, (8) community contacts, (9) contacting groups, (10) the intelligence method, (11) trade shows, and (12) empathy prospecting.

Sometimes good prospects can be located through a perusal of written documents, including the following:

1. *Company records.* This includes information in organization data banks that can provide a very extensive profile of the characteristics of prospects.[4] Less sophisticated company records may consist of lists and/or files of prospects and credit records. Some concerns utilize systems in which representatives of various divisions can pass on leads to others.[5]

2. *Directories.* These provide the names, addresses, and other basic information about individuals or organizations belonging to the association sponsoring the directory or are listed for some other reason.

3. *Telephone books.* The Yellow Pages can be especially useful for classifying prospects.

4. *Published membership lists of associations.* This includes membership lists of trade associations.

5. *List brokers.* These firms collect and sell lists of individuals with specified characteristics, such as lists of public school teachers.

Observation

Observation is the process of looking and listening for evidence of the existence of good prospects. A salesman in a men's clothing store, for instance, is in a good position to utilize observation. Men entering the store who are in the middle and lower age range and who are well dressed might be identified as good prospects.

A seller of heavy-duty construction machinery can also use observation. For instance, in talking to a foreman employed by a local construction company he might find that top management is unhappy with the maintenance of its equipment and that it is not holding up under normal operating conditions. He might therefore be able to sell them a number of units of his own firm's heavy equipment, if it has a good record of few breakdowns on the job.

A wholesale jewelry saleswoman might shop jewelry stores and gift shops from time to time, looking to see which currently offered product lines are not complete. If particular stores lack products, styles, colors, size ranges, or other varieties that her

---

[4]James M. Comer, "The Computer, Personal Selling, and Sales Management," *Journal of Marketing* 39, no. 3 (July 1975): 29.
[5]"The Rollins Connection," *Sales Management* 108, no. 9 (May 1972): 7.

Chapter 5  Finding Prospects

firm offers, the saleswoman knows she has identified a possible prospect.

Cold Canvass

Under the cold canvass method, the sales representative calls upon every possible customer that is located in a given geographic area. In most cases, the representative has little or no information regarding the characteristics and desires of the prospect. Frequently canned sales presentations are employed in conjunction with the cold canvass. This method of prospecting is perhaps best known for its use in door-to-door personal selling to ultimate consumers.

The cold canvass method is not new. Henry John Heinz (founder of the familiar H. J. Heinz Company) made his first major sale in England by calling, on a cold canvass basis, upon "the largest house supplying the fine trade of London and suburbs and even shipping."[6] This sales call was successful and was instrumental in launching the Heinz firm in England.

Representatives of the Realsilk Clothing Company employ the cold canvass. These personnel sell a variety of clothing items to ultimate consumers. Typically, sales representatives are allowed considerable freedom in choosing the neighborhoods in which they sell. The recommended procedure is simply to start at one home, attempt a sale there, then move to the next and other homes down the street. It is expected that, out of every ten homes approached, the representative will be allowed by prospects to make four sales presentations. Out of the four presentations, two are expected to lead to sales.

Cold canvassing is a difficult method of prospecting. Many of the contacts are wasted, because the prospects cannot be qualified (identified as a good prospect) in advance of the sales call. The sales representative has little or no advance information on the prospect, so customized sales presentations are not likely.[7] In addition, cold canvassers are often met with hostility.

Some firms, such as the Fuller Brush Company, have been successful with cold canvassing. Stockbrokers can also benefit by this technique, by, say, canvassing a list of executives with

---

[6]Robert C. Alberts, "Those 57 Varieties of Selling Know-How," *Marketing Times* 21, no. 3 (May/June 1974): 20–23.

[7]It is possible, under some circumstances, for cold canvassers to obtain advance information on prospects. A door-to-door representative, for instance, knows something about the prospects in a neighborhood, based upon visual inspection of the homes in the neighborhood and perhaps upon census data that report income and other characteristics of various areas.

an income tax deferred plan that they believe would interest the executives. In addition, various charitable organizations, such as the March of Dimes, have used cold canvassing to advantage. Consumer hostility to charitable institutions would appear to be less than to business firms, particularly where the objectives of the charity are held in esteem.

The Referral Approach

Under the referral approach, salespersons ask each person they call on to provide the names of friends, acquaintances, and associates who might be interested in the product or service. A life insurance salesperson uses this technique, by asking for referrals at the end of his sales presentations, as follows:

SALESPERSON: Well, this has been an interesting discussion. I'm glad that you have taken a policy with our company.

PROSPECT: Yes, I think you have the best coverage at the lowest cost.

SALESPERSON: Before I go, could you give me the names of any friends or acquaintances who might be interested in a policy with us? You know I can give them insurance coverage superior to that of our competitors, as in your case.

PROSPECT: If you'll give me a sheet of paper, I can give you several names.

The referral approach can be a quick, inexpensive way of acquiring a large group of prospects. As Figure 5-4 illustrates, the number of prospects can build up rapidly. In the illustration, the sales representative has only one prospect, prospect A. However, this prospect provides the names of two friends, B and C, who in turn supply the names of their friends. The outcome is a total of seventeen prospects, and the number will continue to expand, as long as the sales representative continues to ask for new names on each sales call.

Another value of this method, of course, is that sales representatives can use the name of the referrer when they contact new prospects, and the use of a familiar name may be useful in capturing the interest and trust of a prospective customer. For example:

SALESPERSON: Good morning. I'm with Boeing Computer Services, Inc. We specialize in training data processing personnel. A friend of yours, Bob Thompson at Raider Manufacturing Company, decided to use our services and he suggested you also might be interested in a training program.

**Figure 5-4. Chain of prospects from A to Q.**

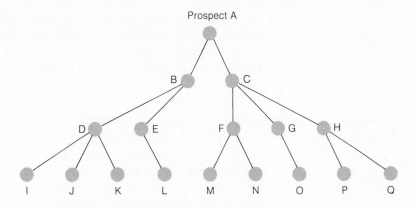

PROSPECT: It's a possibility.

SALESPERSON: Good. Let me go over the main features of some of our programs. First I'll cover the benefits to you, then the costs.

PROSPECT: Sounds like a good idea.

The Introduction Method

In the introduction method, which is an extension of the referral method, prospects introduce the sales representative to other prospects through such means as a letter, a memo or short note, a telephone call, or a personal introduction.

An introduction can be very useful to a salesperson. It is evidence that the prospect making the introduction has some respect for or confidence in the representative, or else he would presumably not be furnishing the introduction. Accordingly, this method is a good way of acquiring the attention, interest, and confidence of potential new customers.

A furniture saleswoman has made good use of introductions to get to know department store buyers. She has found that the buyers in her territory know each other well, both on a professional and on a social plane. This gives the introductions special credibility. Sometimes the introductions are only a short note, such as the following from the buyer at one department store to the buyer at another:

Dear Mary,

I'm sure that you'll find Jill to be very helpful. She's sharp, honest, and a good friend.

Let's get together for lunch sometime soon.

Best, Shelley

Telephone and personal introductions are also useful to this sales representative. Frequently, she takes buyers out for lunch, normally at restaurants that other buyers frequent, so she finds that many of the lunches result in introductions to buyers that she had not met before.

## Follow-up of Advertisements

Inquiries to advertisements are a good source of prospects. The Hewlett-Packard Corporation, for instance, engages in considerable advertising of its electronic calculators in trade and general business magazines. Those readers of the advertisements who are interested in the products are asked to write their names, addresses, and company names on an inquiry format included in the advertisements and to forward the inquiries to Hewlett-Packard. In turn, the inquiries are useful sources of leads to sales representatives.

Often, people who read advertisements will write in and ask for information even when the advertisement does not request inquiries. Thus, suggests the president of O. S. Tyson and Company, companies should "try to use advertising to find out who is interested—to filter out genuine prospects, cultivate those prospects, and make them whistle for your salesmen."[8]

Realtors are extensive users of the follow-up method as a means of generating prospects. Frequently, listed properties are described in newspaper advertisements. People interested in the properties telephone, write, or visit the real estate offices to obtain more information. Such inquirers are often good prospects, because they have demonstrated an interest in a particular site.

## Observing News Stories

A useful technique is to follow news stories in magazines, newspapers, and other publications. Birth announcements indicate good prospects for the sellers of baby needs. Marriage announcements list prospects for life insurance and other "new family" needs. Articles in business publications sometimes suggest that particular firms have specific needs that the salesperson might satisfy (such as reducing operating costs through the use of new production control systems). A subscription to a magazine or newspaper containing news about possible prospects can be an invaluable asset to the salesperson.

---

[8]"Marketing Mix," *Industrial Marketing*, November 1972, p. 42.

**Community Contact Method**

In the community contact method, the salesperson relies upon individuals who have wide contacts with other members of the community containing good potential prospects. The following are logical contacts:

- bank executives;
- successful business personnel;
- chamber of commerce officers;
- service club officers;
- political candidates;
- those who are active in civic affairs;
- sports figures;
- attorneys.

Every community has opinion leaders whose ideas and behavior are emulated by others, and these people tend to have widespread contacts with other individuals.[9] Community leaders are in frequent touch with numerous persons, many of whom may be good prospects.

In some cases, community leaders and other contacts will furnish names of possible customers, as in the referral method. In others, the contacts will go a step further and furnish letters, telephone call testimonials, or personal introductions.

A representative who sells business forms uses the community contact method. He is in frequent touch with community leaders at service club and civic meetings and in informal lunches and coffee breaks. Frequently, these meetings will produce notices of new prospects, such as the following at a coffee break:

ATTORNEY: Have you met any of the Acme Corporation personnel yet? They're moving their corporate headquarters here, you know.

SALESPERSON: No, I didn't know.

ATTORNEY: You should get in touch with them. They'll be looking for a local supply of business forms. Why don't you call Ralph Barlow, the office manager. Mention my name—Ralph and I are good friends.

SALESPERSON: Thanks for the lead. I'll call him this afternoon.

---

[9]Rom J. Markin, Jr., *Consumer Behavior: A Cognitive Orientation* (New York: Macmillan Publishing Co. 1974), pp. 322–25.

Introductions from community contacts are especially useful when sales representatives and/or their organizations are new to the community. Newcomers have not had the time to build up trust and confidence and may have difficulty in attracting the interest of prospects. If the sales representative can convince a banker or some other leader that the new organization promises genuine benefits to the community, very useful introductions may be forthcoming.

Contacting Groups

For some organizations, prospects can be derived by contacting groups made up of people who might be potential customers. Examples of such groups are:

- chambers of commerce;
- advertising clubs;
- service clubs;
- fraternal orders (such as the Elks);
- professional associations (such as the local life insurance underwriters association);
- church organizations.

The general manager of a metropolitan transit system (city bus system) is very involved in contacting groups because it is his job to persuade city residents to ride buses rather than use other transportation. Periodically, the manager obtains permission to speak to groups, such as college students and labor unions, on the benefits of riding the buses. He has found such group contacts valuable in building ridership for the bus system.

Intelligence Method

In the intelligence method, salespeople contact target personnel in the prospect organization to seek information with which they can qualify the organization and thereby plan a custom-tailored presentation. The information they need relates to organization objectives, resources, problems, performance, and personnel.

This method often necessitates contacting many people. During the representative's fact-finding endeavors, an office machines salesman for instance, must talk to a lot of secretaries, office workers, office managers, and purchasing personnel of prospect organizations. Often he finds that one person does not have needed information, but can steer him on to another who does. One office worker may not know how long the type-writers have been in use by the organization, but can suggest that the representative talk to someone who does. The salesman uses the intelligence method to provide information on the:

- type of business;
- size of business;
- type of office machines currently used;
- degree of satisfaction with these machines;
- office machine needs;
- current and expected future financial position.

With this information, the salesman can qualify prospects and plan his sales presentations. Recently, he found as a result of the intelligence method, that a large food processing firm was unhappy with the typewriters it was using. In conversations with several secretaries he learned the typewriters often did not turn out the copy in a form that met the specifications of the office manager. The salesman therefore put together a presentation emphasizing the impressive output of his firm's type-writers, and ultimately this led to a sale and substantial repeat business.

The intelligence method has a danger. The process of contacting various organization personnel and asking them questions may arouse suspicion on the part of buyers and other employees. Consequently, salespeople need to conduct themselves professionally and with tact.

Trade Shows    Various trade and professional groups hold conferences and other meetings to bring together groups and people working in the same professional area. These trade shows present opportunities for organizations selling to the group's members to contact possible prospects. The sellers can set up booths or exhibits to display products and other information. Exhibits of tools are available at the Society of Manufacturing Engineers' meetings, for instance. Manufacturers who sell home furnishings can display their offerings to prospective buyers at the Chicago Home Furnishings and Floor Covering show. Those who visit exhibits are given literature and sales presentations and are encouraged to fill out forms indicating their interest in the sponsoring organization and its products. Many of these inquiries turn out to be a good means of unearthing prospects.

**Empathy Prospecting**

Empathy refers to the ability to put oneself in another's shoes. Empathetic sales representatives are able to mentally imagine themselves to be in the position of prospects and to experience their goals, problems, environment, and values. The sales representative who has empathy is in possession of one of the important requisites to effective communication.[10]

Empathy prospecting begins by identifying possible prospects. The identification process might be carried out by observation, the referral approach, or other prospecting methods mentioned in this chapter. Once the representative has completed the identification, he or she can utilize empathy as an aid to qualifying the potential prospects and to planning sales presentations.

A seller of desk-top computing systems employs the empathy technique to imagine he is in the position of each potential prospect. He asks himself, for instance:

Would I really want to purchase one of our desk-top computing systems if I were this prospect?

Would I have the ability to pay for a system?

What could a sales representative do to gain my attention and interest, if I were the prospect?

What appeals would be effective in convincing me that this brand is superior to others?

What data processing problems experienced by the prospect could be solved or alleviated by owning and using the system?

What objections to the system might I have?

What criteria might I use in evaluating the system, the sales representative, and the company?

The salesman cannot answer these questions definitively, of course, but by putting himself in the potential prospect's place he can produce informed guesses as to probable answers. He has found that this mental process is a useful supplement to other prospecting methods.

Like most other representatives, he does not rely solely upon this or any other one method. The key to prospecting is often in utilizing a combination of methods that fit a particular sales representative representing a particular organization and confronted with a particular environment.

---

[10]James F. Engel, David T. Kollat, and Roger D. Blackwell, *Consumer Behavior* (New York: Holt, Rinehart and Winston, 1973), p. 309.

Figure 5-5. File form
maintained by Ivan
for each prospect.

```
┌──────────────────────────────────────────────────────────────┐
│                                                                │
│                    PROSPECT FILE ENTRY                         │
│                                                                │
│       Prospect name:_____         │
│                                                                │
│       Address: _____         │
│                                                                │
│       Telephone number:_____         │
│                                                                │
│       Position in organization: _____         │
│                                                                │
│       Type of business:_____         │
│                                                                │
│       Major problems:_____         │
│                                                                │
│       _____         │
│                                                                │
│       _____         │
│                                                                │
│       Competitors: _____         │
│                                                                │
│       Credit rating: _____         │
│                                                                │
│       Brands of trucks currently used:_____          │
│                                                                │
│       _____         │
│                                                                │
│       Number of trucks owned: _____         │
│                                                                │
│       Number of each size:                                     │
│                                                                │
│            Heavy duty: _____                   │
│                                                                │
│            Middleweight: _____                   │
│                                                                │
│                                                                │
│       Date of last visit:_____         │
│                                                                │
│       Results of last visit:_____         │
│                                                                │
│       _____         │
│                                                                │
│       _____         │
│                                                                │
│       Comments:_____         │
│                                                                │
│       _____         │
│                                                                │
│       _____         │
│                                                                │
│       _____         │
│                                                                │
│       _____         │
│                                                                │
└──────────────────────────────────────────────────────────────┘
```

**Maintaining
Prospecting
Records**

It is vital that sales representatives maintain records of the prospects they have identified. Records enable the representatives to draw upon past experience and to plan current efforts accordingly. The records should include a file, card, or other form of entry for each potential and actual customer.

Figure 5-5 outlines the nature of the file form utilized by Ivan, the representative who sells heavy-duty and medium-weight trucks to owners of fleets. The form provides spaces for recording the prospect name, address and telephone number, position, type of business, major problems, competitors, credit rating, brand of trucks owned, and the results of the last sales visit. Ivan refers to the files in determining what prospects to call upon at a given time, and in planning the composition of the sales presentation.

**Summary**    Prospecting consists of locating and selecting for sales presentations individuals who both have a need for the salesperson's offerings and are able to purchase. Prospecting is a very important activity. Each year, some old customers are lost. If they are not replaced by new customers, that affects sales revenues.

The amount of time and effort devoted to prospecting varies from one selling position to another. Reasons for emphasis upon prospecting include large turnover among firms in the target consumer group and policies of supplier organizations.

Sales representatives can increase their productivity through prospecting. It reduces unproductive calls and allows the salesperson to plan sales presentations based upon information about individual prospects. Prospecting yields various types of information, which allow a representative to:

1. identify and locate potential customers;

2. design an effective sales presentation;

3. evaluate the prospect's need for the salesperson's product; and

4. evaluate the prospect's ability to purchase.

There are several specific prospecting methods, including the following, outlined in this chapter:

1. Examining written documents—such as company records, directories, telephone books, published membership lists of associations, and list brokers.

2. Observation—looking and listening for evidence of prospects.

3. Cold canvass—Calling upon every possible customer that is located in a given geographic area.

4. Referrals—Asking each prospect called upon to provide names of friends, acquaintances, and associates who might be interested in the product or service.

5. Introductions—Asking each prospect called upon to provide introductions to other prospects.

6. Follow-up of advertisements—Calling upon inquirers to advertisements.

7. Observing news stories—Looking for possible prospects in the reports of magazines, newspapers, and other publications.

8. Community contacts—Asking those who have widespread contact with other members of the community for names of prospects and introductions.

9. Contacting groups—Making presentations to groups of potential prospects and taking the names of group members who are interested in the organization.

10. Intelligence method—Obtaining prospecting information through employees of the potential-prospect organization.

11. Trade shows—identifying possible prospects through inquiries generated by exhibitions at trade shows.

12. Empathy prospecting—Putting oneself in the position of potential prospects and mentally experiencing their goals, problems, environment, and values.

Sales representatives should maintain records of the prospects they have identified. These records, which can appear in files, cards, or other forms, are useful in determining which prospects to call upon at a given time and in planning the nature of the sales presentation.

**Discussion Questions**

1. What is prospecting? What information does the sales representative seek in prospecting?
2. Indicate why prospecting is important to the sales representative.
3. Describe the observation method of prospecting.
4. What is meant by a cold canvass? What are some of the difficulties associated with this method?
5. Outline the essentials of the referral approach to prospecting. What are the advantages of this technique?
6. How does the introduction method differ from the referral method?
7. How does the sales representative prospect through follow-up of advertisements?
8. Set forth the essentials of the community-contact prospecting technique.
9. How can prospecting be accomplished through contacting groups?
10. Describe the essentials of the intelligence method of prospecting. What is the danger of this technique?
11. How are prospects derived through trade shows?
12. Outline the main elements of empathy prospecting.
13. Why should records of prospects be maintained?

**Practical Exercises**

1. Assume you are selling aluminum cans for a manufacturer. What prospecting methods would you utilize?

2. Assume you are the administrative aide to the mayor of a large city. The mayor wants a domed sports arena constructed in the city for the use of a local professional football team and other sports groups. In order to fund a bond issue for the stadium, certain target consumers (politicians, journalists, sports figures, community leaders, and businessmen) must be "sold" on the project through personal selling. What prospecting methods would you employ?

**Selling Project**

1. What prospecting methods would you utilize for your product? Explain why you would employ these particular ones.

2. What prospect records would you utilize for your product?

**Case 5**
**John Hodge**

John Hodge is a salesman for the Lynn Distributing Company, headquartered in St. Louis. The firm is a wholesaler that supplies building materials to lumber yards, building material dealers, hardware stores, and contractors in the midwest portion of the United States. The product line is wide, including lumber, roofing materials, floor and wall tile products, nails, cabinet hardware, paints, roof drains, and insulation. The firm is price competitive. It attempts to keep price levels near and sometimes below the industry average.

Lynn Distributing has a sales force made up of twelve people, each of responsible for calling on target consumers in a designated geographical territory. John covers Missouri and a small part of Kansas.

Lynn has been financially successful over the years, and company sales and profits have increased at a faster pace than that of the industry average. According to the president of the firm, the primary reason for the success is the outstanding sales force.

John joined Lynn as a sales trainee a year ago, and after six months was appointed a salesman. Since that time, his progress has been good but not outstanding. He has met his sales quotas, but only by slim margins and in the process incurred heavy traveling and entertainment expenses.

When he was made salesman, John was given the prospect list of his predecessor, which set forth those dealers the latter had developed in five years of serving the territory. The list also indicated how successful the predecessor had been in obtaining the business of each prospect. John's sales manager had instructed him to concentrate on the established accounts on the list during his first year. "Don't worry about prospecting until you get your feet wet," the manager said. "During your second year you can begin the development of new accounts."

John is now beginning his second year of personal selling. He wonders what prospecting methods would best enable him to develop a prospect list.

Outline your recommendations as to useful prospecting methods.

**Suggested Readings**

*Appraising the Market for New Industrial Products,* the Conference Board, Studies in Business Policy, Chicago, no. 123, 1967.

Carney, G. "Finding New Sales and Profits with Your Present Customers," *Sales Management* 107, no. 8 (1 April 1971): 17–20.

Dunn, Albert H., Eugene M. Johnson, and David L. Kurtz. *Sales Management: Concepts, Practices, and Cases.* Morristown, N.J.: General Learning Press, 1974, pp. 88–96.

Cateora, Philip R., and John M. Hess. *International Marketing.* Homewood, Ill.: Richard D. Irwin, 1971, pp. 815–48.

Hill, Richard M., Ralph S. Alexander, and James S. Cross. *Industrial Marketing.* Homewood, Ill.: Richard D. Irwin, 1975, ch. 8.

James, Don L., Bruce J. Walker, and Michael J. Etzel. *Retailing Today: An Introduction.* New York: Harcourt Brace Jovanovich, 1975, pp. 56–69.

"Mallory's Salesmen Double Up." *Sales Management* 108, no. 7 (3 April 1972): 8, 13.

Reynolds, William H. *Products and Markets.* New York: Appleton-Century Crofts, 1969, pp. 150–63.

Risley, George. *Modern Industrial Marketing: A Decision-making Approach.* New York: McGraw-Hill Book Company, 1972, pp. 122–29.

Still, Richard R. and Edward W. Cundiff. *Sales Management: Decisions, Policies, and Cases.* Englewood Cliffs, N.J.: Prentice-Hall, 1976, pp. 56–59.

Vreeland, Richard C. "Customers: A Neglected Sales Force," *Small Marketers' Aids,* no. 83 (September 1962): 1–2.

# 6

# Planning the Sales Presentation

*After reading this chapter you should be able to demonstrate a knowledge of:*

- *the importance of planning for sales presentations*
- *the process of planning for sales presentations*
- *orientation of the plan to the prospect*
- *obtaining preapproach information*
- *essentials of planning and strategy formulation*

New sales representatives are likely to have the impression that once they have information about the prospect organization, the environment, and target consumers, they are ready to sell. This is not the case. First they must carefully plan sales presentations for their individual prospects. They need to determine the objective of the sales call and how that objective is to be attained. In other words, they need to know in advance what steps to include in the presentation.

This chapter describes the importance of planning the sales presentation and outlines the planning process. It also emphasizes the need for orienting the plan to the prospect and obtaining information about the prospect to include in the plan.

**Importance of Planning**

Before making a sales presentation the sales representative should have a predetermined plan as to just what is going to take place. The value of having a plan has been described by one authority as follows:[1]

> You know what you are going to say and how you are going to say it. You do not mumble, you do not ramble, and you do not stumble. You speak with command . . . it makes you positive and vital. It gives you self-confidence and an air of assurance. . . . Your sales approach loses its mechanical aspect. It becomes a living force.

Failure to have a plan can lead to situations such as the following:

SALESPERSON: Good afternoon, Mr. Breech. I'm Brad Edwards from the Sombus Company.

PROSPECT: The name is Beech, not Breech.
SALESPERSON: This product will definitely sell to teenagers.

PROSPECT: Most of my customers are middle-aged and older. I don't want a product that will bring noisy teenagers into my store.

SALESPERSON: Want to talk about the product over a beer?

PROSPECT: I don't drink and don't hang around people who do.

SALESPERSON: We can supply you with our service for only $350 per month. You can't do better than that.

PROSPECT: Already I'm getting the same thing from the Oeta Corporation for $240 per month. Are you sure $350 is right?

SALESPERSON: If you'll just sign here, I can get an order in for you by next week.

PROSPECT: I don't want to be rushed. I'll sign if and when I'm good and ready.

Effective planning can decrease the probability of such embarrassing situations.

---

[1]Earl Prevette, "How to Perfect Your Sales Plan," in John D. Murphy, ed., *Secrets of Successful Selling* (New York: Dell Publishing Co., 1963), p. 252.

**The Planning Process**

Planning has been defined as "the design of patterns of activity to promote the achievement of a set of objectives."[2] Figure 6-1 outlines the sequence of steps involved. First, a sales representative must develop an overall presentation plan that embraces each element in the selling process. Second, the salesperson must develop a refined "story plan" for the individual prospect. The story plan consists of one or more objectives and preconceived means of reaching these objectives in a single sales presentation. Third, the salesperson must develop last minute planning of details for the sales presentation. These details cover such matters as when the presentation will be held and what materials (such as order forms and product models) are to be taken along on the sales call. In this chapter we will cover each of these three planning steps.

**Figure 6-1. Three stages in planning the sales presentation.**

**The Overall Sales Presentation Plan**

In personal selling, one of the most important objectives is to help satisfy needs of customers. The six elements of the selling process—the six activities undertaken to promote the achievement of this and other objectives—are as follows:

1. Carry out the preapproach. Gather information about a prospect who will be called upon in the future. Essentially, the preapproach is a fact finding process.

2. Contact prospects and obtain permission to make a presentation. (This is sometimes called the "approach.") The contact stage is a forerunner to the presentation.

3. Make the presentation. The presentation consists of the efforts of representatives to describe and illustrate how their products and services will satisfy prospect needs.

4. Handle objections. Objections are reasons for not agreeing with the propositions advanced by the sales representative.

5. Close the sale. Accomplish the goals of the presentation.

---

[2]Wroe Alderson and Paul E. Green, *Planning and Problem Solving in Marketing* (Homewood, Ill.: Richard D. Irwin, 1964), p. 608.

6. Serve the customer after the sale, as by checking to see if the product is performing according to the expectations of the customer.

Figure 6-2, which was reproduced at the beginning of part 2, outlines the various elements involved in the selling process. The lines leading from "information on the prospect" to the various boxes mean that information about the prospect should be employed in planning *all* of these activities. Later in this chapter we will provide details on the use of specific information inputs to develop a well-formulated plan.

## Carrying Out the Preapproach

In first element of the selling process, the preapproach, the salesperson acquires information and makes plans for a specific call upon a particular customer. The preapproach takes place prior to the actual sales call. Since the salesperson's objectives are to acquire information and to prepare for the call, much of

**Figure 6-2. Outline of elements involved in the selling process.**

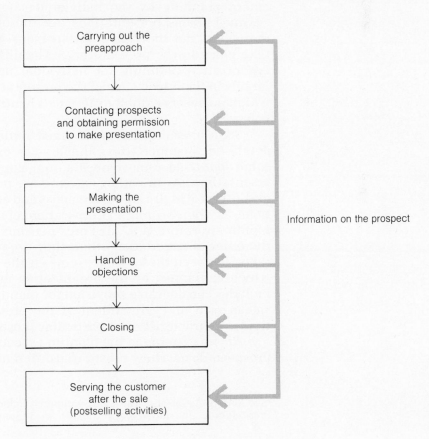

Carrying out the preapproach

Contacting prospects and obtaining permission to make presentation

Making the presentation

Handling objections

Closing

Serving the customer after the sale (postselling activities)

Information on the prospect

the material we covered in chapter 4 (information needed by the salesperson) is relevant at this stage.

## Contacting Prospects and Obtaining Permission to Make a Presentation

The second element is to get in touch with each prospect and obtain his or her permission to make a presentation. This step is one of the most critical selling tasks. Sometimes prospects are not in when the representative calls. At other times, they are "too busy" or "not in the mood." This element is too vital to be left to chance, so a sales representative should have a well-conceived approach.

## The Presentation

In the presentation the sales representative makes a persuasive appeal to the prospect, relying on some combination of speaking, listening, gesturing, demonstrating, and other actions in order to communicate effectively.

Every sales presentation is planned by the sales organization's management to some degree, yet it also involves to some extent planning by the individual salesperson. Planned or "canned" sales presentations are those where organization managers, not individual salespersons, determine what will take place in the presentation.[3] The differences in extent of organization planning for individual presentations are due largely to the importance of the presentation and the degree to which prospects exhibit differences in attitudes, opinions, and behavior.

Some presentations are planned by management in minute detail—for instance, the canned sales presentations used by some door-to-door encyclopedia, magazine, and cookware representatives. At the other extreme are presentations made to executives of high-ranking business and nonbusiness organizations, as when Grumman Corporation representatives try to sell fighter aircraft to U.S. Air Force personnel. These are more in the order of negotiations than they are organization-planned talks. Between these two extremes is the typical presentation, which is planned by the organization in many respects, but includes considerable provision for planning by the individual salesperson and adjustment of the presentation to the particular characteristics of particular prospect.

At one extreme in the planning spectrum are cases where prospects do not show substantial differences in attitudes, opin-

[3]See Marvin A. Jolson, "The Underestimated Potential of the Canned Sales Presentation," *Journal of Marketing* 39, no. 1 (January 1975): p. 75.

ions, and behavior, and so individual presentations are not highly important to salespersons and their employers. Here a canned presentation is likely to be appropriate; individual presentations need not be tailored to individual prospects. Quadrant C in Figure 6-3 identifies this situation; door-to-door magazine salespersons typify this quadrant.

**Figure 6-3. Differences in the degree of planning for individual presentations.**

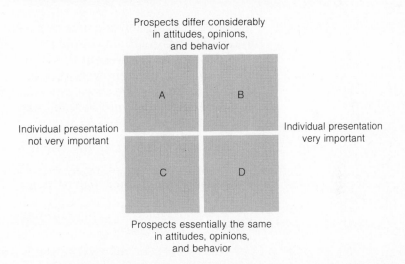

Prospects differ considerably
in attitudes, opinions,
and behavior

Individual presentation
not very important

Individual presentation
very important

Prospects essentially the same
in attitudes, opinions,
and behavior

In quadrant A, prospects differ substantially from one another and the individual presentation is not very important. This situation calls for a higher degree of salesperson planning for individual presentations than does quadrant C. That is, canned presentations are more likely to be effective. An example of quadrant A is the wholesale representative who calls upon large numbers of diverse kinds of prospects and who spends only small amounts of time on each call. Those who sell maintenance and supply items (such typing paper, glue, staples, sweeping compound, and rags) are in this category.

Quadrant D calls for a higher degree of individual planning than does quadrant A. In quadrant D the individual presentation is very important, but attitudes, opinions, and behavior do not differ markedly. Typical are the wholesale sales representatives who sell only to one specific class of prospects (such as manufacturers of phosphate fertilizer) and who spend considerable amounts of time on one presentation because a sale will net large revenue.

Finally, in quadrant B prospects differ considerably and individual presentations must be carefully tailored to individual prospects. In this quadrant would be the Philip Morris and R. J. Reynolds representatives who called upon Bulgarian officials and obtained their permission to export Marlboro and Winston tobacco to the Bulgarian state tobacco monopoly.[4] Here individual company sales personnel planned in detail a presentation that was tailored to the specific characteristics of the Bulgarians and their environment.

Handling Objections

Part of the selling job consists of handling objections, and the means of handling them should be anticipated and planned. In some cases sales representatives use "canned" responses to objections, but, as with presentations, the degree of individual tailoring increases the more prospects differ from each other.

Some door-to-door sellers use canned responses to objections:

PROSPECT: The price of this item is more than I care to pay.

SALESPERSON: You get what you pay for. This is the best vacuum cleaner on the market. Just try it out.

PROSPECT: I really don't have the time to read magazines, beyond those I currently get.

SALESPERSON: An informed person is a successful person. These magazines will help you succeed in your profession, in social relations, and in achieving the things you really want.

At the other extreme are responses to objections that are tailored to individual prospects. For example:

PROSPECT: I'm not sure we're going to be in the market for fire extinguishers this year. We may just keep using those we already have. They're adequate.

SALESPERSON: Let's take a look at several of your extinguishers. It may be that they have deficiencies that would make our product more appropriate for your company.

In chapter 9 we will provide a detailed discussion of the process of handling objections.

Closing

In closing, the sales representative attempts to achieve the purpose of the presentation, such as (1) make an immediate sale, (2) improve the attitude of the prospect toward the organi-

---

[4]"Bulgaria: Marlboro Country in the East Block," *Business Week*, no. 2418 (9 February 1976): 42.

zation, or (3) get the prospect to try out a product or service for a limited time. As in the case of presentations and objections, closes vary in the extent to which they are tailored to individual prospects. Two canned closes are as follows:

> Now that you've seen all of the various items in our line, which one do you like best?

> I can take your order now and we'll be sure that you get the benefit of our low price offer.

At the other extreme are cases where closes are tailored for individual prospects. For example:

> We've spent a lot of time going through your merchandise line. I can see that handling our products would definitely help improve your sales efforts, especially in selling to middle-income consumers. Shall I write you up an order?

Chapter 10 provides detailed coverage of the closing process.

**Serving the Customer After the Sale**

For most products and services, it is necessary for the sales representative to serve the customer after the sale has taken place. Such actions are called *postselling activities*. The representative may be involved in such functions as making sure that purchasers are using the product properly, training purchasers' employees in how to use the product, assuring purchasers that they have made a wise purchase, and providing maintenance service for the product. Chapter 12 focuses on postselling activities.

**Overview on Planning**

The planning process, then, involves determining the activities that are necessary in order to promote the achievement of a set of objectives. As we said, one of the more important personal selling objectives is satisfying prospect needs. The six activities undertaken to promote the achievement of persuasion objectives are the preapproach, approach, presentation, handling objections, closing, and postselling activities. The sales representative needs information about individual prospects in order to attain the degree of tailoring to prospects that is desired. Thus, we should now discuss how to obtain information about prospects.

**Obtaining Preapproach Information**

The preapproach consists of gathering information about a prospect prior to the time of the sales presentation. One famous salesman tries to put the preapproach in this framework:

Every day is a new day.

Every sale is a new sale.

Each one is distinct from every other one.

Each one demands its own individual approach.[5]

The salesperson should attempt to acquire information, first, about the individual prospect and, second, about his or her organization. If you are calling on a prospect for the first time, it may require considerable effort to acquire preapproach information. Conversely, if you have made previous calls upon the prospect, only limited preapproach information may be needed.

**Information About the Prospect**

The information you should have about the prospect should include the name and personal characteristics.

**Name.** A rather basic bit of information about the prospect is his or her correct name, including how to pronounce it. If the prospect's name is not stated correctly, hostility can arise early in the presentation. One of the fastest ways to alienate some individuals is to mishandle their names.

Sometimes when the pronounciation of a name is not obvious you should ask the prospect's secretary or some other employee in the organization how to say it. Asking for help sometimes has an added dividend in breaking the ice with a noncooperative secretary.

At the ultimate consumer level, knowledge of customers' names can be an element of differential advantage. Some small retailers deal with a limited number of customers on a frequent basis. When the retailer uses the name of customers in addressing them, the latter realize that they are being treated as persons rather than as just customers. In turn, personalized attention is one of the ways by which the small retailer can compete with larger and often more efficient firms.

**Individual Characteristics.** Each individual has personal characteristics that set him or her off from others. These characteristics can provide clues as to the conduct of your presentation. Some of the most important are as follows:

*Age.* An older prospect may value being treated with respect, whereas a younger one may prefer a less formal approach.

---

[5]Elmer G. Leterman, *Personal Power Through Creative Selling* (New York: Collier Books, 1975), p. 79.

*Family Status.*   Some sales representatives utilize statements such as "How is the family?" in the approach stage of presentations.

*Formal Education.*   A prospect with limited formal education may be turned off if you attempt to put on an overly sophisticated composure. Conversely, knowledge of the institution from which your prospect graduated may provide suggestions for approaches, such as "I see your school won the game last week."

*Hobbies and Interests.*   Knowledge of these provides clues for conducting the approach. You can use statements such as "How's the golf game?" or "Done any traveling lately?" to build rapport.

*Geographic Area of Origin.*   If the prospect came from somewhere out of the area, references to "back home" may aid in establishing an atmosphere of informality and friendliness.

*Personality Characteristics.*   Traits such as introversion, gregariousness, dogmatism, conservatism, and anxiety can be important in determining the conduct of the presentation.

*Attitude Toward the Sales Representative, Products, and Organization.*   When negative attitudes exist, you should plan regarding how to convert them to positive attitudes. For instance, you might discover some problem confronting the prospect and offer a solution.

Information About
the Prospect's
Organization

If sales representatives are to act as problem solvers for prospects, they must be familiar with prospect organizations and the ways they operate. For instance, one firm, Jack Levin and Associates, buys novel goods, such as handwoven Peruvian rugs, in clearance sales and sells them to stores wanting sudden surges in sales and excitement for the store.[6] Not all store managers want such goods, however. Thus, Levin representatives are faced with the constant need to find prospects.

Useful information about a prospect organization includes the following:

- type of organization (manufacturer or wholesaler, for instance);
- size (as measured by number of employees, volume of sales, or size of physical plant);

---

[6]"Where Blitz Selling Pays Off," *Business Week*, no. 2417 (2 February 1976): 45.

- product line;
- type of target consumers;
- major competitors;
- current suppliers;
- formal organizational structure;
- pricing policies;
- personal selling policies;
- sales promotion policies;
- distribution policies;
- needs for specific goods and services (as typified by Jack Levin and Associates);
- problems currently faced.[7]

With such information the sales representative is in a position to plan a detailed presentation tailored to specific prospects.

A realtor's experience illustrates this use of detailed information. Figure 6-4 shows the realtor's profile of a prospect named Anthony Terelli, information the realtor gained through extensive preapproach discussions with Terelli and two of his employees. The realtor prepares a profile like this for each prospect considered to have good potential and plans the sales presentation around it. The discussions with the prospect went very smoothly and affably. On each occasion, the two spent a short time discussing the state university football team, and then got down to business.

The realtor and Terelli worked together to discover the problems of Terelli Distributing Company that would be alleviated by a move to a new location. These problems turned out to be the negative effects of the currently owned facility upon the company image and productivity. In particular, the facility made it difficult for the firm to carry out the current policy of fast order processing and delivery service. This was significant, since Terelli's major competitors provided fast service.

A location in the industrial park where the realtor held property listings seemed to fit Terelli's needs, in that it provided

---

[7]According to the head of IBM's Data Processing Division, "In the 1970s we'll sell solutions to customer problems"—quoted in "IBM's 370 and Computer Users: A Marriage Made in Armonk," *Sales Management* 109, no. 4 (21 August 1972): 18.

ample space for future expansion. This feature was important, in light of the aggressive marketing tactics of the company. The realtor explained the advantages of the location in terms of its building the image and productivity of Terelli Distributing, and the outcome was a successful sale and Terelli employees satisfied with their new facility.

**Figure 6-4. Realtor's profile of one of his prospects, Anthony Terelli.**

---

PROSPECT PROFILE

Name: *Anthony Terelli*

Organization: *Terelli Distributing Company*

Type of organization: *Wholesaler of restaurant supplies*

Size of organization: *Small. Has two employees. Covers four-county area*

Product line: *Full line of restaurant supplies*

Target consumers: *Covers all types of restaurants in the four-county area*

Major competitors: *Regina Restaurant Suppliers, Inc.; Lybia Distributing Company, and Belus Restaurant Suppliers, Inc.*

Current location: *Located in small office-warehouse combination on the east side of town.*

Formal organization: *Mr. Terelli is the prime decision maker for his company. The other employees confine their responsibilities to selling or office duties.*

Pricing policies: *Attempts to undercut competitors*

Personal selling policies: *Is aggressive. Demands that his sales representatives be aggressive.*

Distribution policies: *Provides very fast order processing and delivery service.*

Needs: *Mr. Terelli has indicated that he needs a more modern and centrally located office-warehouse facility. Would consider a location in the industrial park.*

Current problems: *Feels that the current facility creates a poor image for his business. The office and warehouse are too small and could be more efficient.*

Age: *36*

Formal education: *Graduated from the State University in 1964.*

Hobbies: *Avid reader of mystery novels. Never misses a State University football game.*

Personality: *Outgoing, friendly, aggressive. Impatient with details.*

Attitudes: *Seems to think that our realty is a good firm to deal with. Treats salespeople with respect.*

---

Obtaining Preapproach Information

Sales representatives who call upon industrial and large institutional prospects often must plan to present detailed product specifications and financial information. Many of these prospects utilize *value analysis* and *vendor analysis* techniques.

**Value Analysis.** While some industrial and institutional buyers look for the products and services with the lowest prices, others employ value analysis, where an attempt is made to purchase items that have the greatest overall value to the buyer. In value analysis a study is made of the purpose of the product or service, then the supplier is sought that can best fulfill that purpose. Value analysis, for instance, might indicate that instead of having clerical workers place stamps on letters the firm should buy a postage meter mailing machine, which permits faster mailing and prevents expenses caused by losses of stamps.

When buyers use value analysis, sales representatives should make an attempt to determine exactly what constitutes the "value" in the eyes of the prospects. The experience of a salesman who sells fork lift trucks is a case in point. Some of his prospects develop detailed specifications for the fork lift trucks that they seek. Usually, these include provisions for unit size, power, carrying capacity, weight, durability, ease of operation, maneuverability, driving comfort, noise emissions, initial cost, and operating costs. In addition, prospects often have specifications regarding the financial, engineering, maintenance, and delivery policies of suppliers. The salesman is careful to obtain specifications used by particular suppliers and build his sales presentation around these specifications. In short, the buyer's use of value analysis forces the representative to build a very detailed sales plan oriented to specific specifications.

**Vendor Analysis.** In vendor analysis detailed procedures are set up for evaluating the suppliers themselves (not their products and services, as in value analysis). The sales representative is well-advised to become familiar with the vendor analysis system employed by individual prospects. Such familiarity enables the representative to plan a presentation tailored to the supplier specifications of prospects.

Figure 6-5 outlines a vendor analysis rating form that could be used to evaluate the suppliers of equipment (such as fork lift trucks). On the rating form are listed the criteria that are used to evaluate vendors. A particular supplier can be rated as "good," "fair," or "poor" on each criterion. The prospect might assign a value of 3 to a "good" check mark, and values of 2 and 1 for "fair" and "poor" check marks. Thus, for the sixteen criteria listed in the figure a perfect supplier would receive a rating of 48 (16 × 3) and a very poor supplier a rating of 16 (16 × 1).

If a salesman of fork lift trucks knows a prospect employs the vendor analysis rating form, he can tailor presentations to feature the criteria set forth in the form. He must prepare a detailed documentation of the company's resources and track record for each criterion. With regard to the "past experience of management," for example, he knows and has recorded on paper, detailed accounts of the responsibilities and attainments of key management personnel over the span of their careers.

**Figure 6-5. Vendor analysis rating form.**

VENDOR ANALYSIS RATING FORM

|  | GOOD | FAIR | POOR |
|---|---|---|---|
| Management abilities: | | | |
|     Past experiences of management | ____ | ____ | ____ |
|     Formal education | ____ | ____ | ____ |
| Production and engineering ability: | | | |
|     Past experience of personnel | ____ | ____ | ____ |
|     Formal education | ____ | ____ | ____ |
|     Manufacturing operations | ____ | ____ | ____ |
|     Equipment used | ____ | ____ | ____ |
| Financial resources: | | | |
|     Profits over past 5 years | ____ | ____ | ____ |
|     Credit rating | ____ | ____ | ____ |
|     Solvency | ____ | ____ | ____ |
|     Liquidity | ____ | ____ | ____ |
| Maintenance capability: | | | |
|     Personnel | ____ | ____ | ____ |
|     Equipment | ____ | ____ | ____ |
|     Policies | ____ | ____ | ____ |
| Delivery capability: | | | |
|     Past record | ____ | ____ | ____ |
|     Policies | ____ | ____ | ____ |
|     Equipment | ____ | ____ | ____ |
| TOTAL SCORE | ____ | ____ | ____ |

w35

**The Story Plan**

The outcome of the planning process is a *story plan*. This is an outline of the objectives of the presentation and how the sales representative plans to attain those objectives. In the case of some door-to-door seling positions, the story plan may be detailed to the extent that it is a canned sales presentation. More commonly, it is general in scope and allows the sales representative flexibility and the ability to develop the presentation as the situation dictates. Sometimes the plan simply consists of various points written on a scrap of paper.

Objectives of the Presentation

Sometimes the objective of a sales call is to persuade a prospect to change existing attitudes, opinions, or behavior. Other possible objectives are to provide service to an existing customer (as by setting up a new display) and to acquire information about the prospect for the use of management or the sales representative. A sales presentation may be designed to achieve several of these objectives, but more commonly attempts to attain only one or two.

Figure 6-6 sets forth a copy of a story plan used for a recent call on a shoe store by a saleswoman for a large shoe manufacturing company. The first section identifies the objective: to convince a buyer who already handles small amounts of company offerings to increase her purchases of such offerings. The representative knows that the buyer believes in splitting her purchases between at least five suppliers. The advantage of this, according to the buyer, is that "You aren't dependent on any one. Then, if one supplier comes on with late deliveries, a bad advertising campaign, or some product defects, you always have the others to lean on for help." The saleswoman's objective, then, is to convince the buyer that the risks of depending solely upon her firm are minimal.

Plans to Attain the Objective

The second part of the story plan consists of the set of means by which the objective will be carried out. The saleswoman has enough preapproach information to know that four benefits should be offered:

- high turnover of company offerings, relative to competitors;
- high profit margins, relative to competitors;
- company delivery policies and track record;
- cost savings of dealing with smaller numbers of suppliers.

The representative did not invent these benefits out of thin air. She knows that the company is capable of providing them.

Figure 6-6. Story plan
for shoe store prospect.

STORY PLAN FOR: *Prospect X*

Objective: *Convince her that she should increase her purchases of company offerings.*

Benefits offered: (1) *High turnover of company offerings,*
(2) *High profit margins of company offerings,*
(3) *The company delivery policy and track record, and*
(4) *Potential cost savings by dealing with a smaller number of suppliers.*

Communicating benefits:
(1) *High turnover — bring in testimonial figures.*
(2) *High profit margins — make computations on paper.*
(3) *Delivery:*
  *A. Policy — show written policy statement*
  *B. Track record — use testimonials.*
(4) *Cost savings — illustrate on paper.*

Further, she has discovered that these are the particular benefits in which her prospect holds an interest.

The last portion of the story plan indicates how the benefits are to be communicated to the prospect. These are as follows:

*1. High Turnover.* The representative has testimonials from other customers regarding the rate of turnover that they have been able to attain. She will show the prospect these turnover figures and compare them to figures for the offerings of competing suppliers.

*2. Profit Margins.* The saleswoman will demonstrate on paper the degree to which her firm's products carry higher profit margins than do rivals. As long as retailers do not cut their prices to extremely low levels, the margins will be substantial.

*3. Delivery Policy.* The company physical distribution manager has prepared a statement of the company delivery policy. The representative will show a copy of this statement to the prospect. She knows that rivals cannot provide the fast and reliable delivery to this prospect that the written policy statement sets forth.

4. *Track Record on Deliveries.* The written policy statement may not be sufficiently convincing, so it should be backed up with facts. Consequently, the representative has acquired testimonials from other retail customers on their delivery experience with the firm. The testimonials show that the company delivered as promised in the policy statement.

5. *Cost Savings.* The representative will demonstrate on paper the cost savings of dealing with a smaller number of suppliers. The savings include lower prices for large orders, smaller transportation charges for large shipments, and reductions in the amount of paperwork required.

The story plan will serve as a guide to the presentation of the representative. She has reviewed it to the extent that it is committed to memory. The result will be a well organized, persuasive attempt that is based upon the problems and needs of her particular prospect.

It is not necessary that the story plan be followed to the letter. Sometimes departures are necessary. In the conduct of the presentation the saleswoman may discover, as a result of feedback from the prospect, that different benefits and means of communicating benefits should be stressed. On the other hand, the story plan provides an informed way to approach the presentation, given the information that is available.

**Prospect Records**

Sales representatives should plan to record the results of their sales calls. The records provide information that is useful in designing future sales presentations. Figure 6-7 provides an illustrative format of the items that might be covered in the typical record file.

By reviewing sales presentation reports the representative can obtain insights on the objectives of past presentations and the results of the efforts to move toward these objectives. If orders were made, the items, amount sold, prices, and inventories held are guidelines to orders that might be expected in the future. The report provides space for recording general comments about the call. Any insights acquired by the sales representative in the course of the call can be recorded here. Before making future presentations the sales representative should review these comments for guidance. For instance, notations such as the following may be relevant:

Prospect does not appreciate jokes.

Prospect liked the inventory analysis I did for him.

Prospect is highly concerned with profit margins.

Prospect will not buy products that are not thoroughly laboratory tested.

Prospect is very cost conscious.

**Detailed Planning for the Presentation**

Part of planning for sales presentations consists of last minute efforts to ensure that everything needed is in readiness. You should make provision for planning (1) the time of the presentation, (2) physically for the sales call, and (3) mental role playing of the presentation.

**Figure 6-7. Report of the results of a sales presentation.**

SALES PRESENTATION REPORT

Prospect name:_____ Position: _____

Address: _____

Telephone number: _____

Objectives of the presentation:_____

_____

_____

_____

Results of the presentation:_____

_____

_____

Orders (if any):

| Item | Amount sold | Price | Amount in inventory |
|------|-------------|-------|---------------------|
|      |             |       |                     |
|      |             |       |                     |

Comments about this call: _____

_____

_____

Each presentation should have a specific time allotted to it. It is best to have an appointment for the call and to have a reasonably good idea as to its expected duration.

Because time is one of the real assets of the sales representative, careful scheduling of calls is a must. A frequent problem is wasted time in between presentations. Often you can make use of such time for nonselling work or to make last minute calls on less important prospects. Assume, for instance, that a representative has the following schedule:

1:30–2:30 P.M., call on prospect Greene.

3:30–4:30 P.M., call on prospect Browne.

It takes only 10 minutes to drive from the office of Greene to that of Browne. The sales representative could spend the 50 extra minutes drinking coffee, reading the newspaper, or visiting with friends. But he could make more productive use of the time, and he does so by filling out reports and records. Such gaps can also be used for:

- making a brief courtesy call to say hello to an old and valued customer;
- delivering pamphlets describing a new product to a prospect;
- calling the home office to find out when a new advertising campaign was to begin;
- mentally reviewing the last sales call to gain insights as to what went wrong.

Such time slots can be very productive. Indeed, unscheduled activities can lead to many unexpected sales, gains in customer goodwill, and insightful thinking. Bob Lin, president of the Schweppes Corporation, which produces mixes for alcoholic beverages, once found his train late, so he took the opportunity to go into a liquor store near the train station and sell the owner on carrying Schweppes.[8]

A simple, yet vital, aid to scheduling is an appointment book. A wholesale grocery salesman carries a small 3-by-5 inch leather covered notebook with him at all times. A page from it appears in Figure 6-8. The book provides enough space for recording calls and other important events for each day. At the end of the day, the representative reviews the schedule to deter-

---

[8]"Sales Management Call Report," *Sales Management* 102, no. 7 (1 April 1969): 80.

mine if he has taken care of all important tasks recorded on the page. The tasks not accomplished are transferred to a later day, usually at a time between appointments.

Physical Planning for the Presentation

At some time before the presentation, the sales representative should take inventory to ensure that all needed materials are on

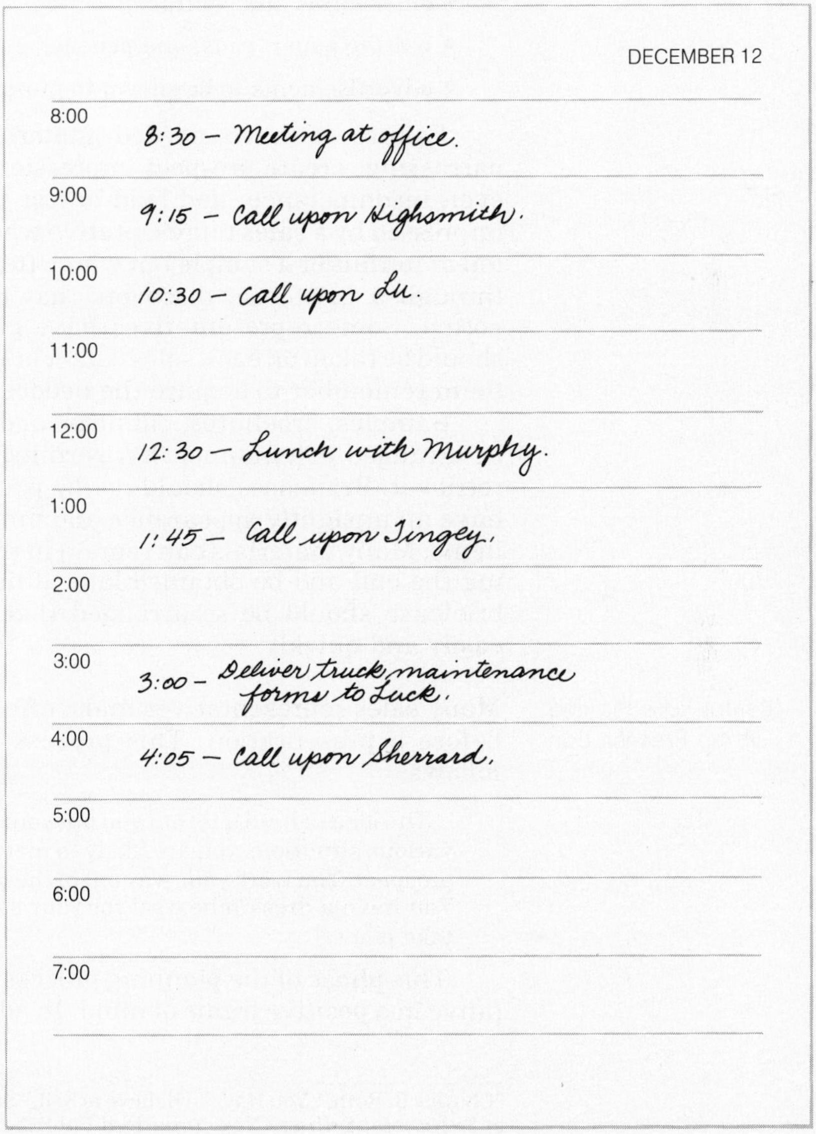

Figure 6-8. Sample page from a salesperson's scheduling book.

DECEMBER 12

| Time | |
|------|--|
| 8:00 | 8:30 — Meeting at office. |
| 9:00 | 9:15 — Call upon Highsmith. |
| 10:00 | 10:30 — Call upon Lu. |
| 11:00 | |
| 12:00 | 12:30 — Lunch with Murphy. |
| 1:00 | 1:45 — Call upon Tingey. |
| 2:00 | |
| 3:00 | 3:00 — Deliver truck maintenance forms to Luck. |
| 4:00 | 4:05 — Call upon Sherrard. |
| 5:00 | |
| 6:00 | |
| 7:00 | |

hand and ready for the presentation. Among such materials are:

- samples of the product;
- brochures and charts;
- portfolios;
- catalogs;
- order forms and contracts;
- writing paper, pens, and pencils;
- advertisements to be shown to prospects.

Failure to have needed materials ready can be embarrassing, create prospect impressions of poor planning and even incompetence, and lead to lost sales. Prospects are not impressed by a sales representative who promises to show written materials or a sample but who, after considerable fumbling through a briefcase, discovers that the materials were forgotten. Some representatives have check-lists of items that should be taken on each sales call. A brief review of the list helps them remember to acquire the needed materials.

Samples, brochures, catalogs, and other materials should be arranged in a manner that permits easy handling and easy retrieval. Briefcases should not be packed so tightly that they have an unsightly appearance and make it difficult to retrieve items. Many materials can remain in the salesperson's car during the call and be obtained later if needed. The items in the briefcase should be so arranged that one can acquire them easily and quickly.

Mental Role Playing of the Presentation

Many sales representatives make effective use of role playing before a presentation. This process has been described as follows:

> The idea behind it is that you put yourself in imagination into the various situations you are likely to meet when in the presence of a prospect. You work your way out of these suggestions successfully. You have a dress rehearsal for your sales interviews before they take place.[9]

This phase of the planning process puts the sales representative in a positive frame of mind. In addition, it helps in antici-

---

[9]Charles B. Roth, "You Have to Believe to Sell," in John D. Murphy, ed., *Secrets of Successful Selling* (New York: Dell Publishing Co., 1963), p. 213.

pating and effectively reacting to problems. The role playing process requires reviewing the story plan, committing the plan to memory, then imagining that the presentation is actually taking place and that it is successful in achieving the objectives of the story plan.

Benjamin McAlpin III, a salesman for the Wall Street firm of F. S. Mosely & Co., utilizes role playing in preparing for sales presentations. According to him, before each presentation "I go into my level and visualize a successful call."[10] By "going into my level" he means mental role playing.

## Summary

The sales representative should have a predetermined plan of action regarding the nature of forthcoming sales presentations. Planning consists of designing activity to promote the achievement of a set of objectives. The activities undertaken to promote the achievement of the objectives are:

1. the preapproach—preparing for an upcoming sales call;

2. the approach—contacting prospects and obtaining permission to make a presentation;

3. the presentation—actually making persuasive appeals to the prospect;

4. handling objections;

5. closing—attempting to achieve the purpose of the presentation;

6. serving the customer after the sale.

These activities vary in the extent to which they are tailored to individual prospects. Generally, when prospects differ considerably in attitudes, opinions, and behavior, and where individual presentations are highly important, the activities are tailored.

Well conceived plans require inputs of information. The salesperson should obtain basic information, such as the name, individual characteristics, and characteristics of the prospect's organization. If the salesperson is selling to industrial and institutional prospects, he or she may have to acquire information regarding the value and vendor analysis systems used by these entities. Value analysis involves attempting to purchase items that have the greatest overall value to the buyer. Vendor analysis consists of using detailed procedures for evaluating suppliers according to specific criteria.

---

[10]"Are You Ready? Here's Mind Control," *Sales Management* 108, no. 11 (28 May 1972): 12.

The outcome of the planning process is a story plan, which outlines the objectives of the presentation and how the salesperson plans to attain those objectives. Some story plans (such as those used in door-to-door selling) are very detailed. More commonly, they are general in scope.

The results of sales calls should be recorded. The records provide information that is useful in designing future sales presentations. Ordinarily, sales presentation reports are constructed shortly after the completion of a presentation.

Part of planning for sales presentations involves last-minute efforts to ensure that everything is in readiness. This requires planning the following:

1. the timing of the presentation;

2. physical aspects of the presentation;

3. mental role playing for the presentation.

**Discussion Questions**

1. What is a plan? Why is planning important to sales representatives?

2. What are the objectives of personal selling presentations?

3. Define each of the following:
   a. The preapproach.
   b. The approach.
   c. Making the presentation.
   d. Handling objections.
   e. Closing.
   f. Postselling activities.

4. What are the factors that determine the degree to which elements of planning are tailored to individual prospects?

5. What information about the prospect should the preapproach yield?

6. What information about the prospect's organization should the preapproach yield?

7. Indicate what is meant by a prospect profile. Of what use to the sales representative is the profile?

8. Define the following and set forth their significance to the sales representative: (a) value analysis, (b) vendor analysis.

9. What is a story plan? What is its value to the sales representative?

10. Indicate the usefulness of written sales presentation reports.

11. Sales representatives should take steps to ensure that all needed materials are on hand and ready for the presentation. What are some of the materials that are needed?

12. What is involved in planning the timing of individual sales calls?

13. Define mental role playing. How does this technique aid the sales representative?

**Practical Exercises**

1. Observe a retail sales representative who is making a presentation. Outline the steps he or she used in the approach. Was the approach effective? Why or why not? What did you learn as a result of this exercise?

2. Did the sales representative in (1) above attempt to tailor the presentation or was his or her effort more in the nature of a canned sales presentation? Comment on the effectiveness of the approach used. What did you learn as a result of this exercise?

3. What individual information about the prospect could the sales representative have used to make the presentation more effective? What did you learn as a result of this exercise?

4. Could the sales representative have benefited through mental role playing presentations such as this one? What should be covered in the role playing? What did you learn as a result of this exercise?

**Selling Project**

1. Assume that you are going to make a presentation of your product to a typical prospect:
   a. What is the objective of your call?
   b. How would you handle:
      1) the preapproach;
      2) the approach;
      3) the presentation;
      4) expected objections;
      5) the close;
      6) postselling activities.

2. Would you tailor your presentations for different prospects? Why or why not?

3. What preapproach information would you seek?

4. What would you include in your story plans?

5. What physical materials would you need for the presentation?

6. What mental role playing activities would you undertake?

**Case 6
Les McColough**

Les McColough directs a Chemaid program in a midwestern city of 158,000 population. The organization is funded by the state and has regional offices (such as that administered by Les) in various cities throughout the state.

The objective of the Chemaid organization is to provide help to persons who have a dependency upon chemicals, including drugs and alcohol. This organization provides benefits to its "consumers" or "clients" in the following manner:

1. Potential users of the service are recruited through advertising, publicity, word-of-mouth, and talks before organizations. Les, for instance, designs advertisements intended to induce chemical dependents to make use of the service.

2. People who respond to the advertisements and publicity are scheduled for interviews with Chemaid personnel. Les conducts the interviews for his unit. The objectives of the interviews are:

a. to determine if the prospect really needs the service; and,
b. if he or she needs the service, to convince the prospect to participate in the program.

3. Those prospects who become involved in the program undertake a series of diagnostic interviews with professional psychologists. These counsellors attempt to determine the nature of the chemical dependence problem and its causes.

4. The clients of Chemaid are then scheduled for therapy. The latter includes counseling with psychologists, group therapy sessions, and emergency help—Alcoholics Anonymous-type aid, where one patient calls another for psychological bolstering when experiencing extreme need for the drug.

5. Those clients who do not drop out of the program (participation is voluntary) eventually "graduate." When this takes place, a counselor decides that the customer is able to take care of the drug problem without further assistance from Chemaid. Graduates are encouraged to contact their former counselors should the problem emerge again, however.

The physical facilities of Les' unit are quite adequate and include a large, modern building stocked with an extensive array of equipment and supplies. Furniture and room interiors are very attractive, and most of the rooms have piped-in music. The location is in a scenic area of the city.

Users of the Chemaid program obtain its services without charge. This is because the governor and legislature of the state are committed to the premise that chemical dependency causes problems for all members of society, not just for those who are dependent.

Les McColough's promotional objectives are several. He uses advertising to make target consumers and their friends aware of the program and to draw target consumers in for interviews. The advertisements stress the effectiveness of the program and the fact that it is free of charge. The "sales presentations" also focus on these attributes. Further, in the presentations, Les emphasizes the high quality of the personnel and facilities and the success rate of the program (percentage of program users who are able to overcome chemical dependencies).

Les feels that his operation is achieving its objective to a large degree. The success rate is one of the highest in the state and is increasing faster than that of any other unit. Numerous program users and their friends and relatives have commented favorably on the program. Allocations of funds from the state headquarters have been ample, indicating that the state level administrators are satisfied with the progress of the unit.

One stumbling block is the "sales presentation" process. Many of those qualified as prospects in the interview have not elected to participate in the program. In fact, Les is very distressed at his inability to persuade those who obviously need Chemaid services to use these services.

Les has no formal training in sales. He once read a book entitled *Be a Super-Salesman*, however, which instructed sales representatives to develop a detailed sales presentation and to commit the presentation to memory. As a result, Les employs a canned sales presentation.

Should Les use a canned sales presentation or should the presentations be tailored to individual prospects? What pre-approach information should he use? Would you suggest the use of story plans? What would you recommend, in terms of planning for:

1. the timing of the presentation;

2. the physical aspects of the presentation (materials needed);

3. mental role playing.

**Suggested Readings**

Berg, Thomas L. *Mismarketing: Case Histories of Marketing Backfires.* Garden City, N.Y.: Anchor Books, 1971, pp. 76–85.

Berlo, David K. "Empathy and Managerial Communication," in Charles Press and Alan Arian, eds. *Empathy and Ideology: Aspects of Administrative Innovation.* Chicago: Rand McNally & Co, 1966.

Coulton, Raymond R. *Industrial Purchasing: Principles and Practices.* Columbus, Ohio: Charles E. Merrill Books, 1962, ch. 8.

Crissy, W. J. C., and Harold C. Cash. "Logic and Creativity in Selling," *The Psychology of Selling*, vol. 8. Flushing, N.Y.: Personnel Development Associates, 1965.

Frank, Paul. "Selling the Professional Buyer," *Sales/Marketing Today* 15, no. 8 (August–September 1969): 64–66.

Heidingsfield, M. S. "The Consumer—An Ever-Changing Marketing Prospect," *Economic Leaflets*, June 1965, pp 1–5.

Kerr, John, and James E. Littlefield. *Marketing: An Environmental Approach*. Englewood Cliffs, N.J.: Prentice-Hall, 1974, ch. 3.

Massie, Joseph L., and John Douglas. *Managing: A Contemporary Introduction*. Englewood Cliffs, N.J.: Prentice-Hall, 1977, ch. 12.

Redinbaugh, Larry D. *Retailing Management: A Planning Approach*. New York: McGraw-Hill Book Company, 1976, chs. 11 and 12.

Stuteville, John R. "The Buyer as a Salesman," *Journal of Marketing* 32, no. 3 (July 1968): 14–18.

# 7

# The Communication Process

*After reading this chapter you should be able to demonstrate a knowledge of:*

- *the meaning of the term communication*
- *the importance of communication to the sales representative*
- *the way the communication process works*
- *components of the communication process*
- *the role of nonverbal communications in personal selling*
- *how the sales representative can make the communication process effective.*

Communication is, of course, one of the more common activities people engage in. That includes all of the following:

- A college sophomore frowns on discovering there is a question on the final exam that covers material in the text that the student failed to read.
- A police officer warns a motorist that crossing traffic lanes in an intersection is dangerous.

- A husband and wife discuss the merits of buying a larger home.

- Two production workers say hello to each other on the way to the bus stop.

- A purchasing agent telephones the catalogue division of a mail-order wholesaler to place an order.

- A cattle buyer raises two fingers to signal an auctioneer that he has made a bid.

This chapter is about effective communication, a significant responsibility of every sales representative. We will define communication and indicate its importance to a sales representative. We will also describe how it takes place and identify the elements of the process. Finally, we will describe "body language" and other kinds of nonspoken communication and show how sales representatives can benefit from well-conceived communications.

## What Communication Is
### Sharing

Communication involves establishing a oneness or commonness with a person or group of people.[1] It consists of sharing perceptions or experiences with others. Everyone has perceptions and experiences stored in his or her memory. Some are very private, since many motives, attitudes, opinions, and beliefs are considered confidential or irrelevant to others and so are not communicated. Where the two circles of *sharing* and *private* intersect—see Figure 7-1—communication takes place: the two individuals share their knowledge.

**Figure 7-1. Communication: shared and private perceptions and experiences intersect.**

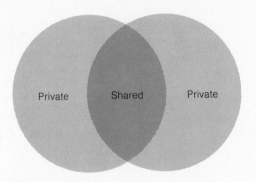

Private          Shared          Private

---

[1]Wilbur Schramm, *The Process and Effects of Mass Communication* (Urbana, Ill.: University of Illinois Press, 1955), p. 3.

**Interpersonal Communication**

Personal selling consists of interpersonal communication—the fancy name for face-to-face interaction between people. This contrasts with mass communication, which involves impersonal communication with groups and consists of advertising, publicity, and other public forms important to marketers.

**The Importance of Communication to the Salesperson**

Communication is important for sales representatives. Since much of their time is spent determining prospect needs and convincing the prospects that their organization's products will help fulfill them, they depend heavily on communication, as in the following:

> SALESMAN: What are you looking for in a new car?
>
> PROSPECT: I want one that's inexpensive and that gets good gas mileage. Gas prices are bound to rise in the future.
>
> SALESMAN: You've come to the right place then. Our cars are certainly inexpensive. In addition, they have a considerable amount of trunk space. Further, these cars accelerate rapidly. Take one out for a test drive.

The prospect did not buy this brand, discouraged by the salesman's comments about ample space and quick acceleration, which seemed to suggest the cars did not attain economical mileage rates and had less interior space and poorer acceleration. The salesman's comments were intended to convey that even though the car attained good mileage, it also had space and acceleration advantages. The salesman failed to notice that the prospect was really very concerned with mileage. As a result, his words did not convey the meaning he intended. What he should have said was:

> You've come to the right place. Our cars are certainly inexpensive to operate. I'll show you some mileage figures for our brand and for some competing makes. By the way, we can also offer considerable passenger and trunk space and rapid acceleration.

The difference between this and the salesman's preceding speech is not great. They differ only in emphasis. The effects, however, were quite different. (He lost the sale.) The point is that he and other sales representatives are faced with the need to be good communicators in order to carry out many of their day-to-day functions.

## The Communication Process

### Communication Is a Process

Communication, as we intend it in this book, is a process. This is in contrast to other uses of the term,[2] in which, for instance, it is used to denote an object, such as an advertisement. Here we mean communication as the *sharing of perceptions and experiences* advertising brings about, rather than the advertising itself.

### Composition of the Communication Process

The communication process involves the following elements:[3]

1. source;
2. message;
3. receiver;
4. feedback;
5. noise;
6. other parties.

Figure 7-2 depicts the communication process in graphic form. The objective of the process is to direct information from the source to the intended receiver. There are seven parts of the process, as follows:

**Source.**  This is the sender of the message, the person who wants to share perceptions or experiences with others. In personal selling, the source is the salespersons and their employers. In advertising, the source is the people who designed the advertising and their employers.

**The Message.**  The message is what the source sends the receiver—the *meaning* or *understanding* the source wants to share. In our earlier example, the car salesman wanted to convey the idea that his make of car provided good mileage, plus ample space and quick acceleration.

**Receiver.**  The receiver is the target of the source's message. In personal selling, the receiver is a prospect or current customer. If the communication by the source work, receivers change their attitudes, opinions, or behavior in the directions intended

---

[2]See Brent Stidsen and Thomas F. Schutte, "Marketing as a Communication System: The Marketing Concept Revisited," *Journal of Marketing* 36, no. 4 (October 1972): 22–23.

[3]For further detail on the process see James Hulbert and Noel Capon, "Interpersonal Communication in Marketing: An Overview," *Journal of Marketing Research* 9, no. 1 (February 1972): 29.

by the source. The receivers may also communicate with other people and carry some portion of the source's message to them.

**Feedback.**   When communications go back from the receiver to the source, they are called feedback. Prospects speak, gesture, motion, and otherwise suggest the directions the source's communications should take. Alert sales people use feedback to alter their presentations.

**Noise.**   Noise is anything that interferes with the flow of effective communication. Noise is that which "tends to reduce the efficiency of the communication system by decreasing the reliability of message reception and requiring many controls to insure its accuracy."[4] Some sources of noise are:

- *Outside interference*—as when a salesperson's presentation is interrupted by a jackhammer outside.

- *Ineffective transmitting by the source*—as when the salesperson slurs or speaks inaudibly.

- *Ineffective reception by the receiver*—as when a partly deaf prospect misses an important part of a presentation.

**Figure 7-2. The communication process.**

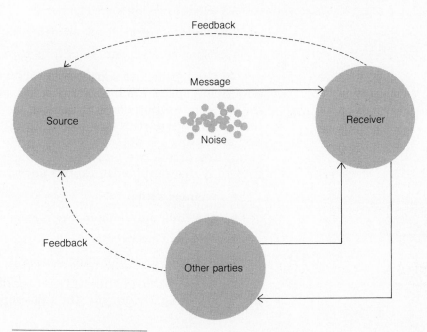

---

[4]M. J. Alexander, *Information System Analysis: Theory and Applications* (St. Louis, Mo.: Science Research Associates, 1974), p. 87.

The sales representative should, of course, take whatever actions necessary to reduce the occurrence of noise or to compensate for its effects—as by speaking loudly over the jackhammer noise or in order to be heard to a hard-of-hearing prospect).

*Other Parties.* Often the receiver communicates the contents of the message to other parties, such as associates and friends. And these other parties may provide feedback to the source. Thus, the prospect may tell a friend about the car the salesman showed her, and the friend may in turn call the salesman. Sales people, therefore, must be aware of the importance of communications from the receiver to other parties.

The Personal Selling Communication Process

The communication process outlined in Figure 7-2 is a general process. It applies to all forms of communication, including advertising, personal selling, publicity, and public relations.

Personal selling has some unique communication aspects, however. Figure 7-3 highlights the differences. The figure:

1. identifies the source and receiver as salesperson and prospect;

2. includes two message elements;

3. includes three feedback elements;

4. has a noise element that affects both message elements.[5]

In the figure, the source and receiver are the salesperson and the prospect. Each transmits messages to the other. Thus, the personal selling communication process is two-way rather than one. Both parties transmit information, receive feedback, and are subject to noise. Sales representatives who think their communications are one-way are likely to be ineffective, for they may overemphasize tactics such as the following:

- a winning smile;

- a powerful and commanding voice;

- an extensive vocabulary;

- an insightful set of mannerisms.

Such tactics do not take advantage of the two-way nature of personal selling. Ordinarily, the sales representative needs help

---

[5]For a useful discussion of the interpersonal communication process, see Rollie Tillman and C. A. Kirkpatrick, *Promotion: Persuasive Communication in Marketing* (Homewood, Ill.: Richard D. Irwin, 1968), pp. 106–115.

**Figure 7-3. The personal selling communication process.**

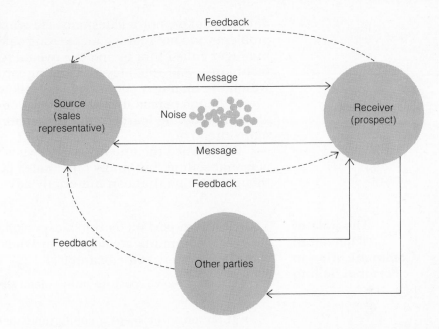

in discovering the prospect's problems and in determining how to help solve these. The best source of help is, of course, the prospect. Behlen Manufacturing Co. dealers ask prospects for a description of the facilities that their proposed new buildings should have. Then the dealers use the description as an aid to selecting a Behlen steel building that fulfills the prospect's needs.

If sales representatives are too busy talking they cannot encourage the prospect to talk. A salesperson who does all of the talking, moreover, is likely to be boring and fail to catch the attention of the prospect, resulting in dialogues like the following:

LONG-WINDED SALESPERSON: Well, what do you think?

DAY-DREAMING PROSPECT: Very interesting. Unfortunately, I have another appointment.

Bill Martin, representative for a manufacturer of oil field tools, is responsible for calling on oil field superintendants, drilling-rig operators and others in a three-county area in California. When Bill first became a salesman he was not sufficiently aware of the need for two-way communication. Although he had read a book on public speaking and one on developing a charming personality, their advice made him only a public speaker, not a salesman. He was not solving prospect problems and not making an exciting sales presentation. Bill's manager called him in and the two talked about Bill's selling techniques and role-played a selling situation, as a result of which the manager counseled less talk and more listening.

Although personal expression was one thing Bill liked best about his job, he learned that by listening he could be much more effective.

Bill learned the importance of two-way communication in personal selling, but many other sales people have not—even though it is one that can materially advance their success.

**The Role of Nonverbal Communication in Personal Selling**

Listening is important for the salesperson, but observing is also. Prospects communicate not only by what they say but by what they do. Here are some examples:

- An aggressive posture may mean that the prospect feels hostility.

- If the prospect keeps a comfortable distance between himself and the sales representative, this may indicate that the former resents the intrusion of the latter.

- The eyes tend to dilate when the prospect is confronted with a salesperson or presentation that is viewed in positive terms. The opposite happens when the salesperson or presentation is regarded negatively.

- A slouched posture may suggest lack of interest in the presentation.

- A rise in the pitch of the words toward the end of a sentence may indicate that the prospect is asking a question.

- If the prospect turns away, so that he or she is no longer facing the sales representative, this may indicate that the prospect wants the presentation to end.

- When a prospect continually rubs ear lobes, chin, or mustache, this may suggest nervousness or anxiety.[6]

There are, of course, no fixed rules regarding the interpretation of particular nonverbal behaviors. (A slouched posture, for instance, may indicate that the prospect is tired and not necessarily that he or she is uninterested in the presentation). Nevertheless, if sales representatives combine the inputs of

---

[6]Julius Fast, *Body Language* (New York: Pocket Books, 1971).

both verbal and nonverbal symbolism, they can often obtain useful feedback regarding characteristics of the prospect and the reactions of the prospect to the presentation.

Consider the example of a sporting goods salesman who makes a point of observing nonverbal symbols before and during a presentation. The salesman was calling on a retail sporting goods store that had just opened up in his territory. In preparing for the call, he had acquired a lot of preapproach information on the prospect, but felt he needed further details on his needs, characteristics, and personality. When the salesman called upon the retailer, the latter was impeccably dressed and conducted himself in a very businesslike and crisp manner. He kept a comfortable distance between himself and the salesman. He also made no attempts at small talk or jokes and the salesman decided that small talk and levity on his part would not be appropriate.

As the salesman showed samples of and talked about his products, he carefully observed the prospect. When the presentation turned to the high profit margins available for his products, the prospect fidgeted and turned away from the salesman. Obviously, this retailer was not concerned about achieving high margins. However, once the salesman mentioned the number of shoppers who would be expected to be attracted to the store if his brand were available there, the retailer looked directly at the salesman and moved closer toward him. The salesman interpreted this as suggesting a concern with the ability of particular brands to draw consumers into the store. As a result, the salesman began asking questions regarding store traffic.

Eventually the salesman uncovered something the prospect had not revealed at the outset—namely, that his marketing strategy depended on there being large numbers of consumers circulating through the store. The salesman was aware of research that indicated two of the products he handled—inexpensive fishing reels and casting rods—were very effective in generating retail traffic. The salesman therefore centered his discussion upon the ability of these two products to build store traffic. The result was a sale and what turned out to be a very good customer for numerous products, in addition to the fishing reels and casting rods. The sensitivity of the salesman to nonverbal communication had paid off.

This and the preceding section have demonstrated the importance of feedback. It is but one of the ways of making presentations effective, however. The following section focuses upon various methods of achieving effectiveness.

## How to Make the Communication Process Effective

There are various ways in which the sales representative can make the communication process effective. These relate to the communication source, message, and methodology.

### Source Effects

Prospects are most likely to be influenced by sales representatives they regard to be competent, reliable, and trustworthy. Certainly, they cannot be expected to become involved in joint problem solving with an individual lacking these qualities. In addition, the salesperson can often communicate well with prospects if the latter view him or her as similar to them in ways that are important. This section deals with these competency, trustworthy, and similarity source effects.

**Competency and Trustworthiness of the Salesperson.** Here the adage "Action speaks louder than words" applies. If salespersons are competent and trustworthy, most prospects will probably perceive these qualities. Conversely, salespersons who lack these qualities will find that many prospects are aware of their failings.

A salesman who handles automotive accessories has a very good image with many of his prospects. They have learned, over time, that he has considerable knowledge regarding how to diagnose problems of retailers who handle this line, and knows his products, competing products, and the policies and operations of his company. He is viewed as an expert advisor in his field. In addition, his actions have demonstrated that he is honest, can be trusted, and is true to his word. This image is very useful in making him a top salesman.

A saleswoman of electronic equipment (transistor radios, stereo sets, CB radios, and the like) realizes that the ways she conducts herself have a major bearing on the image created among prospects. She observes the following guidelines:

- Her posture is always near perfect.
- Her voice is clear and low pitched.
- Her vocabulary is that of an educated person. Slang is avoided.
- She occasionally employs humor, to avoid creating the image of a stiff and overly regimented person.
- She keeps eye contact with prospects.
- She shows courtesy and politeness at all times.
- She avoids undue familiarity, addressing prospects by last (not first) name unless they are close friends.

Feedback from her prospects tells her she has created the desired image. Most prospects seem to like, respect, and trust her, and she feels they have a high regard for what she says and does.

Status symbols can be effective in creating the desired image of the sales representative. These are items that suggest to others the status of their possessor. Included in the status symbols that sales representatives can employ for image-building purposes are the following:

- An impressive company car for the U.S. Steel Company salesman who calls upon automobile manufacturers.

- A four-wheel drive van for the sales representative who sells tools to petroleum producers.

- A conservative suit for the representative who sells securities to mutual funds. According to one authority, "The safest attire for the man who wants to project a respectable business attitude revolves around the classic Brooks Bros.-type suit, in solid or narrow pinstripes, combined with a long-sleeved white shirt and a conservative tie."[7]

- A Pendleton shirt, denim pants, and boots for the representative who sells equipment to loggers.

- An expensive diamond ring for the seller of luxury town houses.

These and other symbols can be instrumental in image building. Obviously, the proper symbols depend upon the perceptions of target consumers as to what constitutes a competent and trustworthy sales representative.

**Competency and Trustworthiness in the Image of the Organization.** If the organization the salesperson is with has a favorable image among prospects, the work of the representative is much easier. Thus, representatives of IBM, Honeywell, and Control Data have an advantage over those who are employed by the Acme Computer Corp. In the same vein, if Dodge is a respected name to buyers of automobile fleets, sales representatives will experience less difficulty in selling Aspens.

In general, sales representatives should do all that they can to influence personnel in other departments to act in a responsible and competent manner, thereby enhancing the image of the entire organization. If an optical supplies salesman is told by

---

[7]Lorraine Baltera, "Success May Be Just a Pinstripe Away: Molloy," *Advertising Age* 13, no. 1 (February 1976): 29.

one of his better customers that a large shipment of eyeglass frames arrived in poor condition because they were poorly packed, the salesman knows that such an instance seriously undermines the source credibility of both the company and himself. To take care of the problem he should first apologize to the customer and promise to attend to the matter immediately, then call the company traffic manager to explain what happened, ask him to take steps to ensure this kind of thing does not happen again, and arrange for fast replacement shipment to the customer. When the replacement shipment arrives at the customer's location, the salesman should be on hand to make sure it was secure and on time, and should follow up this action by taking the customer out for coffee. Such actions will preserve the source credibility of the company in the eyes of the customer. Quick reaction to the problem is very appropriate since source credibility, once lost, can be difficult to regain.

An organization or a sales representative that is unknown to target consumers lacks source credibility. For instance, when an organization begins distributing its products in new areas or when a salesperson is recently assigned to a territory, steps must be taken to build a good image for the organization and sales representative. One of the best ways to do this is through advertising. Advertising can help make prospects aware of the organization and its product line and establish the image management desires.[8]

The owner of John's Realty, a successful enterprise located in the Midwest, is aware of the need for establishing source credibility among prospects who have not dealt with the company in the past (including new members of the community), and so runs an advertisement which appears in the classified section of the local newspaper on all seven days of the week (see Figure 7-4).

**Similarities.** Many consumers have a more positive attitude toward, and tend to buy more from, those they think are similar to them.[9] The similarities are in those behaviors, opinions, values, attitudes, and goals that the prospect believes important. As a result, the following patterns can emerge:

---

[8]David A. Aaker and John G. Myers, *Advertising Management* (Englewood Cliffs, N.J.: Prentice-Hall, 1975), pp. 138–45.

[9]Paul Busch and David T. Wilson, "An Experimental Analysis of a Salesman's Expert and Referent Bases of Social Power in the Buyer-Seller Dyad," *Journal of Marketing Research* 13, no. 1 (February 1976): 3–11.

Figure 7-4. John's
Realty daily newspaper
advertisement.

BUYING or SELLING
A BUSINESS?

If you are, the place to go is JOHN'S REALTY.

We have many listings and an outstanding
sales staff. The firm has been an established
community member for years. You will find
that we are NOT number one. *YOU ARE!*

●

JOHN'S REALTY, 261-4318.

- The president of a small company that manufacturers plastic novelty items used to be a laborer. Thus, he favors sales representatives who appear to have "come up through the ranks."

- The purchasing agent for a school district is very conservative politically and favors sales representatives with this inclination.

- A supermarket chain buyer is sophisticated and worldly. She likes salespersons who also have these characteristics.

- A purchasing officer for the U.S. Coast Guard likes sales representatives who have a good sense of humor and joke with him.

- The owner of a chain of laundromats is an ex-athlete and likes to deal with ex-athlete sales representatives.

- A husband and wife favor buying from retail salespersons who are members of their church.

- A housewife is an accomplished amateur tennis player. She holds a life-insurance policy sold by an agent who is also a good tennis player.

The degree of perceived similarity between prospect and sales representative, then, is one of the influences in the "source effects" field. Significantly, the impact of perceived similarity can be subconscious. That is, some prospects may not be aware of the impact and feel that they are making purchasing decisions that are based upon other criteria. The sophisticated and worldly supermarket chain buyer may insist that she makes purchase decisions that are based entirely upon the prices and the markups on offerings of suppliers, for instance.

It takes skill to discover the similarities that prospects deem to be important. The information may be gathered during the prospecting, preapproach, and sales presentation. During these stages the sales representative may find that:

- the president of the plastics company came up through the ranks and boasts about it;
- the purchasing agent for the school district is very active in a conservative political party;
- the supermarket chain buyer does a lot of world travel, dresses fashionably, and likes to dine at exclusive restaurants;
- the Coast Guard purchasing officer jokes continually;
- the owner of the laundromat chain played college football and made the all-conference team;
- the husband and wife are very active in their church;
- the housewife plays tennis frequently and likes to talk about the sport.

With information such as this in hand, the sales representative is in a position to approach the prospect in a manner designed to bring favorable response. It is doubtful that many representatives would join a particular church or pretend to be an ex-athlete just to obtain the patronage of a particular prospect, of course. Nevertheless, information about similarities allows sales representatives to conduct themselves appropriately. For instance:

- The sales representative who addresses the plastics manufacturing company president might mention that he worked as a laborer on a part-time basis and during summers while in high school and college.
- The sales representative who addresses the conservative purchasing agent for the school district should avoid making any liberal comments that might arouse antagonism.
- A person selling the sophisticated supermarket chain store buyer might strike up a conversation regarding her recent trip to Greece.
- The representative dealing with the Coast Guard purchasing officer might memorize and tell several new jokes.
- The salesperson addressing the owner of the chain of laundromats who played college football might mention that she is an avid skier.
- The representative attempting to sell to the husband and wife active in their church should avoid remarks and behavior that might be interpreted as "unChristian."
- A person selling the housewife tennis player could mention his or her experience with the sport.

Tactics such as these can be useful in producing desired source effects. If the prospect has a favorable attitude toward a sales representative, the latter is more likely to obtain permission to give a presentation and more likely to attain a positive response.

Message Effects    The nature of the message conveyed by the sales representative is a determinant of the effectiveness of the communication process. Representatives should strive to design messages that will promote the achievement of the objectives of the presentation.

**Selection of Words.**   The salesperson is, of course, dependent on words.[10] They are the raw materials of much of the presentation. Words should be chosen that are suitable for particular prospects. In talking to a highly educated buyer, for instance, the salesperson might make a statement such as:

> I'm afraid that your cash flow statement obfuscates the fact that you have an accounts receivable problem.

In talking to a less educated buyer, the salesperson might say:

> Your record keeping system needs improvement. It hides the fact that you might have financial problems in the future.

The selection of words depends on the characteristics and background of the particular prospect.

*Accuracy* in the use of words is a must; words should be chosen that convey meaning effectively. In this regard, you should be aware of both denotations and connotations. Denotations are dictionary definitions of words. Connotations are meanings that particular people attach to words, regardless of their denotations. A seller of steel buildings, for instance, might tell a prospect that the buildings had "ample" storage space. A dictionary definition of "ample" is: "Of large or great size, amount, extent, capacity."[11] But the prospect might interpret the word to mean "just barely large enough" or "only a bit larger than minimum requirements."

*Listening* is important in choosing words. Be continually on the alert for feedback regarding the impact of your words.

---

[10]For a good discussion of this topic see Elmer G. Leterman, *Personal Power Through Creative Selling* (New York: Collier Books, 1975), pp. 201–252.

[11]*The American Heritage Dictionary* (New York: American Heritage Publishing Co., 1973), p. 45.

Ask yourself: Am I getting through? Is the prospect really understanding what I'm saying? What is the real impact of my words? Answers to these questions can be generated only by attentive listening.

A general rule in the choice of words is *simplicity*. When two or more words can be used, the simpler one is likely to be the best. (The exception to this is when words are used for effect, as when trying to impress, say, the sophisticated supermarket chain buyer.) Some examples of simple and not simple words are:

| Simple | Not simple |
| --- | --- |
| Hope | Sanguine expectation |
| Legality | Legitimization |
| Melody | Melodiousness |
| Perfection | Indefectibility |
| Sharp | Setaceous |
| Voice | Modulation |

As this list suggests, the simple words are the most likely to carry meaning effectively.

**Repetition.** One way to improve the effectiveness of a sales presentation is repetition.[12] Sometimes prospects do not respond until they have been contacted a number of times. The sales representative may have to repeat the appeal of the presentation a number of times before the prospect actually internalizes it.

A saleswoman of Continental business insurance uses repetition well. She realizes that many of her calls will not result in immediate sales. Decisions on buying coverage on fields such as property, liability, and crime may take months to make. Further, many prospects may feel their existing insurance coverage is adequate and make no new additions. Because sales to particular buyers are therefore usually infrequent, the saleswoman strives to build a good image for Continental Insurance, herself, and the product line so that when prospects are in the market for insurance they will think of her. Consequently, she is involved in a long term image-building process. This process involves continually repeating the message that the coverage and the company are superior to rivals. Prospects must "learn" this message, and repetition enhances learning.

---

[12]James F. Engel, David T. Kollat, and Roger Blackwell, *Consumer Behavior* (New York: Holt, Rinehart, and Winston, 1973), pp. 340–42.

**Contrast.** Because salespersons are concerned with getting the attention and interest of prospects they must develop messages that stand out from the numerous other promotional messages that bombard prospects. Contrast means to differentiate the message from other elements of the prospect's environment. Messages and sales representatives who appear to be different have a good chance of getting a prospect's attention, interest, and memory. The Sun Life Insurance Company, for instance, contrasts its sales representatives to those of other companies by showing them wearing trenchcoats in advertisements, along with the caption, "Get a Special Agent who has the training and know-how to protect your life and your family's future . . . an agent who looks at life from your point of view . . . because *your* family is the first family."[13] Many prospects will show limited interest and quickly forget about insurance agents unless such methods of contrast are taken to differentiate Sun Life agents from other agents and companies.

One means of being different is through intensity or size. Consumers tend to distinguish items that are unusually large (or small) from the background of average size items. In the following line, for instance, one letter stands out from the rest.

aaaaaaa

A seller of truck axles to truck manufacturing companies achieves intensity contrast through the amount of diligence that he exercises in attempting to discover prospects' needs and in fulfilling these needs. Many prospects are amazed at the amount of effort that he expends in asking questions, probing for answers, and generally trying to discover their precise desires for various specifications. They are equally amazed at the degree of effort exerted in comprehensively evaluating the characteristics of various axles made by the company, in an attempt to identify the appropriate one for them. This difference in intensity gets interest and attention and promotes the memory value of what he says.

Numerous other means of contrast are available. These include the use of colors, motions, shapes, and speeds that differ from those employed by others. They are all alternate ways of being different.

**Drawing Conclusions.** With regard to drawing conclusions, two different techniques can be employed:

---

[13]"Sun Life 'Special Agent' Stars in New Campaign," *Advertising Age* 47, no. 18 (3 May 1976): 67.

1. the sales presentation can focus on factual matters (such as product and supplier characteristics) and allow prospects to draw their own conclusions, or

2. the sales presentation can draw conclusions and suggest courses of action that prospects should take.

The first approach is very much a low pressure technique. It is most appropriate in dealing with two classes of prospects:

1. those who are very skilled specialists in evaluating product offerings (examples are design engineers and chemists), who prefer drawing their own conclusions; and

2. top managers, professionals, and others who feel that it is appropriate for them (not the salesperson) to draw conclusions because of their position of authority.

For most presentations, the sales representative should draw the conclusions. Prospects seek advice and assistance from representatives. Many want specific recommendations. Salespersons who do not provide these are perceived as being indecisive, not well organized, and perhaps not convinced of the merits of their products and/or organization.

A seller of Deming pumps (industrial water pollution control devices) usually provides specific recommendations to prospects. He may advise potential customers that a particular company pump fits their pollution-abatement needs, in light of the guidelines of the federal Environmental Protection Agency and state pollution regulators. Conversely, if it appears that the prospect is already meeting the standards of these agencies, the sales representative recommends that they not purchase pollution-control devices.

Overall, then, the way in which the message is constructed can have a major impact on the effectiveness of the communication process.

Methodology Effects

Various methods can be used to carry out the sales presentation. While chapter 8 will outline a number of these in detail, here we will deal with three techniques that are generally useful:

1. empathy,

2. listening and observing,

3. selecting the proper role.

**Empathy.** As we stated in the previous chapter, empathy consists of mentally putting oneself in the shoes of another. This process is very useful in making the communication process effective. Because the sales representative is attempting to act as a creative problem solver in helping prospects to achieve their objectives, he or she must be able to see problems from the prospect's point of view.

Consider the example of a saleswoman who sells paper copiers. Just before she makes each sales presentation she goes through an "exercise in empathy." The preapproach information that she has gathered makes this practice more realistic than if she were using "cold canvass" methods of prospecting. Before making a presentation, she asks herself:

- What are the objectives of this prospect?
- What problems confront the prospect that inhibit attainment of these objectives?
- What can I do in overcoming these problems?

In the past the paper copier firm employed another saleswoman who did not practice empathy, though she considered herself to be an expert advisor to her customers, one who could quickly size up their needs and tell them what items to purchase. But her main objective was to meet her own needs (selling a large volume of copiers) rather than those of the customers. As a result she often simply "unloaded" several copiers on several prospects who did not need them but succumbed to her persuasive arguments. Because the copiers did not fulfill the buyers' expectations considerable antagonism arose and eventually the woman was asked to resign, since she had consistently failed to meet her sales quota. The point is that she had considerable technical expertise but did not practice empathy.

With the second saleswoman however, new prospects sense that she is genuinely interested in their welfare and tries to do what is best for them. Old customers have found by experience and have heard from their competitors that she has a concern with their welfare. One of the central ingredients of the success of this salesperson is her ability to practice the empathy approach.

**Listening and Observing.**   Earlier we mentioned that listening and observing are useful because they provide the only means of feedback on how the presentation is progressing and the directions it should take. If sales representatives are to be problem solvers for their customers, they must rely upon listening and observing.

**Selecting the Proper Role.**   The third determinant of the effectiveness of the personal-selling communication process is the extent to which the sales representative fulfills the role expectations of the prospect.[14] Role expectations consist of expected behaviors. Thus, one prospect may want the salesperson to act as a supplier of information on what new products are being introduced. Another prospect may feel that sales representatives should be heavy entertainers and should wine and dine their customers. Still another may feel that it is appropriate for representatives to act as consultants who will bring specialized advice and assistance to their customers.

Information gathering in prospecting, the preapproach, and feedback during the presentation may help in indicating the role expectations of particular prospects. When gathering information about the prospect, the sales representative should attempt to include in that information clues regarding role expectations. Feedback during the presentation is especially useful for this purpose. Representatives can ask questions related to role expectations and listen carefully to the responses. Examples of questions to ask are:

- What can I do for you today?
- Can I make some suggestions regarding your displays?
- Would you rather go out for lunch or spend some time going over these files?
- My job is to help you. What kind of help do you need?

Such questions help reveal the role expectations of individual prospects. As sales representatives deal with prospects over a period of time they have opportunities to learn role expectations through experience. One real advantage established representatives have over novice counterparts is their knowledge of the role expectations of particular prospects in their territories.

**Summary**   Communicating consists of sharing perceptions or experiences with others. Personal selling is a form of interpersonal communication, involving face-to-face interaction between individuals.

Communication is an important function of sales representatives. It is through this process that they accomplish many of

---

[14]Frederick E. Webster, Jr., "Interpersonal Communication and Salesman Effectiveness," *Journal of Marketing* 32, no. 3 (July 1968): 9–13.

the objectives of the sales presentation. Communications by representatives can bring about changes in prospect attitudes, opinions, and behavior.

1. *Source*—the person who wants to share perceptions or experiences with others.

2. *Message*—that which is intended to be translated from the source to the receiver.

3. *Receiver*—the target of the message.

4. *Feedback*—communications back from the receiver to the source.

5. *Noise*—anything that interferes with the flow of effective communications.

6. *Other parties*—people who communicate with the receiver about the message.

In personal selling communications, both the salesperson and prospect fulfill a dual role. They are both sources and receivers. As such, there are two channels of message elements and feedback elements. Since the process is two-way, the sales representative has an opportunity to listen and observe, as well as to talk.

Part of communication is nonverbal. People communicate through such means as gestures, posture, and body movement. Salespersons should observe nonverbal behavior and adjust their sales presentations accordingly.

One way to make the communication process effective is through source effects. Sales representatives should attempt to develop an image of competency, reliability, and trustworthiness for both themselves and their organizations. Among the ways of creating this image are the use of appropriate status symbols and the choice of appropriate behavior. Some salespersons attempt to develop an image of similarity with the prospect, knowing that such an image is likely to produce favorable attitudes toward the representative.

Message effects also determine the effectiveness of the presentation. Words that are accurate and suitable for particular prospects should be used. Listening helps in the choice of appropriate words. When possible, simple words should be chosen. The salesperson can sometimes enhance the effectiveness of the presentation through repetition, contrast, and drawing conclusions.

Finally, methodology effects—the means of carrying out the presentation—have a bearing upon its effectiveness. Empathy helps salespersons become creative problem solvers. Listening and observing enable them to make presentations tailored to individual prospects' characteristics and needs. Finally, selection of the role that is appropriate, in the view of the prospect, can improve the sales representative's performance.

**Discussion Questions**

1. Define the term *communication*.

2. Personal selling is interpersonal communication. How does this differ from other kinds of communication?

3. Why is communication important to the sales representative?

4. Define each of the following elements of the communication process: (a) source, (b) message, (c) receiver, (d) feedback, (e) noise, (f) other parties.

5. Indicate how the personal selling communication process differs from the general communication process.

6. What if anything is wrong with the statement, "Good sales representatives are those who have powerful and commanding voices, winning smiles, and extensive vocabularies"?

7. What is the significance of the fact that personal selling is a form of two-way communication?

8. Why is nonverbal communication of importance to the sales representative?

9. How can salesperson's behavior be such that they develop a favorable image in the eyes of target consumers?

10. "Many consumers have a more positive attitude toward and tend to buy from those who are perceived to be similar to them." What is the significance of this statement to the sales representative?

11. How should the sales representative go about selecting appropriate words for sales presentations?

12. Indicate the role of repetition in making sales communications.

13. How can contrast help in making sales presentations effective?

14. Should sales representatives draw conclusions or should they leave this up to the prospect?

15. What is empathy? What does it contribute to sales representative effectiveness?

16. What are "role expectations" of prospects? What is the significance of these expectations to the sales representative?

**Practical Exercises**

1. Hold a conversation with another person. After the conversation, answer the following questions:

    a. Who were the sources?

b. What was the nature of the message(s)?

c. Who was the receiver(s)?

d. What feedback did you receive?

e. What noise entered into this communication?

f. What other parties might become involved in this communication process?

2. What nonverbal communications were used by the person you were conversing with?

3. Did you listen carefully to what the other person said? Can you remember much of what he or she said?

4. What did you learn as a result of the above three exercises?

## Selling Project

Indicate how you could use the following in making the selling of your product effective:

1. action to develop an image of competency, reliability, and trustworthiness;

2. status symbols;

3. developing similarities with prospects;

4. selection of appropriate words;

5. repetition;

6. contrast;

7. drawing conclusions;

8. empathy;

9. listening and observing;

10. selecting the proper role.

## Case 7
## Terry Walters

Terry Walters is a saleswoman for Vesper Importers, Inc., which imports goods from Europe, South America, and Asia and sells them to gift shops, import shops, department stores, and a variety of other outlets in the United States.

Vesper's product line is extensive and varied, and includes clothing, serving dishes, cookware, wall hangings, jewelry, vases, and knickknacks. Management considers the wide product line to be one of the keys to Vesper's success. The firm has experienced continuing increases in sales and profits over the past ten years.

The firm prices its products at levels that are higher than those of most competitors. Management considers this to be justified, because of the high quality of items sold and because of the solid image of the firm among retailers. During the previous year, for instance, Vesper prices to retailers were approximately 20 percent higher than the industry average. In turn, the retailers tended to pass the high prices on to their customers.

Vesper management believes in advertising, and the bulk of it is undertaken through catalogs, brochures, and other mailing pieces that are forwarded to retailers. The purposes of the advertising are:

1. to keep the company name constantly in the minds of retailers;

2. to familiarize retailers with new items; and

3. to pave the way for sales representatives.

Vesper has a sales force of fourteen people calling on prospects along the eastern seaboard and northeastern portion of the United States. The sales force is well trained and receives a combination of salary plus commissions, the amount of which exceed the compensations of sales representatives in competing companies. Turnover among the Vesper sales staff is very low, and of those few who leave the firm, most go into business for themselves, since they consider their experience with Vesper to be a learning experience that prepares them for successful independent business operation.

Terry Walters has been with the company for three years. Her territory is upstate New York, where she serves various gift shops, import shops, department stores, jewelry stores, and resorts. Her income exceeds that of most of her fellow graduates from a private college in the Northeast.

Terry has a six-step formula for selling, as set forth in Figure 7-5. (1) She gathers background information on the prospect, (2) determines the needs of the prospect, (3) shows the prospect an item that will attract immediate attention and interest, (4) attempts to show the prospect how he or she can benefit by buying the item (5) answers objections vigorously, and (6) asks for the sale. The formula has worked well for Terry, and she is considered by her sales manager to be the top salesperson.

Still, she has a problem in that she has been unable to sell to Mr. Turnbaugh, who heads the buying division of the Sol chain of department stores, the largest such chain in her territory. Following is a description of her last meeting with Turnbaugh:

TERRY: Good morning Mr. Turnbaugh. I'm here to attempt to sell you some import items again.

TURNBAUGH: Oh yes, good to see you again. You haven't been around for several weeks.

**Figure 7-5. Terry Walters' six-step selling formula.**

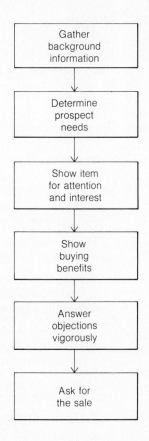

Gather background information

↓

Determine prospect needs

↓

Show item for attention and interest

↓

Show buying benefits

↓

Answer objections vigorously

↓

Ask for the sale

TERRY: That's right. The sales manager has me spending a lot of time developing the southeastern portion of this region. At any rate, I have something interesting to show you. Look at this. [*Hands carved wooden jewel box to him.*]

TURNBAUGH: Where was it made?

TERRY: Yugoslavia. A company in Macedonia puts them out. They employ local artisans who make the boxes for them. Notice the quality. All hand-carved. I can get these for you at only $12 per box if you place a large enough order. On a small-order basis the price would be $14 per box.

TURNBAUGH: I can't use these. We're stocked up in jewelry boxes. They're not turning much at this time of year anyway.

TERRY: All right, I'll check with you in the spring again regarding jewelry boxes. In the meantime, I have some Bulgarian toys that you will be interested in. [*Hands him infant's toy.*]

TURNBAUGH: Interesting looking. Will it sell?

TERRY: Yes. Several gift stores in Mapleton are obtaining good volume with it. One of our representatives has indicated that it sells well as both a toy and as a novelty. It is, of course, part of a line. Here are some photographs of other items in the line.

TURNBAUGH: Do you have a price list?

TERRY: Yes. [*Hands it to him.*]

TURNBAUGH: These are expensive.

TERRY: Yes, but their novelty appeal will allow you to charge a more than normal margin. None of our customers have experienced any problems in getting volume with these toys. Look at the craftsmanship. Your customers will find them to be very durable. Want to place an order?

TURNBAUGH: This is not my buying season for toys. You might check back in the fall.

TERRY: Confidentially, the price on these items will be up by about 35 percent in the fall. I can get you a shipment now. This will give you the jump on those who buy later.

TURNBAUGH: I don't have the storage capability to hold them until the fall. At any rate, the Sol Company is trying to keep inventories to a minimum. It's a new policy.

TERRY: I can get you some volume discounts, by the way. The price list that you have does not mention them.

TURNBAUGH: I think that a purchase now is out of the question.

TERRY: Well, keep these in mind. If you decide to make a purchase, I'll catch you on the next trip. At any rate, I have some other items to show you. Have you ever stocked Italian dinnerware?

TURNBAUGH: No, but I have a full line of dinnerware. I see that its now 3:30. I have a meeting with a store manager in 10 minutes and must run. Good luck in selling these new items.

TERRY: Fine. I'll see you on the next visit.

Critique Terry's communication effectiveness in dealing with Turnbaugh.

**Suggested Readings**

Berlo, David K. "Empathy and Managerial Communication," in Charles Press and Alan Arian, eds., *Empathy and Ideology: Aspects of Administrative Innovation*. Chicago: Rand McNally & Co., 1966.

Campbell, James H., and Hal W. Hepler, eds. *Dimensions of Communication*. Belmont, Cal.: Wadsworth Publishing Co., 1965

Crane, Edgar. *Marketing Communications: A Behavioral Approach to Men, Messages, and Media.* New York: John Wiley & Sons, 1972

Fast, Julius. *Body Language.* New York: Pocket Books, 1971.

Grikscheit, Gary M. "An Experimental Investigation of Persuasive Communication in Selling," *1973 Combined Proceedings American Marketing Association.* Chicago: American Marketing Association, 1974.

Hayakawa, S. I. *Language in Thought and Action.* New York: Harcourt Brace Jovanovich, 1964.

Kerby, Joe Kent. *Consumer Behavior: Conceptual Foundations.* New York: Dun-Donnelley Publishing Corporation, 1975, ch. 14.

Levitt, Theodore. "Communications and Industrial Selling," *Journal of Marketing* 30, no. 2 (April 1967): 15–21.

Parry, John. *The Psychology of Human Communication.* New York: American Elsevier Publishing Co., 1968.

Webster, Frederick E., Jr. "Informal Communication in Industrial Markets," *Journal of Marketing Research* 7, no. 2 (May 1970): 186–89.

# 8

# The Presentation

*After reading this chapter you should be able to demonstrate a knowledge of:*

- *the contact or approach;*
- *means of making the contact or approach effective;*
- *the sales presentation;*
- *various sales presentation techniques;*
- *a recommended sales presentation technique.*

The presentation is that part of the personal selling process where salespersons put their communication skills into effect. You, of course, have been exposed to many sales presentations. Examples of different kinds of presentations are as follows:

COIN SALESPERSON: You should buy this one. It's from the era of Constantine the Great and is in good condition.

VARIETY STORE SALESPERSON: Have you considered a Leica CL camera? It's compact, low in price, and has through-the-lens metering.

GIFT STORE SALESPERSON: A very nice gift for your wife would be Lennox china crystal.

TRAVEL AGENT: A very nice tour for you would be this one to Mexico. It goes through Mexico City, Taxco, and Acapulco.

CHEMICAL COMPANY SALESPERSON: These carbon filters should cut the water pollution from your steel mill considerably.

POWER GENERATOR SALESPERSON: Much of the heat that your plant emits is wasted. We can provide you with on-site electric power generation that uses what used to be waste heat.

POLAROID SALESPERSON: We can provide portrait identification cards for all of your employees at a low cost.

U.S. NAVY RECRUITER: The navy can provide you with career training that is difficult to duplicate anywhere else.

MUSEUM DIRECTOR: I can assure you that if you donate these paintings to the museum they will receive the finest care possible.

This chapter describes the sales presentation, starting with the contact or approach, when the sales representative first gets in touch with the prospect, and then the other elements of the presentation that follow the contact. We will also examine various sales presentation methods that are used and recommend a particular method.

**Elements of the Presentation**

Figure 8-1 outlines the four primary elements of the presentation. First, the salesperson must develop an overall plan for making the contact and the presentation. Second, he or she carries out the contact, actually uses it in conjunction with a particular sales call. Third, the salesperson applies the sales presentation method designed to achieve the objectives of the call. Finally, he or she observes the feedback from prospects, which can result in varying the contact and presentation methods original planned. Let us consider these four steps.

**Figure 8-1. The four elements of the presentation.**

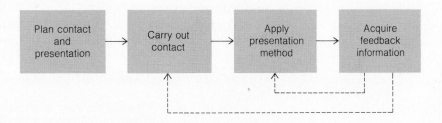

**The Contact or Approach**
Nature of the Contact

In the contact, the sales representative approaches the prospect with the goal of making a sales presentation. The objectives of the contact are:

1. to convince the prospect that he or she should allow the presentation to take place;

2. to set the stage for the remainder of the presentation.

Normally, the contact is more difficult when salespersons are calling upon prospects for the first time than they are in cases where the parties are already acquainted. In the case of first-time calls, sales representatives are strangers. They must convince prospects that the representative and organization have benefits to offer and are trustworthy. In either case, some preliminary nonselling small talk, such as "I can see you have a background of purchasing work in the food-processing industry," is expected by most prospects.[1] Basically, this preliminary conversation should be interesting and pleasant.

Whether the parties are already acquainted or not, the contact is of extreme importance. Many sales are made or lost in the first 30 seconds of the presentation.[2] If the contact is not properly handled, the prospect may not allow a presentation. Or poorly handled contacts can get presentations off to a bad start, as when the prospects become hostile or sales representatives appear unsure of themselves. Failure to practice techniques such as those mentioned in this chapter can alienate both first-time and established prospects and render the remainder of the presentation ineffective.

Dealing with Gatekeepers

In many cases, effective contacting requires getting past a "gatekeeper," a secretary, receptionist, clerk, or other person who protects the prospect from interruptions. Good relations with those individuals can be one of the most important assets of the sales representative. Once the gatekeeper has been gotten around, the sales representative must gain the attention and interest of the prospect.

There are various techniques for getting past gatekeepers. Basically, if the sales representative has confidence and has a

---

[1]"Openings for Every Occasion," *Sales Management* 109, no. 9 (30 October 1972): 6.

[2]Bert Schlain, "How to Handle the First 30 Seconds of the Sale," in John D. Murphy, ed., *Secrets of Successful Selling* (New York: Dell Publishing Co. 1963), p. 68.

positive attitude toward gatekeepers, he or she is likely to be effective in dealing with them. The representative should be friendly but not overly friendly. The gatekeeper should be treated with respect, for he or she may not only control the gate but may be influential in buying decisions. Secretaries have been known to wield considerable influence over their bosses.

Following are some methods that can be used in approaching the gatekeeper:

Good afternoon. Would you please arrange an interview with Mr. Devereaux for me.

Please tell Mr. Devereaux that I am here.

If you cannot arrange an interview for today, I'd like to make an appointment for tomorrow.

Mr. Devereux asked that I bring this sample by to show him.

I know how to take care of that excess inventory problem that your company is experiencing. Bet that your boss would be interested.

Sometimes sales representatives are delayed at the gatekeeper stage. It is important that they convey the idea that the time of the representative is as valuable as that of the prospect. Where waiting is necessary, the salesperson can use the time to complete written reports, plan other calls, and take care of other accumulated paperwork and planning. Where the delay becomes excessive, the representative should approach the gatekeeper and make an appointment for a future date. This communicates the idea that the time of the representative is important—which it is—and helps conserve it.

Gaining the Attention and Interest of the Prospect

Once past the gatekeeper, the sales representative must gain the prospect's attention and interest in the presentation. This can be difficult. Many thoughts and distractions compete for the prospect's attention and interest. For instance, during the contact the following may take place:

- Background noise in the secretary's office distracts the prospect.

- A telephone call interrupts the contact. The caller is a foreman who says that a shipment of chemicals did not arrive on time and this means part of the plant must be shut down for a day or more. The prospect is annoyed.

- Outside a truck is noisily backing into a loading dock, which makes it difficult for the prospect to hear what the sales representative is saying.

- The prospect worries how he will ever get through all the work he has to do and decides to give the representative only five more minutes.

- The prospect's stomach growls. His new diet is wearing on him and he thinks about lunch.

- The prospect remembers he must pick up his daughter's party dress at the cleaners on the way home, because his daughter was furious when he forgot yesterday. He has to leave early.

The sales representative, then, is faced with major obstacles in gaining attention and interest. Fortunately, there are some proven techniques for achieving them.

**Gaining Attention.** Since many stimuli compete for the attention of the prospect, those that stand out from the rest are most likely to receive attention. Some means by which the salesperson may gain attention are as follows:

1. *Surprise*—as when the sales representative walks into the office and places a new product on the prospect's desk or pulls from his briefcase a sound cartridge projector (which looks like a portable TV) for demonstrating the product.

2. *Color*—as when the sales representative wears a colorful sports jacket and trousers.

3. *Distance*—as when the salesperson presents the opening remarks while standing close to the prospect.

4. *Motion*—as when the sales representative strides very slowly to the desk of the prospect. (Simplicity Manufacturing Company representatives use Super 8 mm sound motion pictures to dramatically portray new products.[3])

5. *Volume*—as when the salesperson speaks in a loud voice. (Care should be taken, however, not to alienate the prospect through stunts such as speaking in an overly loud voice and making dramatic entrances into the prospect's office.[4])

6. *Size*—as when a tall sales representative maintains an erect posture and wears high-heel shoes in order to take advantage of his or her natural size.

---

[3]"Simplicity Uses Films, Eliminates Annual Models in Promoting New Marketing Concept," *The Marketing News* 8, no. 23 (23 June 1975): 7.

[4]Elmer G. Leterman, *Personal Power Through Creative Selling* (New York: Collier Books, 1975), p. 118.

All of these attention-getting devices represent means of being different. Once representatives have achieved attention, they are in a position to generate interest in the presentation.

**Attracting Interest.**　It is not enough that sales representatives acquire the prospect's attention. They must also attract interest in the presentation. Interest can be attained by promising a benefit or by arousing curiosity. Possible means of promising a benefit are:

I can save you some money.

Want to know a sure way to raise sales?

You are wide open for a burglary. Our product can provide you with protection.

I can show you a product you can't afford to turn down.

You seem to have maintenance problems. We are specialists at handling these.

We have improved our products in some directions that will be beneficial to you.

There are innumerable ways of arousing curiosity. Some examples:

I bet you haven't seen our new product yet.

I have something to show you.

Do you know why I'm making this call?

Your competitors are buying the product that I'm about to show you.

I have a surprise for you today.

Herb True, president of Team International, gives the following means of getting attention:

1. Questions to arouse interest and curiosity.

2. News—"Would you like to see the results of a heavy dollar research project designed to help you . . .?"

3. Sampling—"How would you like ten days' complementary use of this product/service?"

4. Solutions to problems—"How would you like to solve your most pressing . . . problem?"

5. Honest praise—"Because you're considered an authority on . . ., I'm going to ask for advice."

6. Dramatize—"I need three minutes of your time to explain an idea that might save you thousands."[5]

All six of the techniques either promise a benefit or attempt to arouse curiosity.

Acquiring Information

Sales representatives should use the contact for acquiring information about the prospect. During the few minutes consumed by this phase of the presentation they should make an attempt to listen and to observe. The resulting inputs add to information gained during prospecting and the preapproach. For instance, a seller of small private airplanes might uncover information such as the following during the contact:

- This prospect has no need for a company aircraft at this time. He has just bought an airplane from another company.

- The prospect's currently owned plane looks old. He may be ready to consider the purchase of a new unit.

- This prospect looks very busy and prosperous. I'll have to compliment him on his success.

- This prospect looks very busy and nervous. I'll have to get to the point quickly.

- I see that the prospect has won a skydiving trophy. I'll use that as a conversation opener.

The contact adds to the store of information that the sales representative already possesses about the prospect from the initial prospecting and from the preapproach. Succeeding stages of the presentation will provide even more knowledge. Figure 8-2 illustrates the scope of the information-acquisition process. The objective is to get enough information so that a presentation can be developed that fits the unique needs of the particular prospect.

Having gotten past gatekeepers, attained the prospect's attention and interest, and possessing some information about the prospect, the salesperson is now ready to employ some personal selling methods to carry out the objectives of the call.

---

[5]Herb True, "Get Prospect's Attention: Open with a Bang," *Marketing Times* 21, no. 3 (May/June 1974): 17–19.

**Figure 8-2.
Accumulated
knowledge about the
prospect.**

Prospecting

Preapproach

Contact

Other steps in the presentation

**Sales Presentation
Methods**

There are a number of sales presentation methods, and here we will describe four of the most important:

1. the canned sales presentation;

2. formula selling;

3. need-fulfillment selling;

4. professional selling.

The Canned Sales
Presentation

Canned sales presentations are standardized. They are not tailored to the characteristics and needs of specific prospects. Rather, the salesperson memorizes the presentation and applies it to all prospects.

If the idea of canned sales presentations seems to have some negative connotations, the approach is not necessarily ineffective for all salespersons and all situations. It may be appropriate when individual sales presentations are not exceedingly important and when prospects do not differ considerably. One research study indicated that the canned presentation can be superior to tailored presentations, in terms of arousing more prospect interest and excitement and in producing more purchase intentions.[6] In this study eighty-six under-

---

[6]Marvin A. Jolson, "The Underestimated Potential of the Canned Sales Presentation," *Journal of Marketing* 39, no. 1 (January 1975): 75–78.

graduate students were exposed to a canned sales presentation and ninety-four students to an ad lib presentation. The product was *Great Books of the Western World* (produced by Encyclopedia Britannica). The students exposed to the canned version found the presentation to be more exciting, amusing, and enjoyable than did the other students. Further 42.3 percent of those exposed to the canned presentation expressed a definite intention to buy the product, as compared to only 25 percent of the group exposed to the noncanned presentation.

The canned presentation has several advantages. (1) It can be carefully planned in advance. The salesperson is in a position to use words, phrases, and sentences that have been developed and tested. (2) The presentation can be organized around audiovisual materials, such as films, slides, portfolios, charts, graphs, and videotapes. (3) The sales representative need not grope for words, phrases, and sentences that are meaningful to the prospect. This is a benefit to the employer, since training costs may be minimized. It is less difficult to have sales representatives memorize a planned sales talk than it is to train them to be creative problem solvers. Further, the organization does not necessarily have to hire creative personnel to render memorized sales talks. (4) Finally, sales representatives who are using a canned presentation often have considerable self-confidence, since they do not have to worry about determining what to say to prospects. All that is necessary is to recite what has been learned.

Memorized presentations are not uncommon at the door-to-door level. Some magazine and encyclopedia representatives employ this technique with considerable success. The Realsilk Company, a producer of clothing items, employs canned sales presentations for its salespersons. Representatives memorize sentences and words to be used in the contact and throughout the presentation and practice and memorize product demonstrations. (One demonstration involves handing a ladies' stocking to the prospect and asking him or her to attempt to tear or stretch it.) In addition, the representatives memorize phrases to answer objections and to close the sale. In short, much of the Realsilk representative's presentation is planned and committed to memory prior to the sales call.

For many selling jobs memorized presentations are not appropriate. Representatives cannot act as creative problem solvers if they are merely reciting previously memorized words and phrases. Individual prospects' characteristics and needs differ considerably and cannot be expected to be met by a standardized approach. Further, prospects may be alienated if they feel that what the sales representative is saying and doing is part of a plot to achieve the goals of the marketer and not as a means of satisfying the needs of the prospect. "People usually do not trust other persons who try to influence them," says one psychologist. When you know in advance that someone is going to try to change your attitudes, you tend to resist."[7] Many selling situations, therefore, require methods other than the canned approach. One of them is formula selling.

Formula Selling

Formula selling makes use of some set of preconceived objectives in order to carry out the selling task. Probably the most widely used formula is the AIDA approach, which states that the sales representative should strive to achieve the following objectives:[8]

1. *Attention,*

2. *Interest,*

3. *Desire,*

4. *Action.*

A salesperson who uses the AIDA formula first attempts to gain the prospects' *Attention,* then to gain their *Interest*—in both cases using the methods we described in the contact stage of the presentation—to develop their *Desire* for the product or service, and finally to induce them to *Action,* such as purchasing the product.

The formula approach does not require the use of a canned sales presentation. Sales representatives have not memorized their sales talks; they have, however, memorized the formula and have certain key words, gestures, and other preconceived means of achieving the four objectives.

John Meyers, a real estate salesman, uses the AIDA method. The essence of his approach to the presentation; outlined in Figure 8-3, is written on a card, which he consults in planning individual sales presentations.

To gain Attention, John attempts to "Be different—be more informed, faster, bigger, etc." His voice is naturally deep, and with practice he has found he can make it even deeper, which

[7]Elton B. McNeil, *The Psychology of Being Human* (San Francisco: Canfield Press, 1974), p. 381.

[8]E. Jerome McCarthy, *Basic Marketing: A Managerial Approach* (Homewood, Ill.: Richard D. Irwin, 1975), pp. 391–92.

| | |
|---|---|
| ATTENTION: | Be different. Be more informed, faster, bigger, etc. |
| INTEREST: | Promise a needed benefit, such as quality home construction. |
| DESIRE: | Show how that benefit can be attained through our firm. |
| ACTION: | Invite the prospect to action—as by saying, "Shall we close the deal?" |

works reasonably well as an attention getting device. Many prospects direct their attention his way when he speaks.

To gain Interest, John attempts to "Promise a needed benefit—such as quality home construction." He has developed a practice of carefully looking over each property he lists and deciding what outstanding benefits it offers. Some listings are in fact very well constructed, so "trouble-free living" is one benefit he promises. Other benefits might be large size, good location, or low interest rates on the mortgage.

John believes that the way to gain the prospects' Desire is to show how wanted benefits can be attained through him. This requires discovering what specific desires the prospect holds and then relating these to specific properties and to the realty company. John asks numerous questions aimed at determining the desires of prospects—for example:

Do you want a large home?

How many bedrooms do you need?

Would a property located on a lake interest you?

About what price range are you considering?

Is a location near your place of work important?

Once the desires are discovered, John indicates what property listings seem to offer the wanted benefits. He also explains that any transaction will be handled with expertise by the well-qualified personnel of his brokerage firm. This technique seems to work well, but it must be supplemented with a number of devices to bring about Action. For examples, he may say to the prospect:

Why don't you make an offer? Other prospects are interested in this property and they may beat you to it.

You can be in this property in only a month if you buy it now.

If you make an offer, I'll take it right over to the owner and present it to him tonight.

While some of the action devices work well, John must use caution, for some prospects become alienated if they feel John is pushing them. Thus, he attempts to be as subtle as possible in suggesting action.

**Disadvantages of the AIDA Approach.** The AIDA method has some significant disadvantages. One is that the sales representative may not operate as a creative problem solver for the prospect. Basically, the formula is designed to attain the objectives of the sales representative rather than those of the prospect. Thus, reliance upon the formula can produce selling techniques that are not attuned with the marketing concept. John Meyers, for instance, found that using the AIDA framework led him to be more concerned with selling properties than with satisfying customers.

Another weakness in the AIDA approach is that it does not necessarily involve the prospect in the decision making process. The sales representative is the one who is creating attention, interest, desire, and action. Conversely, the prospect is the passive recipient of the sales representative's efforts. Prospects are more observers than participants. They are treated as objects to be manipulated, rather than as sales representatives' partners in determining the best way to overcome the problems of prospects. Because of this orientation, the AIDA method is sometimes ineffective.

A third disadvantage of formula approaches is that they can lead the sales representative to undue reliance on the use of gimmicks and "magic words," such as the following:

- When meeting a new prospect smile broadly and give a firm handshake. This is good for developing attention.

- Say "I have something that you have never seen before" to develop attention and interest.

- Say "We can save you money" to incite desire.

- Hand a pen to the prospect as a means of suggesting that he or she should sign a contract for an order.

Such devices are not necessarily bad. Sales representatives who use them, however, may come to view their roles as that of manipulating devices, rather than as problem solvers for prospects. This is not likely to be in the best interest of customers. Further, customers may develop the impression that the representative is not trying to help them but is simply trying to sell them something. Such an impression certainly does not enhance the source credibility of the sales representative.

**Summary of the Formula Approach.**   Overall, formula methods have some contributions that are useful to the sales representative. These methods suggest various ways of attaining effective persuasion. A number of organizations have found that formulas are useful in training new representatives. Still, their disadvantages are sufficiently great to dictate consideration of other methods. One of these is need fulfillment selling.

Need-Fulfillment
Selling

Neither the canned sales presentation nor the formula methods focus upon the needs of prospects. Instead, both emphasize the needs of sales representatives and their organizations. In need-fulfillment selling sales representatives first attempt to discover the needs or desires of the prospect.[9] Then they endeavor to satisfy these needs by providing the desired benefits.

**Implementing the Method.**   Figure 8-4 outlines the three steps involved in need-fulfillment selling. First, sales representatives attempt to determine the needs of the prospect. Among the major ways of doing this are asking questions, listening, and observing. Second, salespersons determine what benefits are required in order to satisfy the needs. Finally, they attempt to supply these benefits.

Martin James is a seller of scrubbing systems, devices used to screen out sulfur dioxide and other emissions from industrial installations and so reduce air pollution. Martin relies heavily upon the need-fulfillment technique, although he has modified it somewhat. He attempts first to determine the needs of the prospect, which is not easy to do. He cannot simply ask "What are your pollution abatement needs?" and obtain the required answers. Some prospects are probably not aware of their needs. Others are aware but are unwilling to reveal them or cannot seem to articulate them. As a result, Martin relies upon a series of questions and upon considerable listening and observing. For example:

> PROSPECT: I need a light-duty scrubber, one that just meets federal and state minimum requirements and does no more than this.

---

[9]For a discussion of how to discover needs and desires see David J. Luck, Hugh G. Wales, and Donald A. Taylor, *Marketing Research* (Englewood Cliffs, N.J.: Prentice-Hall, 1974), pp. 228–37, 242–44.

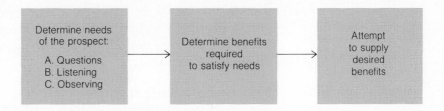

**Figure 8-4. Three steps of need-fulfillment selling.**

| Determine needs of the prospect: A. Questions B. Listening C. Observing | Determine benefits required to satisfy needs | Attempt to supply desired benefits |

MARTIN: Why do you feel that only a light scrubber is required?

PROSPECT: Our emissions are not great. In fact, they are probably the lowest in this community.

MARTIN: I get your point. Are local utility companies fulfilling your power needs effectively?

PROSPECT: They really aren't. As a matter of fact, we've had to cut back production several times, simply because we couldn't get fuel.

MARTIN: A heavy-duty scrubber might help, in this regard. We have one model that permits recycling of some of the gas that normally would be lost. This provides the user with an additional source of fuel. Would this interest you?

PROSPECT: It certainly would. Let's look at some of the specifications on your heavy-duty models.

Together, through a process of questioning, listening, and observing, Martin and the prospect were able to ascertain an important need of the latter. Most of the comments made by Martin were designed to instigate thinking and fact finding by the prospect.

Once the needs are identified, the sales representative, working jointly with the prospect, attempts to discover the benefits that satisfy the identified needs. The salesperson also attempts to determine the best means of providing these benefits. As it turned out, the prospect needed a source of reducing air pollution and a second fuel provider. The light-duty scrubbers would have not furnished fuel. Martin had a heavy-duty scrubber in his product line that effectively cuts air pollution, yet was not overly expensive, in comparison to the offerings of competitors. These characteristics were exactly what the prospect sought and as a result he ultimately bought the model.

**Limitation of the Need-Fulfillment Approach.** The need-fulfillment casts the sales representative in the role of one who helps prospects discover, articulate, and fulfill their needs, but it is not complete. It does not go far enough, in terms of providing all of the guidelines that sales representatives should have. The professional selling approach, however, does provide these guidelines.

Professional Selling Professional selling combines some of the best of the elements of each of the methods described earlier and adds a few more. The technique involves:

1. a determination by sales representatives that they are creative problem solvers for prospects;

2. a dedication to fulfilling the needs and desires of prospects;

3. a willingness to work with prospects and to gain their participation in the selling process;

4. utilization of the AIDA method;

5. asking questions and observing;

6. empathy;

7. maturity.

**Creative Problem Solving.**   Professional sales representatives view their role as that of creative problem solvers for prospects. In this light, the Mead Corporation adheres to the following philosophy:

> A professional paper salesman is an expert in problem solving, a consultant to both graphic arts and industrial customers, able to make sound recommendations about their advertising, packaging, and other requirements.[10]

Prospects have problems when there is a gulf between a desired situation and an actual situation. The role of the creative problem solver is to build a bridge between these two situations, as illustrated in Figure 8-5. Salesman Richard K. Ransom of Hickory Farms of Ohio, franchiser of cheese and sausage stores, is effective in building bridges. According to one source, "He'll walk into a store that the owner thinks never looked or operated better and find a dozen things wrong in as many seconds."[11]

Problem solvers are concerned with the needs and desires of the prospect, rather than the needs and desires of sales repre-

---

[10]*Annual Report*, Mead Corporation, New York, 1974, p. 16.

[11]Steve Blicksten, "Flattening the Averages at Hickory Farms," *Sales Management* 108, no. 12 (12 June 1972): 27.

sentatives and their organizations. Representatives who embrace this role practice the marketing concept—that of satisfying consumers at a profit. They are actively involved in helping the prospect to identify actual and desired situations and in determining how to move from the former to the latter. The term "creative" means that the sales representative seeks to conceive of means of problem solving that may not be readily apparent. Following is a scenario where an air conditioner sales representative engages in creative problem solving in calling upon a prospect (an insurance company purchasing agent):

PROSPECT: Our company wants to replace the air conditioning unit of our office building. Basically, we want low cost. We simply cannot afford to go overboard in buying a luxury installation.

SALESPERSON: Yes, in the face of inflation, it's foolish to overspend and buy more than you need.

PROSPECT: I'm attracted to your product because I've heard that it is attractively priced, relative to the competition.

SALESPERSON: All of our products are competitively priced. On the other hand, we place a lot of emphasis upon low operating costs and trouble-free maintenance. Our quality, then, is better than some of our rivals, but our purchase price is higher than some. If you want a low purchase price and are unconcerned with operating costs and maintenance, the Ajax Company may be the answer. Their initial costs are low, but I would be concerned with these other factors.

PROSPECT: You have a good point. We don't want to buy a cheap unit that results in high operating and maintenance costs.

SALESPERSON: Our X-342 unit may be just what you need. Its price is low, yet it is not expensive to operate and requires little maintenance.

PROSPECT: Let's look at some specifications for that item. It may be what we need.

This prospect had a problem—that of determining the air-conditioning unit qualities that he sought. The talk with the sales representative permitted him to develop his thoughts and

**Figure 8-5. Creative problem solving.**

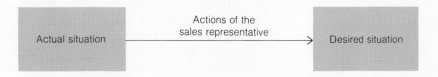

Actual situation — Actions of the sales representative → Desired situation

to realize that he really wanted low operating and maintenance costs, in addition to low initial price. The sales representative did not hedge—he pointed out that the Ajax Company would provide the low initial price. But he also brought out the importance of low operating and maintenance costs, which turned out to be important to the prospect. This buyer profited considerably from the creative problem-solving abilities of the representative.

**Fulfilling Prospects' Needs and Desires.** Professional representatives are dedicated to fulfilling the needs and desires of prospects, as representatives who use need-fulfillment selling are also. This means that professional salespersons seek to identify needs, look for benefits that will satisfy the needs, and attempt to provide the desired benefits. Consider this example, in which the prospect is an oil-company employee who purchases automobiles for the company fleet:

PROSPECT: Basically, we're interested in your Acme line.

SALESPERSON: It's an excellent make. Why are you focused in on Acme?

PROSPECT: We want an impressive automobile for our company executives and salesmen to drive. The Acme seems to be a good bet.

SALESPERSON: The Acme is impressive looking. It has a rather classic cut. Is that what you want?

PROSPECT: Not necessarily. We want something that will help in sustaining and building our company image.

SALESPERSON: Would you be interested in a make with more modern lines?

PROSPECT: Yes. That really would be more in keeping with the image that we want to project.

SALESPERSON: That being the case, let's look at some of our Zeus models. They have a modern design and may be more in line with your thinking.

PROSPECT: Yes, I'd be very interested in considering the Zeus make. Let's go and see some of your stock.

Ultimately, the prospect purchased a number of Zeus model automobiles and was pleased with the results. Company executives and sales personnel liked the new automobiles and felt that the purchasing agent had made a good choice. Essentially, the reason for this choice was that the sales representative was dedicated to discovering and fulfilling the needs and wants of the buyer.

Participating with
Prospects in
Selling

Professional selling requires that the salesperson work *together* with prospects in the selling process. Representatives do not sell *to* prospects. Rather, they sell *with* them.

Professional salespersons have the attitude that they want to help solve prospects' problems. Significantly, the sales representative must convey the idea to the prospect that the two are jointly seeking solutions to these problems. Sales representatives are much like consultants—their objective is to bring expert advice and assistance to the prospect. Like the consultant, however, the salesperson needs the assistance of the client to determine how the advice and assistance might be applied.

Much of the sales representative's role is that of guiding the thinking of prospects. This requires asking relevant questions that direct prospects toward the solution of their own problems. In fact, the sales representative cannot easily "sell" the prospects in such a way that they arrive at a particular decision. Rather, the prospects must "sell" themselves.

Professional selling should be considered in relation to *conflict selling*. Figure 8-6 shows the two concepts. Conflict selling takes place when the representative attempts to sell *to* the prospect—that is, attempts to convince the prospect to make a purchase in order to fulfill the *representative's* goals. The expected result is resistance from the prospect, and thus the two parties are locked in conflict.

In professional selling the two parties work together to achieve the interests of the prospect. Each can contribute something in the direction of promoting these interests. Prospects will make decisions, however, only when they have convinced themselves that this is the proper course of action. The following dialog, between a sporting goods sales representative and a sporting goods retailer, illustrates the process of allowing prospects to sell themselves:

SALESPERSON: Are you facing any major problems these days?

RETAILER: Yes. Competition is getting tougher. The new shopping center has two stores that carry sporting goods. The competition's killing me.

SALESPERSON: How are you trying to meet it?

RETAILER: Mainly by more advertising, but I don't have the funds to keep advertising at this pace. And my competitors do more advertising than I do anyway.

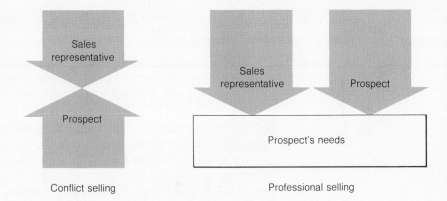

**Figure 8-6. Efforts expended in conflict and professional selling.**

Sales representative

Prospect

Conflict selling

Sales representative

Prospect

Prospect's needs

Professional selling

SALESPERSON: Have you considered any other means of meeting competition?

RETAILER: Yes, I'm going to begin appealing more to younger people. Maybe this is the answer. The competition seems to be aiming at all age groups. If I make a special effort to satisfy youth needs I may gain an edge in that market.

SALESPERSON: How are you going to appeal to young people?

RETAILER: I'll emphasize goods that young people like in my advertising. I'll also hire some high school or college students to work as sales clerks on a part-time basis.

SALESPERSON: What goods will you emphasize in your promotion program?

RETAILER: Probably backpacks, skis, ski equipment, tennis equipment, and golf equipment. I'm making a major shift into cross-country skis. The sport is really picking up in the youth groups.

SALESPERSON: I don't see very much ski equipment on display here.

RETAILER: I want to talk to you about that. What do you have available?

SALESPERSON: I'll show you a number of lines and you can decide which ones to order. We carry quite a variety of offerings in the cross-country field.

[*The two go over catalogs and price lists for half an hour.*]

RETAILER: I like your Trak and Skilom lines. Norwegian skis really are the best. Let's write up an order. I want to stock up now, since the buying season will soon be past.

SALESPERSON: Fine, I'll write it up.

This was obviously a very successful sales call. In a skillful manner, the salesperson had allowed the prospect to "sell himself" on the desirability of the purchase. The role of the sales representative was mainly to encourage the prospect to explore his needs and to act as an expert adviser on the quality of various lines and models. Contrast this to the following approach, one likely to produce conflict:

SALESPERSON: I have some new items you'll be interested in. We brought out some new fishing reels that are a must in any sporting goods store.

RETAILER: I'm not really interested in more fishing reels at this point. In fact, I'm making a major thrust toward the youth market. They're mainly interested in other sports.

SALESPERSON: You may be making a mistake. Many of the local college students are avid fishermen. Look at our Pursues line. It has some unique benefits that cannot be ignored by anyone who's a serious fisherman.

RETAILER: Yes, I'm familiar with the line, and really do not need more fishing reels.

SALESPERSON: If you buy now I can get you a good price.

RETAILER: I have no real need for these items. Look at the clock. It's almost 3:00 already and I have a lot of things to do. See you around.

This presentation is bound to produce conflict. The sales representative decided that the prospect needs fishing reels and attempted to impose his judgment on the prospect. Such an approach is bound to be ineffective since it does not allow the prospect to act as a participant in the selling process—to sell himself. The sales representative would probably not only not get an order for fishing reels but would likely seriously alienate the prospect.

Utilization of the AIDA Method

Professional selling utilizes adaptations of the AIDA method. This does not mean that sales representatives should memorize certain words and phrases calculated to bring about attention, interest, desire, and action. Rather, these four stages should be regarded as goals the representative wants to achieve in making the presentation. In turn, he or she can include means of reaching the four goals in the story plan.

Figure 8-7 depicts a story plan that Ivan (the seller of light- and medium-weight trucks) uses. Each of the four goals is presented at the top of the form. In planning the presentation Ivan determines how he will reach each goal and writes this in the appropriate column. This process aids him in organizing his thinking in developing a well-planned presentation.

Asking Questions and Observing

Professional salespersons make considerable use of asking questions and observing, qualities we stressed earlier, since this helps them tailor their presentation to specific prospects. The questioning process also allows sales representatives to act as creative problem solvers and permits the prospect to participate actively in the selling process.

**Figure 8-7. AIDA story-plan form used by Ivan.**

STORY PLAN FORM

Prospect's name: _Marty Dugan_

Date: _1-12-78_

| Attention | Interest | Desire | Action |
|-----------|----------|--------|--------|
| 1. Mention his name. | 1. Say I'm here to help him. | 1. Describe product benefits. | 1. Have him test-drive a company heavy-duty truck. |
| 2. Introduce myself and mention name of Marty's friend, Mary Radovich. | 2. Mention fact that some of his drivers are complaining about frequent breakdowns of existing trucks. | 2. Describe company services. | 2. Ask for a sale. If that fails, give him more facts. |
| 3. Speak loudly. Marty is hard of hearing. | 3. Mention fact that his competitor (Calypso Trucking Co.) has just purchased four new company trucks. | 3. Show on paper how company trucks can save him money and speed up his deliveries. | 3. If he will not make a decision now, ask for another interview within a week. |
| 4. Keep posture good. He is an ex-Marine colonel. | | | |

When salespersons do not listen and observe, the prospect may become inattentive or antagonistic without their knowing it. Sales representatives must stay attuned to how an interview is progressing in the mind of the prospect, so that they can depart from the story plan, if necessary.

Ivan found it necessary to depart from the AIDA "Desire" (step 3) techniques he listed in Figure 8-7. His questions brought out responses by the prospect, Marty Dugan, that indicated he had a negative image toward the truck producer:

IVAN: Well, I've described the product benefits and our services and have shown on paper how this model can save you money and speed up your deliveries. Want to take a test drive?

MARTY: Yes, I guess so.

IVAN: You don't seem enthusiastic. Do you have doubts about this model?

MARTY: Not really.

IVAN: Are there other questions that I could answer?

MARTY: To tell you the truth, I'm not too sure that I should do business with your firm. One of my friends had some bad experiences with it. He had difficulty in getting parts deliveries on time. Also he found the billing procedure confusing. I don't want to get into these sorts of problems.

IVAN: Your friend's experience was unfortunate. This may have been due to misunderstandings on the part of company personnel and him. If he is still having problems, give me his name and I'll take up the matter myself. In the meantime, do you know Ed Warson or Bill Black?

MARTY: Yes, both competitors and good friends.

IVAN: Both of them have said that I can use them for testimonials. Will you call them and ask them about their experiences with my company? You'll be pleasantly surprised to find that they have been very happy with our services.

MARTY: Okay, I'll call them. Meanwhile, will you see if you can help my friend who had the problems with your company.

IVAN: Of course. Give me his name and telephone number. I'll get on it today.

Ivan used his listening and observing to pick up the negative attitudes of Marty. This led to substantial departures from the story plan. If Ivan had merely delivered a canned sales talk or mechanically lectured around a formula, he probably would never have known about the negative attitude and so could not have been in a position to eliminate the negative element.

Empathy

As we said before, empathy is the process of mentally putting oneself in the shoes of another. Sales representatives who employ this technique imagine that they are the prospect when they are planning and carrying out the presentation. This is an aid to acting as a creative problem-solver and in helping to meet the needs and the desires of prospects.

Mary Larson, representative for a producer of fashion clothing, practices empathy when before making a sales call she asks herself:

> If I were this prospect, what would my major goals be? What would my major problems be? What buying benefits would I seek? What kind of sales representative would I respond to? Why would I buy from a particular supplier?

Over a period of time, Mary has found that empathy is very effective. It allows her to see sales transactions from the prospect's point of view. It also makes her work more interesting. She enjoys the empathy exercises because they have improved her relationships with individual prospects, and many have become close personal friends.

When Mary first began selling, she was very formal and businesslike. Because she had not learned to practice empathy, her sales presentations were rather stiff and mechanical. She also felt extremely tense, both before and during the presentations. In a selling seminar, Mary learned how to utilize empathy and found that when she used it she was no longer tense nor were her prospects. Indeed, she found herself developing genuine affection for many prospects and felt that they liked her. Empathy is thus one of the most important ingredients for successful selling, not to mention for establishing favorable interpersonal relationships with others.

Maturity

Mature means "complete and finished in natural growth or development."[12] The mature individual has literally grown up. He or she has control over emotions, adjusts to society, and is not self-centered. By these definitions, clothing saleswoman Mary Larson is mature, even though she is relatively young.

---

[12]*The American Heritage Dictionary* (New York: American Heritage Publishing Co., 1973), p. 807.

**Control Over Emotions.** Mature salespersons can control their emotions. This means they can avoid undue anger, self-pity, pursuit of pleasure for its own sake, and other potentially undesirable emotions—at least insofar as it affects their jobs. Mary has this capability. She realizes that effectiveness on the job requires that she control, not be controlled by, emotions. Sometimes this requires substantial patience and understanding. For example:

> PROSPECT: I've been a buyer for years and I know what I'm doing! Don't tell me what will sell in this city. You don't know what you're talking about!

> MARY [*after mentally counting to ten*]: No one would dispute the fact that you have an excellent idea of what sells in this city. I'm very impressed with your knowledge. Let's look at the lines my firm has just introduced. I bet that there are several that fit into the needs of your customers.

Mary's natural reaction was anger. But by controlling her emotions she made a successful sale. At other times she has resisted the desire to quit work early and spend an afternoon on the tennis courts. In short, she is dedicated to her work and does not allow emotions to interfere.

**Adjustment to Society.** Mature people have the ability to adjust to society; they are adaptable. When cultural values and ways of life change, they are willing to consider change on their part. Mary, for instance, was raised to believe that buying on credit was not acceptable. She has changed her attitude, however, since many of her customers buy on credit, both as purchasing officers for their companies and as individual consumers.

**Lack of Self-Centeredness.** Mature people are concerned with doing their jobs well rather than being overly occupied with personal feelings and activities. No one is *un*concerned with his or her own well-being, of course, but some are less concerned than others. As Figure 8-8 indicates, self-centeredness is a matter of degree.

Mary is very concerned with the job, and her attitude places her somewhere in the right-hand portion of Figure 8-8. She is willing to undertake activities for the company, such as filling out reports, that do not benefit her directly. Further, she puts in long hours when it appears that these are necessary in order to service her accounts. In short, Mary is job oriented. This is one of the reasons why she is one of the top sales producers in the firm.

**Figure 8-8. Maturity and concern with self and job.**

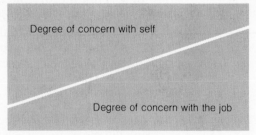

Relatively immature sales representatives

Relatively mature sales representatives

Degree of concern with self

Degree of concern with the job

Conclusions on Professional Selling

Professional sales people are creative problem solvers for their customers. They are dedicated to fulfilling their prospects' needs and desires and draw them into participating in the selling process. Such representatives utilize the AIDA method, ask questions and observe, practice empathy, and are mature. People with these qualities and attitudes are likely to be successful as sales representatives.

**Summary**

This chapter has been concerned with the sales presentation. The first part of the presentation is the contact or approach. The objectives are to convince the prospect to allow the presentation and to set the stage for the remainder of the presentation. Sometimes gatekeepers such as secretaries must be surmounted. Once past the gatekeeper, the representative attempts to gain the attention and interest of the prospect and acquires information about the prospect. There are various sales presentation methods and this chapter covered four of the most important.

1. The canned sales presentation, is standardized. It is used most commonly in situations not requiring a high degree of selling skill, as in door-to-door operations.

2. In formula selling, the representative strives to attain some set of preconceived objectives. One widely used formula is AIDA, for Attention, Interest, Desire, Action. The representative attempts to achieve these four objectives in the order listed. The formula approach allows the salesperson to tailor the presentation to specific prospects. Its disadvantages, however, are that it does not lead the salesperson to be a creative problem solver, does not involve the prospect in the decision-making process, and sometimes leads the salesperson to undue reliance upon gimmicks.

3. Need-fulfillment selling requires that the salesperson discover the needs or desires of the prospect and then attempt to satisfy them. This requires considerable skill in determining needs or

desires and an ability to work closely with prospects. While the method has much to offer, it does not provide all of the ingredients needed for professional selling.

4. The professional salesperson attempts to be a creative problem solver for prospects. He or she is dedicated to fulfilling their needs and desires. Such a salesperson is willing to work together with prospects and to gain their participation in the selling process. This representative makes use of a variation of the AIDA method. Finally, he or she asks questions and observes, practices empathy, and is mature. People who use this method have a high probability of sales success.

**Discussion Questions**

1. What is the contact or preapproach? Set forth the goals of the contact.

2. How can the salesperson deal with gatekeepers?

**Questions**

3. How can the salesperson gain the attention and interest of the prospect, once he or she is past the gatekeeper?

4. Why should representatives attempt to gather information at the contact stage?

5. What is meant by a canned sales presentation? What are its advantages and disadvantages?

6. Describe the AIDA formula. What are its advantages and disadvantages?

7. What is need-fulfillment selling? What advantages does it offer over canned sales presentations and AIDA techniques?

8. What are the essentials of professional selling?

9. How can the salesperson act as a creative problem solver for prospects?

10. What ways do professional salespersons attempt to fulfill prospects' needs and desires.

11. What is meant by "participating with prospects in selling"?

12. How does the professional salesperson use the AIDA method?

13. What is the importance of empathy in professional selling?

14. What are the ingredients of maturity in selling?

**Practical Exercises**

1. Develop a simple sales presentation using the AIDA approach. Try to "sell" a friend on some idea that he or she does not agree with. Possible ideas are:

    a. Let's forget our studies and go to a movie tonight.

    b. Loan me $10.

    c. I can't attend a meeting, will you go in my place?

What did you learn as a result of this exercise?

2. Observe the selling techniques of a retail salesperson. What method did the sales representative use? Was he or she effective? Why or why not? What did you learn as a result of this exercise?

3. Assume that you are going to practice need-fulfillment selling to convince a friend on some idea that he or she does not agree with. Try to determine the relevant needs and desires of that friend. What did you learn as a result of this exercise?

**Selling Project**

1. Develop a contact for selling your product to a hypothetical prospect. Include provision for getting past gatekeepers, for attaining prospect attention and interest, and for gathering information.

2. Develop a sales presentation plan for this same prospect, using the professional selling method.

**Case 8**
**Ronald Terrill**

Ronald Terrill works for a manufacturer's representative, the Arion Company. Arion sells tools to firms involved in exploring for sources of crude oil. Since the enterprise is a manufacturer's agent, it receives income (commissions) only when sales are made. Arion sells the products of over nineteen producers to accounts located in the southwestern part of the United States.

This case describes one of Ronald's sales presentations. He is calling on Mr. Hugh Winter, an oil field superintendent. The superintendent is in charge of all exploration efforts of a large California oil company.

RONALD: How do you do, Mr. Winter. As I said on the phone, I now represent the Arion Company in this area. My predecessor, Tom Blore, was transferred to Texas.

WINTER: Glad to meet you. Have a seat. What's Arion have that's new?

RONALD: Well, we have some diamond drilling bits, the G114 line. They do about the same job as the old G100 model, except that the G114 is 20 percent cheaper. Take a look at the technical specifications in my catalog.

WINTER [*after reading the specifications*]: Interesting. We never have used the 100 model. I've had excellent success with the products of the Nestor Corporation. They're especially good in servicing us. We can get overnight delivery on emergency orders.

RONALD: Arion has fast delivery, too.

WINTER: In this business speed is a must.

RONALD: Well, if you think you might like to try a G114 model, give me a ring. We'll ship them right out.

WINTER: Fine.

RONALD: How are you fixed for casing?

WINTER: We've ordered all that's needed for at least four months. I don't know what we'll be doing after that. We're thinking about drilling on some leases in Bakersfield.

RONALD: I'll check with you in a couple of months to see what your plans are. We've been selling a lot of casing in this area. Our prices are competitive. In fact, the recent steel price increases didn't affect us as much as they did many competitors. The Orion Company, for instance, raised their prices by over 10 percent on casing. Ours rose only 2 percent.

WINTER: Good. Limited price increases are always good news for oil explorers, in times of inflation.

RONALD: We have an excellent management. At the production level, our manufacturing processes are as efficient as they come. Yet our quality-control standards are high. We're also efficient in marketing. Our transportation costs are very low compared to our competitors'. In addition, we have some highly efficient warehousing operations.

WINTER: That's interesting.

RONALD: Yes. Well, back to the product line. We have some good pump models. Do you need any?

WINTER: I just signed a delivery order with the Nestor representative. We won't be needing new pumps for some time to come unless our drilling activity increases substantially.

RONALD: We have some very good pumps. Have you used them?

WINTER: I don't think so. We bought the bulk of these from Nestor. They make a good pump.

RONALD: Yes, they do. We make some good ones too. At one time I was assistant superintendent for the Odin Company's operations in Wyoming. We used Arion pumps almost exclusively and had good luck with them. I hope you'll consider them in the future.

WINTER: It's possible we will when the need arises.

[*The conversation is interrupted by a secretary who enters the room.*]

SECRETARY: Mr. Winter, you're wanted on the telephone.

WINTER [*after finishing the call*]: I've got to leave. One of our drilling rigs has developed some problems. It's been very enjoyable talking with you.

RONALD: The feeling is mutual. I'll look forward to further contacts with you in the future.

Critique Ronald's effectiveness in dealing with Winter.

**Suggested Readings**

Blickstein Steve. "Get Stupid: Do It My Way," *Sales Management* 108, no. 10 (15 May 1972): 19–24.

Canfield, Bertrand R. *Sales Administration: Principles and Problems*. Englewood Cliffs, N.J.: Prentice-Hall, 1962, ch. 19.

Field, George A. "Dysfunctional Role Conception: The Weakest Link in Selling," *Southern Business Review* 1, no. 1 (Spring 1975): 1–7.

Gray, Frank. "Lifters, Leaners, Learners," *Salesman's Opportunity* 103, no. 4 (March 1974): 43.

Kerby, Joe Kent. *Consumer Behavior: Conceptual Foundations*. New York: Dun-Donnelley Publishing Corporation, 1975, ch. 9.

Micali, Paul J. *The Lacy Techniques of Salesmanship*. New York: Hawthorn Books, 1971, ch. 3.

Mueller, Conrad G. *Sensory Psychology*. Englewood Cliffs, N.J.: Prentice-Hall, 1965, chs. 3 and 4.

Robinson, Patrick J. and Bent Stidsen. *Personal Selling in a Modern Perspective*. Boston: Allyn and Bacon, 1967. ch. 8.

Smaltz, Peter R. *Salesmanship: A "Get-up-and-Go" Guide to Effective Selling*. Paterson, N.J.: Littlefield, Adams & Co., 1959, chs. 11, 12, 13, and 14.

Wasson, Chester R. *Consumer Behavior: A Managerial Viewpoint*. Austin, Texas: Austin Press, 1975, ch. 6.

# 9

# Objections

*After reading this chapter you should be able to demonstrate a knowledge of:*

- *what the term* objections *means*
- *the significance of objections to salespersons*
- *types of objections*
- *how objections can be handled*

Objections are a common element in any culture. Courtroom lawyers raise objections to the statements of competing lawyers. Parents object when children return home late. Theater audiences object when films break during a showing. And prospects object to what sales people tell them.

Figure 9-1 outlines five steps in handling prospects' objections:

1. Representatives construct plans for dealing with objections prior to making sales calls.

2. While in the process of making the calls they may find it necessary to encourage the prospect to voice objections.

3. They determine the nature of the objections, thus providing insights as to how to handle them.

4. The determination of how to handle objections is facilitated by various guidelines.

5. These culminate in the actual handling of objections.

6. Finally, salespersons' experiences in handling objections result in feedback, which is useful in planning for ways to meet future objections.

In this chapter we will define objections and point out their importance and meaning to sales people. In addition, we will provide a classification of various kinds of objections. Finally, we will furnish suggestions as to what sales representatives can do when confronted with objections.

## What Objections Are

The verb "object" means "to present a dissenting or opposing argument."[1] In selling, objections are arguments raised by prospects in opposition to the points made by the sales representative. For example:

This motor doesn't have enough power for my needs.

Your deliveries are too slow.

I won't need any new items in this line for at least several months.

It costs too much.

We tried this product last month and didn't like it.

The credit terms you offer aren't as good as those furnished by company X.

Your product is too big. It takes up too much space!

## Kinds of Objections

Objections are of two kinds:

1. excuses, and

2. genuine objections.

**Excuses.** Excuses arise when the prospect is confused. He or she cannot make a decision and, as a result, attempts to escape from the situation by escaping from the sales representative.

Jill Willis is a representative of the Acme Corporation, which sells cameras and photographic equipment to ultimate

---

[1] *The American Heritage Dictionary of the English Language* (Boston: American Heritage Publishing Co., 1973), p. 904.

**Figure 9-1. Five steps in handling objections.**

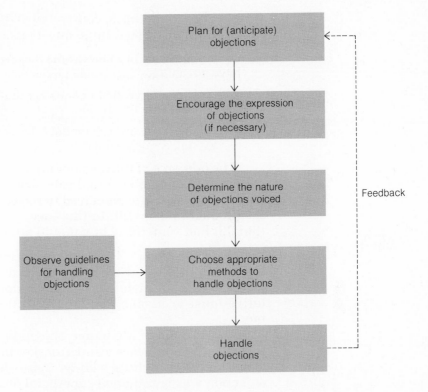

consumers through retailers. Recently, Jill called on, for the first time, a camera store buyer who had just been transferred from another store and so was not familiar with Jill or her company. Accordingly, the buyer felt uncertain about dealing with the unfamiliar.

Jill was halfway through her presentation of an instant camera line when the buyer interrupted that it was obvious Acme had nothing to offer that the store did not already have. In fact, the buyer saw nothing wrong with the company, product line, or Jill. Rather, he felt uncertain about his new job, was experiencing fear of failure, and just wanted to get rid of Jill (whom he perceived as a threat).

Jill realized this was an excuse rather than a genuine objection, since she had witnessed cases of buyer uncertainty and attendant excuse making in the past. Jill's technique for handling such situations is to ask some tactfully worded questions to help prospects clarify their thinking and realize that their opposition to the presentation is due to uncertainty. First, she attempted to put the buyer at ease by complimenting him on the way he had built up a comprehensive line of photographic items. Then she asked three questions:

> Could you tell me in what ways do the products you currently stock have advantages over Acme products?

> You might be interested in knowing that Acme is one of the top-selling brands in this region.

> You might consider the potential sales gain you would experience by stocking Acme products.

The outcome of the questioning process was a reduction in uncertainty and an eventual sale. The buyer realized that his resistance was due to perceived risk and not to defects in Acme, the product line, or Jill. In this case, the buyer became aware that Jill had something of value to offer.

**Genuine Objections.** There are, of course, real reasons for resisting the points raised in the sales presentation. Thus, if a prospect says "Your deliveries are too slow," the sales representative must overcome this argument before the prospect will buy.

An example of a genuine objection is when a wholesale-food salesperson hears a supermarket buyer say that "dry dog foods just don't sell as well as those that are canned." This objection was based upon superficial observation of past sales figures and not upon facts. The salesman countered the objection with fact. He produced sales figures for both dry and canned dog food that his company's marketing research department had developed. The research indicated that sales of dry dog food were, in fact, high and growing, relative to sales of canned products.

**The Significance of Objections to Sales Representatives**

You might think that sales representatives should try to discourage objections. After all, these are negative comments regarding the products, company, or representative. On the contrary, sales personnel should often *encourage* objections.

Unless prospects raise objections, sales representatives cannot really act as a creative problem solvers. They cannot determine the questions, attitudes, and degree of uncertainty experienced by the prospect. Indeed, one of the more *difficult* types of prospects are those who will not raise objections.

Consider the example of Bill Harris, who sells offset newspaper presses for the Harris Company (which his father owns). Bill is not a good salesman since he cannot elicit objections from prospects. Recently, for instance, he came across a prospect who would not raise objections. This prospect agreed with everything that Bill said and was very agreeable and hospitable. After the presentation was completed, however, the prospect indicated that he was not interested in the Harris line. Bill was at a loss. What could he say to convince the prospect that Harris products had a great deal to offer? This inability to draw out objections cost Bill many potential sales.

**Types of Objections**

There are many kinds of objections, and in this section we will discuss nine of the most common:

1. the price is too high;

2. the product is not of adequate quality;

3. the prospect has a sufficient stock of goods already;

4. the advertising and sales promotion of the product are inadequate;

5. the services rendered by the salesperson's company are inadequate;

6. deficiencies in the sales representative's company are apparent;

7. the prospect is too busy to listen;

8. the prospect wants time to think the offer over;

9. the prospect is loyal to a competing supplier.

**The Price Is Too High**

The common objection that "the price is too high" may conceal the fact that prospects really are interested in what benefits they will receive from the product or services and that price tends to be a secondary consideration. Hence, when this objection arises, a sales representative often can emphasize benefits.

Rodney Thompson sells Poisedon microfilm systems to industrial buyers. When he is told "the price is too high," he often counters by focusing on the benefits Poisedon buyers receive. Figure 9-2 is a list of such benefits which Rodney has had typed out on bond paper. He refers to the listing frequently throughout a typical sales presentation. When someone says the price is too high, Rodney refers to this list and covers the benefits that seem to be most applicable to the prospect.

**The Product Is Not of Adequate Quality**

Sometimes prospects will indicate that the quality of the product is not good enough. This often means they believe the benefits they expect are not adequate in relation to the price or in relation to the benefits offered by competitors.

WHAT BENEFITS DO POISEDON SYSTEM USERS OBTAIN?

1. Records of transactions are filed properly.

2. Errors in filing are avoided, so the user avoids the embarrassment of mistakes.

3. Users avoid the extra cost of unnecessary monthly billings to customers.

4. Users can copy and refile a record in its correct place in as little as 26 seconds.

5. Users can answer customer questions about billings quickly and easily.

6. When the system is employed, records are never misplaced.

7. Poisedon systems require little maintenance.

8. Poisedon systems are guaranteed for almost twice as long as any competing unit.

9. Repair parts for the system are readily available.

10. Company maintenance personnel are readily available.

If the benefits do not, in fact, match the needs and expectations of the prospect, this may mean that the sales representative has not done an effective prospecting job, and steps should be undertaken to improve the prospecting function. At any rate, when benefits do not meet needs, the salesperson should not continue to press for a sale, for the result of selling something that will not fulfill the prospect's expectations is likely to be ultimate ill will and bad word-of-mouth publicity.

Sometimes, however, the sales representative perceives that the prospect has misperceived the quality of the product or service and not grasped the fact that the offering has benefits he or she desires. The sales representative who detects these misperceptions can then stress the relevant benefits. Rodney Thompson often refers to the list of benefits and points out how Poisedon microfilm systems excel over competing systems in which the prospect is interested. For instance, when one prospect misperceived that Poisedon units were slower than those of most competitors, Rodney pointed out that a Poisedon system could copy and refile a record much faster than any competing make.

**The Prospect Has a Sufficient Stock of Goods Already**

Prospects who are retailers, wholesalers, manufacturers, and nonbusiness organizations sometimes indicate they are stocked up in the product in question. That is, they possess a level of inventory that prohibits further purchases of the product, at least for the time being.

To this objection, sales representatives can ask, "Why are you stocked up?" It may be that currently owned products are not selling or are not needed, thereby resulting in excess investment in unneeded assets. Should this be the case, sales representatives can point out (where this is the truth) that their company's product will not accumulate in inventory but will sell and produce revenues—something the dead inventory will not do.

For instance, when a wholesale grocery sales representative was confronted with a supermarket buyer who said he was stocked up in instant coffee and could not possibly add to the line at present, the representative knew that the brand stocked by the store was not selling well anywhere in the United States. He knew it was probably not heavily advertised, was high priced, and did not have the flavor many consumers wanted. The salesperson therefore suggested drastic price cuts for this brand, so the supermarket could rid itself of its inventory, and replacement of that brand with the wholesaler's popular brand. The buyer and the salesperson worked with some sales and cost figures and came up with the comparative analysis depicted in Figure 9-3. The analysis indicated the superiority of the sales representative's plan, in terms of increasing the contribution to overhead that the supermarket currently receives.[2] After going through the analysis, the buyer placed an order for the wholesaler's brand of instant coffee.

**The Advertising and Sales Promotion of the Product Is Inadequate**

Prospects who are wholesalers or retailers may object that a sales representative's firm is not devoting enough money to advertising and sales promotion of the product. Some wholesalers and retailers, in fact, use rules of thumb, whereby they are unwilling to stock products unless they are backed up by particular amounts of promotion.

---

[2]Contribution to overhead consists of sales, minus the cost of goods sold and direct costs of each product. See Don L. James, Bruce J. Walker, and Michael J. Etzel, *Retailing Today: An Introduction* (New York: Harcourt Brace Jovanovich, 1975), pp. 485–87.

Figure 9-3. Comparison
of supermarket
contribution to
overhead with currently
stocked and
wholesaler's coffees.

Expected sales and costs if only the currently used
brand is stocked

| | |
|---|---|
| Revenues from currently used brand (over 6-month time period) | $12,000 |
| Inventory and related costs for currently used brand | $ 7,000 |
| Contribution to overhead | $ 5,000 |

Expected sales and costs if the wholesaler's brand
is stocked and the currently used brand is sold at
bargain prices (as proposed by the sales representative)

| | |
|---|---|
| Revenues from currently used brand (over 6-month time period) | $10,000 |
| Inventory and related costs for currently used brand | $ 8,000 |
| Contribution to overhead | $ 2,000 |
| Revenues from wholesaler's brand (over 6-month time period) | $25,000 |
| Inventory and related costs for wholesaler's brand | $14,000 |
| Contribution to overhead | $11,000 |
| Total contribution to overhead under the sales representative's plan | $13,000 |

A good rebuttal to this objection is to draw attention to elements of the marketing mix other than promotion. Most items that are not promoted as heavily as are competitors' products have compensating features. Marketing management allocates funds that could have been spent for promotion to produce high product quality, low prices, fast delivery, or other benefits to wholesalers and retailers. The sales representative can emphasize these other features.

Consider the example of Ray Wright, representative for Blight Toy Company, a large manufacturer and marketer of a wide line of toys. Ray's function is primarily to act as an order getter by calling upon department-store and variety-store buyers. At one time a variety store buyer complained that "The Acme Company must do twice as much television and magazine advertising as Blight does. I never seem to see your ads." Ray knew that Acme did, in fact, spend much more on advertising. But he also knew that Acme's deliveries tended to be slow and unreliable. The following discussion ensued:

RAY: You're right, Acme does advertise more. On the other hand, how fast can they deliver a shipment, on the average?

PROSPECT: Generally, they take about a month, depending on the time of year, of course.

RAY: We can deliver to you within one week, except during the Christmas buying season, when it goes up to two weeks. Further, I've heard that Acme deliveries are somewhat unreliable. Have you found this to be the case?

PROSPECT: Yes, I have. It seems like I'm always on the phone to the Acme salesman, trying to find out the status of our orders.

RAY: You won't have that trouble with us. We're never more than one day late and, as you know, a few days can make a big difference, especially during the holiday season.

PROSPECT: Yes, late deliveries, particularly before Christmas can be devastating.

By drawing attention to Blight's delivery policies, in relation to Acme's, Ray was able to effectively overcome the "inadequate advertising" objection.

Services Are Not Adequate

Some prospects raise the objection that the company services are not adequate, whether credit, delivery, repairs, maintenance, or returns of defective merchandise. When such objections arise, the sales representative should take steps to determine whether or not they are true. If, for instance, a customer complains delivery dates have not been met, the representative can check order and shipping dates with warehouse personnel to see if this is so. If the delivery was slow or unreliable, efforts should be made to ensure it will not happen in the future. The representative, for instance, might ask the sales manager to pressure warehousing personnel to improve their performance. Delivery reliability is an important purchasing criterion for a number of industrial buyers,[3] as well as for many purchasers of consumer goods. Where deliveries have been unreliable, the sales representative should complain to shipping personnel, report the situation to sales management personnel, or take other steps to improve this important customer service.

---

[3]Richard M. Hill, Ralph S. Alexander, and James S. Cross, *Industrial Marketing* (Homewood, Ill.: Richard D. Irwin, 1975), pp. 105–106.

Oftentimes inadequate services are beyond the control of the sales representative's company. Slow deliveries may be due to a union strike. The firm may not be able to grant as much credit as do competitors because of limited funds. Slow repair and maintenance services may be due to the fact that the repair and maintenance facilities are deluged with work. When service inadequacies cannot be overcome, the sales representative should just be a patient listener. Many prospects want to complain about service inadequacies just to get the matter off their chests. If the sales representative listens to the complaints and then explains why services are such as they are, considerable ill will can be averted.

Some prospects, however, have unreasonable service demands. An office supply salesperson, for instance, may have a customer who insists on deliveries within three days after placing an order, service beyond the capability of the company (as well as the company's competitors). To overcome this kind of objection the salesperson might carefully explain why such a delivery schedule is impossible, and mention compensating benefits (such as the high quality of company products) which were, in fact, of more value to the customer than extremely fast service.

## Company Weaknesses

Some prospects may find fault with company personnel, policies, lack of (or bad) reputation, size, lack of financial resources, and the like.

Some of these objections are excuses rather than genuine objections, and so can be overcome by listening to the prospect and by emphasizing compensating benefits. A machine tools salesman, for instance, has found that some prospects object to the fact that his company is smaller and not as well known as several of his competitors. He often counters this by explaining that his sales force works much harder to service customers than do the competitors' employees.

The sales representative sometimes is faced with a real challenge, in that a prospect feels very negative about the company. This attitude, of course, presents a major barrier to successful selling. Further, the attitude can be dangerous when the prospect conveys his or her feelings to others, thereby creating hostility and distrust toward the sales representative's organization.

An appliance saleswoman in a department store has come across shoppers who have doubts about the company. They have heard that the store does not provide good maintenance services, that its credit terms are unreasonable, that store employees will try to force the customer to buy credit life insurance, and similar complaints. The saleswoman answers such objections by denying them when they are false and by referring to the positive aspects of the store. She emphasizes the excellent delivery services, good credit terms, repair services, and other benefits.

## The Prospect Is Too Busy to Listen

When prospects are genuinely too busy to listen to a sales presentation, the sales representative should make an appointment for another call. Oftentimes this problem would not have occurred in the first place if the representative had made an appointment prior to the call.

When the "too busy" objection is merely an excuse, various tactics can be employed. Some salespersons handle it like this: "All that I need is a few minutes of your time. I have a lot of calls to make this morning and will need less than fifteen minutes to show you our line."

Another way to overcome the "too busy" objection is to promise a striking reward. The representative of a sporting goods wholesaler, for instance, uses statements such as these to overcome the objection:

I have a new backpack that will bring many students into your store.

Wait until you see the new touring skis that the Ajax company has produced. There's nothing like them on the market and their sales reflect this.

I hate to see you miss out on carrying our new line. It is just what you need for pushing up summer sales.

These and similar promises of reward are useful in inducing busy prospects to find time to hear presentations. The possibilities of reward tend to incline the prospects to place higher priorities upon listening to the salesperson than they would in the absence of the promises. The sales representative should, of course, be sure that the promises are genuine and are not just bait to lure the prospect into a sales presentation.

## The Prospect Wants Time to Think the Offer Over

After a sales presentation has been made, the prospect may indicate that he or she requires time to think about the purchase, to gather additional information, or to compare the offering with those of rival suppliers. Certainly, this is a valid statement for many prospects. The sales representative could generate considerable ill will by attempting to push the prospect into a prematurely early decision. For expensive products, such as new buildings, computer installations, and machinery, buyers need time to contemplate a purchase, to compare the offerings with those of competitors, and to compute the effect of a purchase upon the financial position of the organization. Sometimes prospects need time to make arrangements for acquiring the funds that will be used to make the purchase. These various deliberations and actions frequently consume considerable periods of time, yet are vital prerequisites to a purchase.

But the "need for time" objection can also be an excuse. The sales representative should therefore ask questions designed to reveal the true reason for the delay. If the reasons can be uncovered, the representative is in a position to provide answers to them. Prospects who indicate they need time may have made up their minds that they are not going to purchase the offering because they have heard, for instance, that the supplier is slow in processing orders. If the sales representative can uncover this true objection, he or she is in a position to provide answers to it.

Another tactic for overcoming the "need for time" objection is to stress the dangers of delay and/or the possible rewards of a rapid decision. A jewelry salesperson who calls upon retailers follows this practice. She indicates such things as:

> We can provide you with good credit terms now, but this may not be the case next month.

> The price of this digital watch will go up before long. Better get it while you can at this price.

> We may experience difficulty in providing fast delivery after the 21st, since a Teamsters' strike may take place then.

## The Prospect Is Loyal to a Competing Supplier

There are cases where a prospect indicates that the organization buys from another supplier and is loyal to that supplier. Possible rebuttals to this objection are:

> Why not buy part of your needs from us? The two brands can both be stocked.

> Certainly, your loyalty is to be admired. On the other hand, why not give us a fair chance to prove what our product can do for you?

This last rebuttal appeals to the prospect's sense of fair play.

**Ways of Handling Objections**

In the previous section we focused on various common objections and ways of answering them. Now let us go into some of the specific means of handling objections—namely:

1. the "yes, but" method,
2. answer a question with a question,
3. propose trial use,
4. boomerang method,
5. direct-answer method,
6. demonstration,
7. comparative-item method,
8. the "it's in your hands" method,
9. comparison with rivals' products,
10. case-history method,
11. ask questions.

**The "Yes, But" Method**

A very effective technique is the "Yes, but" method.[4] This involves agreeing with the objection, then making another statement that tends to offset it. This technique allows the sales representative to agree with prospects, yet show them their objections need not prevent a sale. Examples of the "yes, but" tactic are:

Yes, I see what you're getting at, but have you considered how much money you can save by using this product?

Yes, your point is well taken, but look at the other advantages of this item.

**Answer a Question with a Question**

Sometimes prospects raise objections that are difficult to answer, placing pressure on the sales representative to provide a response. The salesperson can redirect the pressure back to the prospect by answering the question with a question. For example:

PROSPECT: How could I ever justify a $1,000-per-month lease for this property?

SALESPERSON: You want a location that will bring in more profit than is now the case, don't you?

---

[4]Robert L. Shook and Herbert M. Shook, *The Complete Professional Salesman* (New York: Barnes & Noble Books, 1974), p. 147.

PROSPECT: Are you telling me that these coats really are the latest in fashion? Our store attempts to stay in the forefront.

SALESPERSON: Just last week *Women's Wear Daily* had a long article about these coats being in fashion. Did you see the article?

**Propose Trial Use**

Some buyers experience uncertainty to the extent that they are afraid to make a purchase at present. Uncertainty is likely where the prospect perceives risk,[5] such as:

1. money risk—as in the case of an expensive item such as an automobile;

2. physiological risk—as in the purchase of items that might affect health or safety (examples are medicine and motorcycles);

3. psychological risk—as in the purchase of items closely related to the prospect's self-image (examples are some clothing and jewelry).

Prospects can overcome uncertainty, in many cases, if they are offered the use of the product without charge for a specified period of time. Ivan the truck salesman has used this technique extensively. After using a truck for three or four days, some prospects decide that they must have it.

**Boomerang Method**

This tactic converts prospects' reasons for not purchasing into reasons *for* purchasing. The boomerang method can have a very heavy impact upon prospects. For example:

PROSPECT: I don't think that my customers will buy a dog food that has the word "gourmet" on the label.

SALESPERSON: According to our marketing research, the word "gourmet" is a key ingredient in selling to customers such as yours.

PROSPECT: You are selling too many sportshirts that are blue.

SALESPERSON: Our research shows that blue is going to be very popular in this city this year.

The boomerang method requires considerable diplomacy. If handled untactfully, it can offend prospects.

**Direct-Answer Method**

This technique requires that the sales representative provide a specific response to the exact question raised by the prospect.

---

[5]For a discussion of the impact of risk on buying see Joe Kent Kerby, *Consumer Behavior: Conceptual Foundations* (New York: Dun-Donnelley Publishing Corp., 1975), pp. 111–18.

An example is when the salesperson promises rewards greater than those now received.[6] Generally, this is a strong method, requiring less tact and diplomacy than many of the others, yet effectively answering the objection. The direct-answer method can, however, arouse antagonism on the part of prospects. Examples of this method are:

PROSPECT: Your automobiles consume too much gas per mile.

SALESPERSON: No, our mileage is better than that of any competitor, according to EPA standards.

PROSPECT: I've heard that the water supply for homes in this part of the city is inadequate.

SALESPERSON: No other part of the city has a water system with a capacity as high as this. If you buy this home, you will never lack water pressure.

Demonstration

Frequently, the best way for a sales representative to overcome an objection is to demonstrate the use of the product. This is perhaps the superior means of showing that an objection is not applicable. When an industrial buyer asserts that a milling machine is dangerous, for instance, the salesperson can demonstrate how the safety guards work, thereby proving that danger from this element is not present. When a shopping-center manager indicates that an electric floor sweeper is noisy, the sales representative can demonstrate that it is quiet. When a consumer indicates that a Hewlett-Packard programmable desk-top calculator is difficult to operate, the sales representative can show that this is not the case.

Comparative-Item Method

When this method is employed, the sales representative shows the prospect two or more different products, models, styles, colors, or other variations. When a prospect objects to a feature of one variation, the salesperson rejects it and substitutes another variation. For instance:

PROSPECT: I really don't care for the fourteen-day tour of Scotland, but the "deluxe" excursion into Scandinavia has some nice features.

TRAVEL AGENT: You've made a good choice. I can sign you up for the June 1st group.

---

[6]Dillard B. Tinsley and Vinay Kothari, "Unfreezing Your Prospects," *Sales and Marketing Management* 117, no. 5 (2 June 1975): 51.

SALESPERSON: What style do you prefer, the traditional or the modern?

PROSPECT: The modern.

SALESPERSON: Good, I can have it delivered this afternoon.

Obviously, the comparative-item method can antagonize prospects. Further, when used improperly, it is unethical sales practice. Sales representatives should use it with discretion.

The "It's in Your Hands Method

This is a specialized technique. It requires surrendering when prospects raise especially potent objections and telling them, "I just have to leave the purchase decision up to you—what more can I say?"

This technique, if effective, arouses sympathy for the sales representative. In essence, the salesperson is asking the prospect for assistance in making the sale. The danger inherent in the "it's in your hands" method is that some prospects will perceive the sales representative as being inept and nonprofessional.

Comparison with Rival Products

A very effective way of answering objections is to compare the product with the competition (many advertisements do this, as in Avis versus Hertz). Salespersons can point out the major advantages of their goods and explain the benefits that are forthcoming from these, compared to those of competitors. This technique is especially effective in industries where competition is very intense. Examples of the comparative tactic are:

SPORTING GOODS RETAILER: Your high powered hunting rifles are expensive.

SALESPERSON: Taking into account the quantity discounts we offer, they are less expensive than those of any other manufacturer.

FARMER: I do not believe your brand of fertilizer contains enough phosphate.

SALESPERSON: I've checked with the local agricultural extension agent. Our brand meets the phosphate requirements of your soil better than any other brand.

Case-History Method

This technique requires describing how another prospect purchased the product or service and benefited accordingly. Case histories add realism and believability to the answer to the objection. This is especially important for sales representatives who are not acquainted with the prospect, who represent an unknown company, or who are selling a new product. Some examples of the case history approach are:

FARMER: I've never heard of your company before. It's not my practice to try unknown insecticides on my crops.

SALESPERSON: Ted Gillette over in Tyler County used this product last year. He indicated to me that it was twice as effective as Brand X, which he previously used.

PROSPECT: You are a new salesman for this company. I'd never deal with someone who lacked experience in helping me determine my inventory needs.

SALESPERSON: Last week I made a study of the merchandising needs of the Kimby Hardware chain. They were very satisfied with the study. You might want to call Mr. Kimby in order to verify this.

Ask Questions    Some novice salespersons take the view that, in handling objections, they should engage themselves primarily in making assertive statements. This is not necessarily the case, since a very good means of handling objections is to ask questions. The answers to the questions provide the sales representative with the insights needed to effectively react to the objections. Further, questions force prospects to clarify their own thinking. Sometimes prospects raise objections that are not clearly formulated in their own minds. Answering questions forces them to devote thought to their needs and desires and the ability of the product to fulfill them. For instance:

PROSPECT: I just don't feel that our store can make money by selling your product.

SALESPERSON: Certainly your concern is understandable. For my own information, could you tell me why you don't see our product as profitable?

PROSPECT: With a margin as low as you have on that product, I'll barely be able to cover overhead expenses.

SALESPERSON: I see. Your doubts are regarding the margin. It is true that our margins are lower than those of some competitors. Our distributors make money because this product attracts customers into the store and because it has a high turnover. Let me show you some figures taken from retailers who handle our products now and who used to stock competing products. That will illustrate my points.

PROSPECT: I'd be interested in looking at those figures.

| Which Method Is Best? | No one of the methods of handling objections works best for all sales representatives and with all prospects. Rather, each salesperson is faced with the need to determine which set of methods are most appropriate for him or her, in conjunction with particular prospects. The sales representative should be familiar with the various methods and should exercise care in choosing those that fit his or her selling techniques and the characteristics of particular prospects. |

**Guidelines in Handling Objections**

There are four general guidelines that are useful in handling objections:

1. avoid arguments;
2. determine the real objection;
3. tailor the means of handling objections;
4. make use of objections.

Avoid Arguments

At all costs, the sales representative should avoid arguing. This type of dialog creates an emotional climate that is not conducive to joint problem solving. The process of arguing causes each party to become defensive and to set up psychological barriers against the other. Both are likely to resort to emotional rather than to problem-oriented behavior.

Meredith Dalton is an employee of a cosmetics producer who serves retailers, including department stores, fashion clothing stores, and gift outlets. On one occasion Meredith became involved in an intense argument with a prospect, who had said her brand of floral scented shampoos literally did not adequately clean the hair. Meredith disagreed completely and countered by insisting that the company produced floral shampoos that had been proven through marketing research to be superior in cleaning power to that of any competitor. The prospect insisted that she had heard otherwise from the sales representatives of competing manufacturers. In the ensuing discussion, Meredith reduced the arguments of the prospect to shreds. In the end, the prospect asked her to go, feeling very offended by Meredith's comments.

Later, Meredith reflected on the conversation with this prospect. She had succeeded only in convincing her that the company's brand of floral shampoos was not for her store. By winning the argument she had lost a potential good customer. On the other hand, if she had lost the argument, she also would have lost the customer. Argumentation seems to be an unproductive technique that should be avoided in any event.

| | |
|---|---|
| Determine the Real Objection | The sales representative should take steps to determine the exact nature of the objection before attempting to react to it.[7] Sometimes this is difficult, however. Prospects may not be willing to reveal the objection that is really in their minds and instead just provide generalizations, such as "I don't think this is for me," or "I'm just not interested." |

Determine the Real Objection

The sales representative should take steps to determine the exact nature of the objection before attempting to react to it.[7] Sometimes this is difficult, however. Prospects may not be willing to reveal the objection that is really in their minds and instead just provide generalizations, such as "I don't think this is for me," or "I'm just not interested."

Oftentimes the sales representative must go to considerable effort in uncovering the real objection. The uncovering process requires skill in asking questions that will encourage prospects to disclose their real objections. At this point in the presentation, the sales representative should be doing most of the listening and the prospect most of the talking. The salesperson can encourage the prospect by making statements such as:

I really don't understand the full nature of your objection. Could you explain further what is meant by it?

As I understand it, your objection is that the price is too high. Am I correct in interpreting your statements in that way?

Why do you feel this way about the product?

That's interesting. Can you amplify on this point?

The process of encouraging the prospect to talk and in the process to reveal the real objection may be time consuming, but it can be rewarding to sales representatives. Once they know the real objection, effective handling of the objection is possible. Without this knowledge, they have a good chance of choosing an ineffective method of response.

Tailor the Means of Handling Objections

The discussion of "means of handling objections" may have created the impression that successful sales representatives develop skills in particular tactics and always employ these same tactics in answering objections. This is not the case. The representatives should adjust the tactics to the characteristics of particular prospects. A tactic that works for one may not work for another.

Take this example in which a woman prospect at a fairgrounds exhibit area examines a Kuempel chime clock, then says she does not like the Kuempel style, walnut, tooling, and most other characteristics.

"You know, lady," the salesman responds, "I have just decided I don't think I want to sell you one of our clocks."

---

[7]See Paul J. Micali, *The Lacy Techniques of Salesmanship* (New York: Hawthorn Books, 1971), pp. 116–23.

She looks shocked. "What?"

"There's only one reason why people buy one of our clock kits and that's because they think they will enjoy building and owning a Kuempel clock. I wouldn't want you to have one if I thought you wouldn't like it."[8]

At this the prospect's attitude changed from hostility to humility. She asked another series of questions, and ultimately purchased a clock. Obviously, however, this method would not be effective for all prospects.

The sales representative who has determined the real objection is in a position to create a means of handling it that fits the characteristics of the particular prospect under consideration and the nature of the objection. For instance, a representative might use the following tactics for the specified circumstances:

- For a prospect who lacks self-confidence—the "yes, but" method.

- When a difficult to answer objection is voiced—answer a question with a question.

- For a prospect who is experiencing considerable uncertainty about the performance of the product—suggest trial use.

- For a prospect who is not overly sensitive and likes frank answers—the boomerang and direct-answer methods.

- For a very skeptical prospect—demonstration.

- For an indecisive prospect—the comparative-item method.

- For a prospect who experiences sympathy for the problems of others—the "it's in your hands" method.

- For a prospect who favors a competing brand—the "comparison with rivals products" tactic.

- For a prospect who is not familiar with the sales representative, product, or organization—the case-history method.

- For the prospect who has not clearly formulated the objection in his or her mind—ask questions.

Thus, sales representatives need to develop an arsenal of tactics for responding to objections. The tactics should not be used randomly, however. Rather, the representative should carefully choose the particular method or combination of meth-

---

[8]Doug Maxwell, "Selling Worth Telling," *SME Newsletter: Sales and Marketing Executives of Minneapolis* 7, no. 7 (26 January 1976): 4.

Chapter 9  Objections

ods that have the greatest chance of working effectively in each situation.

Make Use of
Objections

As we mentioned earlier, sales representatives should not view objections as barriers or obstacles that block the selling effort (as depicted in the top part of Figure 9-4). Rather they should consider objections as indicators of the directions that the sales presentation should take (as outlined in the bottom of Figure 9-4). When prospects voice objections, they reveal something about themselves and their attitudes, opinions, and values. The sales representative should take advantage of these revelations.[9]

Objections, then, are not to be "handled," in terms of overcoming and then forgetting about them. The effective sales representative often encourages the voicing of objections, considers them in choosing the directions the presentation should take from there on, and then attempts to provide an answer that will satisfy the prospect. The prospect receives satisfaction when objections are handled in this manner. The sales representative is acting as a creative problem solver, rather than as an arguer.

Ivan (the representative of a large manufacturer of trucks) sells to business and nonbusiness organizations. The brand name which Ivan handles is Minerva. He uses objections in the creative manner described above. At one time he was experi-

---

[9]See Earl Prevette, "How to Turn Objections into Sales," in John D. Murphy, ed., *Secrets of Successful Selling* (New York: Dell Publishing Co., 1963), pp. 158–68.

**Figure 9-4. Two views of objections.**

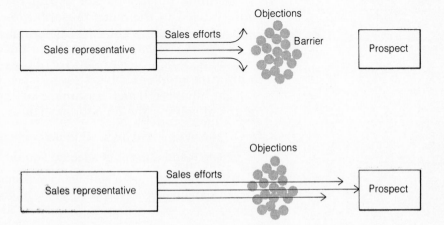

encing considerable difficulty in interesting a truck-fleet owner in Minerva trucks. In fact, he had been calling upon the prospect for three years and had not yet made a sale, despite the fact that he appeared to be a good prospect.

On a particular call Ivan questioned him at length and discovered that the real objection was that the fleet owner had the impression that Minerva trucks were not durable. This was important, since his drivers tended to put a severe strain on the equipment, in an attempt to improve upon the delivery times of competing organizations.

This insight on the real objection guided Ivan to the steps necessary in order to change the owner's opinion regarding durability. (He discovered that the prospect had developed the opinion as a result of conversing with other fleet owners.) Ivan showed the fleet owner extensive information, collected by the company engineering department, on the expected life and number of breakdowns of Minerva trucks. Ivan also had the owner drive a Minerva truck over an old highway having a very uneven surface and traversing steep grades. After the drive one of the owner's mechanics examined the truck and found that the grueling drive had not affected its performance in any way. The fleet owner then began to order Minerva trucks. Ivan had used the objection to set the stage for a profitable sale.

**Summary**     Objections are arguments raised by prospects in opposition to the points made by the salesperson. Excuses are one kind of objection. These are attempts of the prospect to escape from the salesperson and the situation. The sales representative should help the prospect overcome uncertainty, as through a series of tactfully worded questions, in order to surmount excuses.

Genuine objections are actual reasons for resisting the points raised in the sales presentation. Much of the chapter dealt with handling genuine objections.

Effective sales representatives encourage the voicing of objections. When they are aware of the objections they can act as creative problem solvers for prospects.

The chapter listed a number of types of objections and means of solving the objections. These were as follows:

1. The price is too high. (Emphasize benefits.)

2. The product is not of adequate quality. (Emphasize benefits.)

3. The prospect has a sufficient stock of goods already. (Focus on sales and profits of the salesperson's products.)

4. The advertising and sales promotion of the product is inadequate. (Draw attention to other elements of the marketing mix.)

5. Services are not adequate. (Improve the services. Patient listening. Explain the reasons for inadequate services.)

6. Company weaknesses. (Listening. Emphasize compensating benefits.)

7. The prospect is too busy to listen. (Make an appointment. Say "This will only take a few minutes." Promise a reward.)

8. The prospect wants time to think the offer over. (Be patient. Try to determine the real reasons for the delay. Stress the dangers of delay and/or the rewards of a rapid decision.)

9. The prospect is loyal to a competing supplier. (Say "Why not buy from two sources?" or "Give us a fair chance.")

The chapter mentioned eleven ways of handling objections. These were as follows:

1. The "yes, but" method—agree with the objection, then make another statement that tends to offset it.

2. Answer a question with a question—direct pressure brought on by a difficult question back to the prospect by asking him or her a question.

3. Propose trial use—offer the use of the product without charge.

4. Boomerang method—convert reasons for not purchasing into reasons for purchasing.

5. Direct-answer method—provide a specific response to the exact question raised by the prospect.

6. Demonstration—demonstrate the use of the product.

7. Comparative-item method—reject a variation the prospect objects to and substitute a favored variation.

8. The "it's in your hands" technique—tell the prospect, "I give up, the purchase decision is up to you."

9. Comparison with rivals' products—explain the benefits of the product in contrast with those forthcoming from rival offerings.

10. Case-history method—describe how another purchaser benefited from the product or service.

11. Ask questions—to provide insights for the salesperson and aid in clarifying the thinking of the prospect.

The chapter set forth four guidelines for the handling of objections. These were:

1. avoid arguments;

2. determine the real objection;

3. tailor the means of handling objections;

4. make use of objections (in contrast to attempting to avoid them).

**Discussion Questions**

1. What are objections?

2. Define the two types of objections. How should the salesperson handle each type?

3. "Effective sales representatives encourage the voicing of objections." Explain why this statement is true.

4. Explain how each of the following types of objections might be answered:

   a. The price is too high.

   b. The product is not of adequate quality.

   c. The prospect has a sufficient stock of goods already.

   d. The advertising and sales promotion of the product is inadequate.

   e. The services rendered by the salesperson's company are inadequate.

   f. Deficiencies in the salesperson's company.

   g. The prospect is too busy to listen.

   h. The prospect wants time to think the offer over.

   i. The prospect is loyal to a competing supplier.

5. For each of the following ways of handling objections, set forth a situation (hypothetical or real) where the "way of handling" is used.

   a. The "yes, but" method.

   b. Answer a question with a question.

   c. Propose trial use.

   d. Boomerang method.

   e. Direct-answer method.

   f. Demonstration.

   g. Comparative-item method.

   h. The "it's in your hands" method.

   i. Comparison with rival products.

   j. Case-history method.

   k. Ask questions.

6. Which of the ways of handling objections are most effective? Explain your answer.

7. Why should the salesperson attempt to avoid arguments?

8. How can the salesperson determine the "real" objection?

9. Explain how a salesperson tailors the means of handling objections.

10. How do sales representatives make use of objections?

**Practical Exercises**

1. Attempt to persuade a friend or acquaintance to do something or to change an attitude or opinion. (You might, for instance, attempt to persuade the prospect to try a new soft-drink brand or to have a more positive opinion toward some political candidate.)

    a. Did the prospect raise excuses or genuine objections?

    b. Were you successful in eliciting genuine objections?

    c. How did you handle the objections?

    d. What did you learn from this exercise?

2. Act as the prospect for a clerk in a local retail store. Raise excuses and genuine objections in the process of talking with the sales clerk.

    a. How did the clerk handle the objections?

    b. Was the clerk effective? Why or why not?

    c. What did you learn from this exercise?

**Selling Project**

What types of objections would you expect to receive in selling your product or service? What means of handling these objections would seem to be most effective? Explain.

**Case 9
Darrell Slater**

Darrell Slater is a salesman for the Diana Corporation, a producer and marketer of office furniture for manufacturers, wholesalers, retailers, other business enterprises, and non-business organizations. The company sells its products in all fifty states, Canada, and Mexico.

Diana office furniture is of high quality. Target consumers are those organizations that want furniture that is aesthetically pleasing, impressive, functional, and comfortable. Company prices are approximately 10 percent above those of its major rival. The firm advertises heavily in *Business Week,* in various trade publications, and through direct mail. The sales force consists of seventy-two salespersons, each of whom covers a geographical sales territory.

Darrell Slater graduated from a state college five years ago and joined Diana as a sales trainee. As a salesman, his performance has been about average, according to the sales manager. Darrell earns a comfortable living, working just hard enough to provide an adequate income but not so hard as to interfere with extensive sailboating, water-skiing, and other recreational activities with his family and friends. His territory is in Georgia, and he operates out of the Atlanta office, which is staffed by a regional sales manager and ten salespersons.

Marcia Roth is the office manager of the Pluto Corporation, a large producer of lawn mowers, garden tractors, snow blowers, and other outdoor equipment for ultimate consumers. Recently, she had a requisition for new office furniture in the home office approved. She consulted several producers of office furniture and found their offerings just didn't create the "right atmosphere" for the main Pluto office. Her latest inquiry into furniture is with Darrell.

Darrell heard that Ms. Roth had telephoned to ask about Diana offerings, and he called upon her the next day. The presentation involved asking a series of questions regarding Pluto's needs, then explaining the benefits of the Esquire line of Diana products. This line was the most expensive produced by the firm, and seemed to fit Pluto's needs.

Darrell has found that the boomerang method of answering objections works very well for him. Accordingly, when Ms. Roth indicated that the Esquire line was perhaps a bit too traditional for Pluto, Darrell countered with "Good traditional furniture will give the Pluto office an aura of solidarity, comfort, and luxury." Later, Ms. Roth said, "I don't really care for the gold colors. They don't seem to match the color scheme of our office." Darrell handled this objection by stating. "I could sell you a different color but really would dislike doing that. Visitors to the office will be impressed with the gold. The trend today is to mix colors." Still later, Ms. Roth suggested that the Esquire line products did not form as many modules (combinations or clusters of pieces of furniture) as she would prefer. Darrell indicated that too much flexibility was a problem. "It leads office personnel to want to change the furniture alignment every other week," he reported.

Darrell did not get the sale. How could he have better handled the objections?

**Suggested Readings**

"A Westinghouse Deal Hits a Canadian Snag," *Business Week*, no. 2392 (4 August 1975): 21.

Dodge, H. Robert, "The Role of the Industrial Salesman," *Mid-South Quarterly Business Review* 9, no. 1 (January 1972): 11–15.

Dreyfact, Robert, "How to Be One-up on Customer Objections," *The American Salesman* 9, no. 1 (January 1964): 45–49.

Goldstein, Arthur, *Secrets of Overcoming Sales Resistance*. West Nyack, N.Y.: Parker Publications, 1969.

"Wall Street Learns It Pays to Listen," *Sales Management* 109, no. 11 (27 November 1972): 14.

# 10

## Closing

*After reading this chapter you should be able to demonstrate a knowledge of:*

- *the meaning of the term* closing
- *the importance of closing*
- *obstacles to closing*
- *the nature and employment of* trial closes
- *when to attempt a close*
- *specific closing methods*
- *general guidelines for closing*

You have witnessed many closes to sales. Some typical examples are:

- "Now, if you'll just sign the order blank, we can get you a Key Telephone System installed within a week."

- "If you order now, the desk-top computing system will come at a much lower price than if you order later."

- "I've summarized the benefits of our duplicating machines. Are you interested?"

- "Which of these stainless steel carving sets do you prefer?"

- "In summary, the Honda Civic is an excellent automobile. How much can you pay per month?"
- "Well, then, will you head the Sunday school youth group?"
- "Will you give us the money for the gymnasium repairs?"

In this chapter we will define closing, identify various barriers to closes, and point out certain principles that can be employed to surmount these barriers. We will also deal with feedback to the sales representative, which indicates that a close is appropriate, and describes the use of trial closes. Finally, we will set forth various closing techniques and general guidelines that indicate which directions the close should take.

Figure 10-1 sets forth the steps in the closing process. The salesperson develops an overall plan for closing, prior to the sales call. The plan includes provisions for detecting and reacting to obstacles, determining when the close should take place, and choosing the methods to be employed. General guidelines are available to help the salesperson make these deliberations.

**Figure 10-1. Steps in the closing process.**

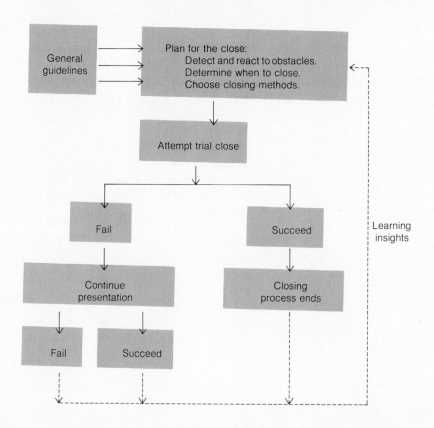

Chapter 10 Closing

A trial close may be attempted, where the sales representative determines the feelings of the prospect regarding a purchase. If the trial close is successful and a sale is made, the closing process ends. If it is not successful, the sales representative continues the presentation and attempts a close later. The closing process provides the representative with learning insights that will enable him or her to better plan and conduct future closes.

**What Closing Is**

Closing consists of asking for an order. As indicated in Figure 10-2, it is the last step in the sales presentation. All of the previous steps lead up to the close. If the presentation is successful, the sales representative closes effectively and obtains an order. At this point the presentation has been completed and its primary objective has been attained.

**Figure 10-2. Positioning of the close in the presentation.**

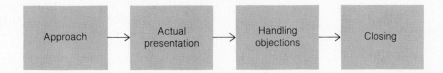

**The Importance of Closing**

Closing is one of the more vital steps in personal selling. Representatives who cannot close are simply not good salespersons. They have considerable skill in prospecting and in handling the preapproach, approach, presentation, and in overcoming objections, yet many fail in closing.[1]

Sometimes, sales representatives are effective in attracting attention. They present stimuli that induce a prospect to be attentive to their presentation. They skillfully build interest in the product or service and then generate the prospect's desire for the offering. The last step in the AIDA persuasion-buying process is action, and this is where the close comes in. The sales representative must translate desire into action. Thus, closing is the capstone to the entire selling process.

**Obstacles to Closing**

There are various obstacles or barriers to making effective closes. The prospect is responsible for some of them, while the sales representative is responsible for others.

---

[1]Albert H. Dunn, Eugene M. Johnson, and David L. Kurtz, *Sales Management* (Morristown, N.J.: General Learning Press, 1974), p. 100.

The personal characteristics and attitudes of prospects account for some of the obstacles to closes. Specifically, prospects may:

1. avoid decision making;

2. be subject to inertia;

3. be fearful about the outcome of a purchase.

**Avoiding Decision Making.**   In the case of many prospects, it is easier to defer decision making until a later point in time. Ultimate consumers, for instance, frequently delay decisions regarding major dollar purchases, such as those for TV sets, automobiles, and homes. This allows them to further consider whether or not a purchase should in fact be made. Often, of course, the process of deferring the decision results in a failure to purchase. The prospect may have a strong desire for the product or service in question but still want to delay the decision. This puts off into the future the psychological burden of having to make a choice today. For example:

> SALESPERSON: The Green Giant plant care line seems to fit your needs, as we have discussed them. Shall I write up the order?

> RETAILER: No, not just now. I need to think about this for a while. Check with me when you are in this area again.

There is a strong liklihood that when the sales representative calls back upon this retailer the latter will have lost much of his interest in the plant-care line.

**Inertia.**   Inertia has been defined as "resistance to motion, action, or change."[2] Those who experience inertia prefer the status quo. They follow the course of least effort and attempt to avoid change, since it requires activity as well as risk. The status quo, on the other hand, appears to be less arduous and more secure. For example:
example:

> SALESPERSON: We've pretty well decided that an AMC Pacer is what you like best. Let's sign a contract and put you behind the wheel.

> PROSPECT: I don't think so. After looking at these models I've decided to stick with the old model. It's good for a few more years.

---

[2]*The American Heritage Dictionary of the English Language* (New York: American Heritage Publishing Co. 1973), p. 672.

**Fear About the Outcome of a Purchase.** Prospects tend to fear the implications of many purchases. "Risk is present because once the purchase is made the buyer will often be stuck with the consequences, whether good or bad."[3] One possible implication is the loss of funds. That is, the prospect may fear that, after the purchase, he or she will find a better use for the money. Other implications are that the product will not work properly, that the buyer will not be able to operate it correctly, and that a more desirable product will be discovered in the future. Overall, fear and uncertainty tend to inhibit buying.

> SALESPERSON: I can have this SL27 lawn tractor delivered within twenty days.

> PROSPECT [*to himself*]: Can I really afford this? What if I can't make the payments? What if I can't operate it properly?

Obstacles Posed by Salespersons

Salespersons sometimes are the sources of barriers to effective closes. The representative may:

1. not ask for the sale;

2. be unknowledgeable;

3. fail to conduct previous steps effectively.

**Not Asking for the Sale.** Some sales representatives conduct good preapproaches, approaches, and presentations, yet when it comes to asking for the sale, they are unable to perform. Very often the reason for this is that they lack the courage to make this request. This is unfortunate, since courage is one of the prime attributes of effective sales representatives.[4] Yet these salespersons simply are not willing nor able to ask prospects, "Will you make this purchase?"

**Unknowledgeable Representatives.** The sales representative may not know how to conduct a good close. There are many dos and don'ts in closing, as we will show. If salespersons are unaware of them, they are unlikely to carry out workable closes. One principle, for instance, is that representatives should not carry out closes in such a manner that they appear to be unduly

---

[3]Joe Kent Kerby, *Consumer Behavior: Conceptual Foundations* (New York: Dun-Donnelley Publishing Corp., 1975), p. 111.

[4]Henri Saint-Laurent, "What It Takes to Star in Selling," *Salesman's Opportunity* 103, no. 4 (March 1974): 29.

anxious to make a sale. Neophyte representatives may violate this principle.

**Failure in Previous Steps.**   The close is dependent upon previous personal selling steps. If prospecting, the preapproach, the approach, or the presentation were not handled well, the close is not likely to be successful. Consider prospecting, for instance. It may be that the prospect does not have a need for the product or does not have the means of paying for it. If these conditions hold, even a very skillfully rendered close cannot be expected to produce a sale. Conversely, if prospecting and other previous steps were conducted adroitly, the close may come about naturally and easily.

**Trial Closes**     Trial closes are those that the sales representative attempts at various points throughout the interview to determine if the prospect wants to make a purchase. Often the prospect is ready to buy, but salespersons fail to recognize this and thereby talk themselves out of a sale. Trial closes help in preventing such occurrences.

Some trial closes are *actions* on the part of the sales representative. Picking up a product and beginning to wrap it is such an action, for instance. So is opening up a briefcase and taking out an order form. These behaviors are suggestions for actual purchase. If they work—lead to a sale—sales representatives have accomplished their goal. If they do not work, salespersons can continue on with the presentation and attempt another close later.

Other trial closes are *verbal*. They consist of words. Here the sales representative asks for the sale in an indirect manner, so that if the trial close does not result in a sale the presentation is not damaged. Examples of such trial closes are as follows:

Would you want delivery next week?

We can do the installing of this product or you can do it yourself.

Do you like the C1 model better than the C4?

We can arrange for credit on any purchase above $50.

If you'd like, we can air-freight your order.

The sales representative may attempt several trial closes in the course of one presentation. The objective is to see if the prospect is ready to buy, but to do this indirectly and subtly. Later, when the presentation has advanced to a further state of development, the salesperson can go into the final close—one that is less subtle.

## When to Attempt a Close

A question for the sales representative is "When should a close be attempted?" If one is too early, the presentation is incomplete and the prospect may not be ready to buy. If one is too late, the sales representative may have talked himself or herself out of a sale.

The prospect's readiness to purchase normally fluctuates from high to low levels and vice versa, as illustrated in Figure 10-3. The salesperson, then, should be on the alert for evidences of high readiness, as identified by point A.[5] At the time associated with A, an attempted close would more likely succeed than at other points.

**Figure 10-3. Readiness to purchase at various times in the presentation.**

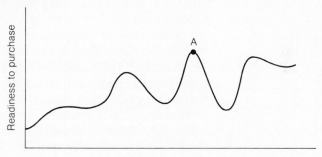

One indicator of when to close is a "green-light signal." This consists of actions or words of the prospect which suggest that the sales representative should close.[6] In the previous chapter we indicated that professional sales representatives utilize feedback from prospects in carrying out the presentation. The green-light signals tell representatives it is time for a close.

Sometimes representatives carry the details of the presentation too far. They mention buying benefits, ask questions of the prospect, demonstrate the product, and carry out other tasks designed to build attention, interest, and desire for the offering.

[5]See Elmer G. Leterman, *Personal Power Through Creative Selling* (New York: Collier Books, 1962), pp. 100–103.

[6]Robert L. Shook and Herbert M. Shook, *The Complete Professional Salesman* (New York: Barnes & Noble Books, 1974), pp. 162–64.

They fail to detect signals that the prospect is ready to buy, and the prospect is literally oversold. Attention to the green-light signals can prevent this problem from occurring. Some examples of these signals:

> If I purchased this furniture, when could you deliver it?

> What are your credit terms? I would need credit to buy this article.

> What quantity discounts does your company offer?

> Am I right in stating that you have a two-year guarantee?

> This product might fit my needs very well.

> Maybe this product would help cut my maintenance costs.

Or the green-light signals may be in the form of actions: the prospect smiles or nods his head in agreement with the salesperson.

These various signals are indicators of a state of readiness to respond favorably to the close.

Another indicator of when to close is the perception of the individual salesperson regarding his or her own performance. Sometimes the sales representative does an outstanding job of demonstrating a product, describing particular product features, handling an objection, or some other selling activity. A close might be effective if it follows outstanding performance by the sales representative. Assume, for instance, that the prospect has just been exposed to a demonstration that portrays the product as different, exciting, and potentially rewarding. The prospect's readiness to purchase may be quite high, and this would be a good time for a close.

In sum, then, determining when to attempt a close should involve:

> 1. looking for green-light signals;

> 2. following up parts of the presentation that were outstanding with attempted closes;

> 3. generally not waiting too long before attempting a close, lest sales representatives talk themselves out of a sale.

**Specific Closing Methods**
A number of closing methods are available, each with its strong and weak points and each applicable in some situations but not others. Sales representatives are likely to find that they are good in carrying out some of the methods but ineffective in attempting others. Similarly, they will find that a method that works with one prospect is ineffective when employed with another.

Sales representatives need experience in order to discover what methods they are best equipped to utilize. Normally, beginning representatives utilize one or more of the standard methods that they have learned in organization training sessions or through senior sales representatives who act as advisors and coaches. As representatives develop on-the-job experience, they can experiment with various methods and determine which tend to work best.

Prospects differ with regard to their responses to different methods. One may respond to a high-pressure close, where the sales representative makes it difficult for the prospect to say no. Another may respond only to low-pressure closes, where the representative is subtle in asking for an order. Thus, representatives who have experience in serving particular prospects have an advantage over novice salespersons, in that the former know what types of closes work with particular prospects.

Novice representatives and those who are calling on new accounts are not without prospect information that is useful in choosing closing methods. They have gathered information in prospecting, the preapproach, the approach, and the presentation that can be used in selecting a closing method. Further, company files may contain information on prospects that other sales representatives have gathered in the past. The information on hand might suggest, for instance, that the prospect under study is highly intelligent and has dealt with sales representatives for years. Some of the more obvious canned sales presentation closes would not be appropriate for this individual. Rather, a more subtle and sophisticated close would be in order.

This section covers the following closing methods:

1. the comparison method;

2. the assumption method;

3. the report method;

4. the choice method;

5. the single-obstacle method;

6. the summary method;

7. the concession method;

8. the emotional method;

9. the "buy now" method;

10. the "ask for the order" method.

The order in which the methods were listed does not imply that some are more important than others. Each is appropriate for particular sales representatives and particular prospects, but not for others.

The Comparison
Method

This technique requires that the sales representative make a comparison of the features of the product or service with the features of a well-known competing product or service. The representative demonstrates verbally that his or her offering is superior to that of rivals. This does not mean that the salesperson disparages the offerings of competitors. Rather, an attempt is made to show that the product or service of the organization is superior in various ways that are important to the prospect. For instance:

PROSPECT: I'm having a difficult time deciding which location to lease. Your industrial park listing is attractive. The problem is that some others are too.

REALTOR: Let me provide you with some facts:

One, our park is located near two interstate highways and a railroad line. No other site in the state can duplicate that.

Two, our park has plenty of space. It is not crowded like the Parson and Apollo parks.

Three, check our lease rates. This is premium property, yet it comes at lower rates than most other sites, including the Apollo park.

Four, we have all of the utility hookups ready to go. You can move in without delay. Parson locations can take months to get all of the utility hookups completed.

Five, we're located near retail and industrial properties, not miles from nowhere, like the Apollo park.

In summary, we have some choice benefits to offer. In plain terms, they are much better than anything the competition has available. I don't want to run down the competition—they are good. The point is that we are better.

PROSPECT: I'm sold. Let's sign a lease on that corner location.

The realtor's close was to summarize the benefits of the property, in comparison to the offerings of other industrial parks. He vividly described what his park had to offer, in comparison to the benefits offered by other industrial parks. This summary description of benefits had a powerful effect upon the prospect. He realized that the realtor's package held more potential value than the other alternatives.

The comparison method is especially useful when the salesperson's prospects have difficulty in evaluating various brands and discovering the relative merits of each. This is the case, for instance, when consumers are comparing different insurance policies or when medical doctors are comparing two or more drugs. Comparison closing helps prospects in making a choice as to which is most appropriate for them.

This technique is also useful when the sales representative's organization is competing with well-known rivals (as when the Acme automobile rental company must compete with Avis and Hertz). Much can be gained by showing that the product offering is superior to those of competitors who have established names in the eyes of consumers. Thus, if the organization is small and less established, relative to other organizations, this method can be very useful. In the realtor's case, both the Parson and Apollo industrial parks were very large and large numbers of businessmen held them in high esteem.

## The Assumption Method

In the assumption method sales representatives act as though the prospect had already decided to purchase the product or service in question. They do not raise the question of *whether* the prospect is going to buy or not. Rather, they focus on details of how to carry out the transaction. Instead of asking for the sale, the representative might state:

> We can deliver within two weeks, or can delay if you are not ready for delivery that soon.
>
> Do you want to set this up as an installment loan or as an accounts-receivable?
>
> Would you like to take this article with you?
>
> We can have the attorneys draw up the legal documents for this sale while we have a cup of coffee.

This method is applicable when the sales representative is convinced that a particular product or service will fullfill the needs and desires of the prospect. The preapproach, approach, and presentation have revealed that the prospect could benefit materially from a purchase, and the sales representative is convinced that this would overcome one or more problems faced by the prospect. Hence, the issue of whether to buy or not is not raised—only details of the transaction are mentioned.

This method, of course, is effective only in cases where the prospect is favorably disposed toward the product or service. It would not be appropriate if the prospect was not convinced of the merits of the offering. Further, it is unlikely to be effective if the prospect is aware that the sales representative is using the technique. For example:

SALESPERSON: Do you want immediate delivery?

PROSPECT: What do you mean, "Do I want immediate delivery?" I have not decided to buy this product. You're trying to push me into a decision I did not make.

The Report Method    This technique requires that sales representatives use analogy. They describe a situation where another prospect had a problem similar to that of the prospect at hand and the former benefited from the salesperson's offering.

PROSPECT: I'm not convinced that your nylon carpeting is just what I need to cover the selling areas of our company stores.

SALESPERSON: This reminds me of the buyer from another chain of stores. He doubted the durability of Acme nylon.

PROSPECT: Sounds like me.

SALESPERSON: Yes, his company's stores had a lot of foot traffic and needed carpeting that was very durable, under the pressure of that traffic.

PROSPECT: Now you're describing my situation.

SALESPERSON: This buyer installed our "Authority" brand of carpeting in four stores and tested its durability over a period of one year. The stores chosen were those with the greatest amount of foot traffic in the chain. The carpeting held up and he decided to use it for all stores in the chain.

PROSPECT: Are they still using the "Authority" brand?

SALESPERSON: Yes. In fact, we made a delivery to a store in Atlanta only last month. The store was about the same size as this one and probably had about the same amount of foot traffic.

PROSPECT: You've convinced me. I'll try your carpeting in five of our stores. If it works out, we'll probably decide to use the brand in all of the new stores we build.

This sales representative observed an important rule associated with the report method. Names of others should not be mentioned unless the others have given their assent to being mentioned. Considerable ill will can result from revealing confidential information about others (the "other buyer" in the example, for instance). Therefore, the carpeting sales representative kept the name of the other customer confidential.

**The Choice Method**

The choice method involves asking the prospect which of two or more product or service variations offered by the sales representative are preferred. The salesperson does not raise the question of whether or not the prospect is going to make a purchase.[7] The presumption is that a purchase will be made and the only question is what product or service package to buy:

Would you rather purchase the red or the green one?

Do you want a month's supply or a two-weeks' supply?

Do you prefer the electric over the gasoline-powered model?

Would the X21 series fit your needs better than the X29 series?

I can order all four of these designs if you prefer a complete package over only a limited offering.

Both consulting projects A and B would work well for you. Which do you prefer?

This method is advantageous where the prospect is generally favorably disposed toward the offerings of the sales representative, yet is experiencing difficulty in reaching a purchase decision. The representative aids prospects in reaching a decision by offering them a choice. Psychologically, this places the prospect in charge of the situation. The prospect is involved as a decision maker in the selling process. In turn, the salesperson withdraws from the decision process and delegates this responsibility to the prospect. The role of the sales representative is to describe the alternatives available to the prospect and then to leave it up to the latter to make the choice. This widely used technique is adaptable to a variety of selling situations.

**The Single Obstacle Method**

This technique is appropriate when prospects have only one reason for not purchasing the product. They are favorably disposed toward the offering, but a single obstacle stands in the way of a purchase. This obstacle might be a price that is perceived as being too high, negative feelings about the quality of the product, or doubts regarding the servicing capabilities of the marketer.

---

[7]For a good discussion of this method, see Paul J. Micali, *The Lacy Techniques of Salesmanship* (New York: Hawthorn Books, 1971), pp. 101–102.

The sales representative begins by inducing the prospect to admit that the obstacle is the sole reason for not purchasing:

> The one reason that we cannot come to an agreement is that you're dubious about paying this price, right?

> Is it safe to say that you haven't signed the contract because of doubts regarding my company's delivery policies?

Once the prospect admits that the single obstacle is preventing a purchase, the sales representative makes a vigorous attempt to eliminate that obstacle:

> This price is not that high, if you compare it with competitors' prices. Besides, we offer better quality products.

> We can give you special delivery that will take only two days.

In closing, the sales representative reminds the prospect that the only previous reason for not purchasing was the single obstacle and that the obstacle has now been overcome:

> Well, we found that you had doubts about the price of our product, but we've found those to be unfounded. Your only objection was regarding price. Now that we've removed that doubt, let's write up the order.

> Your only reason for not buying was the delivery policy of my company. We've found a way around that. Would you rather have delivery on Tuesday or on Wednesday?

The Summary Method

The summary method is a strong technique. It involves providing a summary of the benefits already covered in the presentation: "In summary, this product will bring to you:"

> Increased store traffic—one of your major goals.

> A higher margin on costs—which when added to increased traffic, means higher profits.

> Less need for shelf maintenance—relieving your employees for other duties.

> The prestige of stocking a nationally known brand—something that will impress your customers.

> The assurance that you are dealing with a financially strong and dependable supplier.

A sales/advertising consultant and former salesman describes an instance of the summary method.[8] In this case a

---

[8]George Anderson, "Tell Him What You Told Him," *Marketing Times* 19, no. 1 (January/February 1972): 12.

salesman was calling upon the consultant. While addressing the prospect, the salesman pulled a piece of scratch paper out of his pocket and wrote on the paper:

- Economy—$40 to $50 a week saving.
- Convenience—20 hours a week time saved.
- Quality.
- Maximum service.

He mentioned each benefit as he wrote. Just as he finished his summary, he tossed the sheet of paper to me. Without seeming to use a mechanized tool, he had that summary under my nose all during the close. "That was a good selling technique," I said.[9]

The summary technique has considerable impact. It brings together all of the benefits and presents them as a unit. Thus, prospects are confronted with a number of possible reasons for making a purchase. If they are having trouble convincing themselves that the purchase is in fact justified, the summary may be effective. Consider the following situation.

A life-insurance salesman has discussed his company's "whole life" (a combination of life insurance and savings) insurance offerings at length with an executive. In the course of the discussions, the salesman has mentioned numerous benefits that the insurance company could bring to the executive and his family. The executive likes the idea of purchasing whole life insurance in addition to that which he already owns. Still he is reluctant to pay additional premiums. Is it really worth it? Perhaps the funds could be better placed elsewhere, such as in the bank, in common stock, or in bonds. Overall, the executive wants to buy the insurance, in order to provide protection for the family, but cannot bring himself to make the decision.

SALESMAN: We've talked about a number of benefits which our firm could bring to you:

One is the protection element. Our policy will guarantee that your entire family will have financial security in the event of your passing away.

Another is the savings and investment element. Some of the premium money will be invested, thus providing funds you can use on retirement or at some later date.

---

[9]*Ibid.*

Another is that we are a mutual company. This means that you, the insured, will also be an owner of the company. You'll receive quarterly dividends and have the opportunity to vote at stockholders' meetings.

As mentioned earlier, our premiums are very reasonable, compared to those of others. We keep our costs down and invest our monies wisely.

We've talked about the personalized service our company offers. Our sales representatives and other personnel are available to serve you, not just to collect premiums.

So, what is your feeling at this time about the policy that we were considering?

PPROSPECT [*after reflecting for several minutes*]: You have convinced me. I think it's the right thing to do.

The summary of benefits provided the executive with reasons for justifying the decision to himself. Without this justification, the prospect could not have brought himself to purchase the policy, despite his favorable attitude toward the company and its products.

The Concession Method

In the concession method, the sales representative makes his or her presentation and then makes some concession to the prospect. The concession consists of benefits in addition to those that were originally proposed. Some examples are:

If you place an order now, I'll give you these items for $5.99 per case.

I don't ordinarily do this, but if you order ten cases or more, I'll toss in a free one.

How would you react to a price of $15.69? That's 60 cents off the regular price.

If you place the order I have suggested, I'll give you this very attractive portrait at no charge.

I really feel that this product would fulfill your needs. My feeling is strong enough to offer you a 10 percent price reduction on this order.

You drive a hard bargain. Place this order and I'll do an audit of your inventory at no charge.

The H. O. Penn Machinery Company (New York city dealer for Caterpillar products) has made use of concessions. Their sales representatives in 1972 could offer customers a free hand-pallet truck worth about $200 if they would rent a Towmotor fork-lift truck for one, two, or three months, depending upon its size.[10]

The concession method appeals to those who want to obtain a bargain, to obtain concessions that are not part of the standard package of benefits. Buyers who acquire concessions feel that they have the ability to accomplish that which others cannot. A concession represents a victory and evidence that the buyer is able to attain benefits that are not achieved by others. The idea of getting something "free" as a result of one's shrewd bargaining abilities appeals to many prospects.

There are disadvantages to this technique. Granting a concession may be viewed as evidence that the product or service being sold is inferior and cannot be sold without giving concessions. Providing extra benefits can lead to a sense of defeat on the part of sales representatives, thereby damaging their morale and enthusiasm. Further, the prospect who obtains a concession may press for more, thus putting the sales representative on the defensive. Finally, concessions often result in financial costs (an example is a price decrease) to the company. This technique, then, has merit, but should be used judiciously.

## The Emotional Method

As its name implies, this technique involves appealing to the emotions. Examples of emotions that might be emphasized are:

- status
- love
- fear
- competitiveness
- recognition

The emotional close is appropriate for some products and services but not for others. It is appropriate when the product or service fulfills some need or desire that is emotional in nature. Some examples are:

This automobile is designed for those who want to show their station in life.

You should buy life insurance—you owe it to your family.

Your plant needs a better fire alarm system—the effects of a fire can be devastating.

---

[10]"Up with Fork Lifts," *Sales Management* 108, no. 3 (7 February 1972): 15.

Your company should have a computer such as this. None of your competitors have one yet.

Using this conveyor-belt system in your warehouse will bring you recognition as one of the real forward-looking firms in this region.

Obviously, the emotional method can lead to unethical behavior. Playing on emotions can cause prospects to make purchases that are not in their best interests. A vacuum cleaner salesperson, for instance, might play on emotions by telling a prospect "Don't you care about your wife's health? You must buy this vacuum cleaner or your home will be full of germs." And the prospect ends up paying large sums of money for vacuums not much superior to others. Thus, ethical sales representatives will guard against using this method in such a way that consumer dissatisfaction results from the purchase.

The "Buy Now" Method
In this method the sales representative tells prospects they may not be able to acquire the product or service in question.[11] This challenges the prospect to attempt to get the product or service, despite what the sales representative has said. Some examples are:

We have only two of these left in stock. If you want one, better take it now.

These products will be available at the quoted price for only a limited time period. Then the price goes up. You should consider buying now.

Your competitor is large enough to qualify for our volume discounts. Your purchase size may not be large enough to enable you to qualify.

I can't ensure that your order will be filled. Demand for this product has been so high that we have difficulty in keeping up with orders.

Users of the "buy now" method attempt to instill a sense of urgency and insecurity in prospects. If the method is successful, the latter will demand their share of the product.

The technique can be used in an unethical manner, of course. This happens when the sales representative goads the prospect into an unneeded purchase by raising a sense of urgency that is not justified by facts. The method is not patently unethical, however. Sometimes apathetic prospects must be

---

[11]Bert Schlain, "Closing the Sale," in John D. Murphy, ed., *Secrets of Successful Selling* (New York: Dell Publishing Co., 1963), pp. 124–35.

stimulated into purchasing needed items through this technique.

The "Ask for the Order" Method

This technique requires that the sales representative ask for the order, in a straightforward manner. It is often employed when other methods have failed, and all that is left is to request an order. Some examples of the application of this technique are as follows:

Should I go ahead and fill out the order form?

I can set aside four cases for you.

When shall I send the installation engineers over to your establishment?

I'll forward your order to the home office today, okay?

Could I have a down payment?

This product fits your needs—shall we order it?

The "ask for the order" technique works best when applied to prospects who appear to be sold on the product or service in question. When prospects want the offering, the logical thing to do is to ask for the order. If the prospect is not sold on the offering, this method is risky, however. All the prospect has to do is to say no, and the sales interview is essentially over. It is difficult for the sales representative to recover from a flat no response to this technique. The recovery is less difficult with the other methods mentioned in this chapter.

Summary of the Methods

Figure 10-4 summarizes the ten closing techniques covered in this chapter.

Failures in Closing

Sometimes, of course, the close does not result in a sale. When this happens, the sales representative should attempt to pave the way for future calls. Often representatives must make numerous calls upon a particular prospect before a sale materializes. When a rejection occurs, they should be courteous, thank the prospect for the time spent listening to the presentation, and set the stage for future calls. Sometimes it is appropriate to make an appointment for another sales interview at a future date. Or the salesperson may issue statements such as:

I'll look forward to seeing you again.

I'll be making another visit in three weeks.

If you need anything, I'll catch you on the next time around.

**Figure 10-4. Summary of ten closing methods.**

| METHOD | ESSENTIALS OF THE METHOD |
|--------|--------------------------|
| 1. Comparison | 1. Compare features of the offering with features of a well-known competing offering. |
| 2. Assumption | 2. Behave as though the prospect has already decided to purchase the offering. |
| 3. Report | 3. Describe a situation where another prospect with an analogous problem benefited from the offering. |
| 4. Choice | 4. Ask the prospect which of two or more offerings are preferred. |
| 5. Single obstacle | 5. Get the prospect to admit that only one obstacle is preventing the sale. Then eliminate the obstacle. |
| 6. Summary | 6. Summarize the benefits already mentioned in the presentation. |
| 7. Concession | 7. Make a concession (such as in price) to the prospect. |
| 8. Emotional | 8. Appeal to the emotions. |
| 9. Buy now | 9. Indicate to the prospect the he or she may not be able to acquire the offering.later. |
| 10. Ask for the order. | 10. Simply ask for the order. |

The important thing is to orient the close that did not bring an order toward the future. A subsequent visit to the same prospect may result in a sale.

Every sales representative experiences multiple closing attempts that do not work. Successful salespersons use these experiences as learning situations. Rather than despairing and reacting negatively, they attempt to identify what went wrong and to avoid the consequences in the future. Further, successful representatives tend to view closing failures in a healthy manner. They realize that not all presentations will result in sales and that these nonsales should not be allowed to create pessimism or anger. In other words, they have mature attitudes regarding presentations that did not result in sales.

## General Guidelines for Closing

Certain guidelines and principles tend to increase the probability of effective closes. Specifically, the sales representative should:

1. be confident;

2. strike a balance between appearing to be too eager and appearing unconcerned;

3. assure prospects that they are doing the right thing;

4. ask for the order.

Be Confident

One of the most important principles of selling is that the sales representative should be confident. Confidence tends to be contagious, and if the representative has this mental attitude, it is likely to be passed along to the prospect.[12]

If the salesperson has conducted the preclose selling steps in a competent manner, confidence in closing probably will come about naturally. The prospecting stage will have revealed that the prospect needs the offering and is able to pay for it. The approach and preapproach will have prepared the representative for the presentation. In the presentation the representative will have acted as a creative problem solver for the prospect.

If the preclosing steps are handled ineptly, however, confident closing is unlikely. Assume, for instance, that prospecting revealed that a prospect did not greatly need the representative's offering but the latter went ahead with the call despite this evidence, as a means of filling in time between two other important calls. In this situation, the sales representative probably will find it difficult to be confident. His or her insincerity tends to produce mental doubts that the prospect is inclined to detect and react to.

Balance Between Eagerness and Unconcern

Salespersons who are good at closing do not appear to the prospect to be overly eager to make the sale, on the one hand, and unconcerned about it, on the other. Rather, they strike a balance.

Overeager salespersons appear to be inexperienced and inept. They are likely to create the impression that the purpose of the sales call is to make a sale rather than to serve the customer. Thus, the sales representative should exercise some restraint in closing.

Conversely, unconcerned representatives often arose prospect hostility. The salesperson must show a reasonable amount of aggressiveness in pressing toward a sale. Unconcern is likely to be viewed as evidence of a feeling of superiority or of lack of interest in serving customers. Few prospects are attracted to

[12]Shook and Shook, *The Complete Professional Salesman*, pp. 162–64.

sales representatives who treat them as inferiors who do not deserve full attention and interest.

Assuring the Prospect

Prospects who are contemplating a purchase are subject to some degree of doubt and uncertainty. "Am I doing the right thing in buying this home?" "Will I be sorry later?" "What if it has defects in the wiring, plumbing, heating system, or other elements I have not uncovered?" "Am I paying too high a price?" These and other doubts frequently arise. Effective closes include provision for dispelling prospect doubts and uncertainties.

A useful means of assuring the prospect is to emphasize the benefits the product or service will convey:

> You can be assured of little or no maintenance or trouble with this home. We have thoroughly inspected it and, of course, have a one-year guarantee for major installations.

> If you purchase this home, you will have received a real bargain. Other similar properties in this neighborhood have sold at much higher prices.

> I consider this home to be a real investment. Its value will rise steadily over the years.

> A nice element about this home is that you will not have to worry about future assessments. All of the sewage facilities, water lines, sidewalks, and curbing are in, unlike other areas of the city.

Asking for the Order

As we mentioned earlier, a relatively common problem is that sales representatives simply do not ask for the order. They become involved in demonstrating the product, describing its benefits, taking steps to build the organization's image, and other activities but never get down to the essential procedure of asking for the order. This seemingly elementary action sometimes is not undertaken. Therefore, an important guideline is: "Ask for the order!"

**Summary**

Closing consists of asking for an order. It is the last step in the presentation. Those representatives who cannot close effectively cannot be very successful.

There are various obstacles to making effective closes. The prospect is responsible for some of these. Prospects may avoid decision making, be subject to inertia, and be fearful about the outcome of a purchase.

Sales representatives are the cause of some obstacles to

effective closing. The representative may not ask for the sale, be unknowledgeable, or fail to conduct the previous steps in an effective manner.

Trial closes are attempts to determine if the prospect wants to make a purchase. These should be employed throughout the interview. Trial closes are both actions of sales representatives and verbal statements.

Sales representatives face the problem of when to attempt a close. The answer lies in the prospect's readiness to purchase and in the extent to which the salesperson has accomplished something that is likely to be perceived by the prospect as different, exciting, or potentially rewarding.

Green-light signals for closes are actions or words of the prospect which suggest that the sales representative should close. These signals should be attended to when they appear, since failure to act upon them can produce oversold prospects.

This chapter has described ten specific closing methods, each useful for particular sales representatives and particular prospects:

1. Comparison method—compare the features of the product or service with the features of a well-known competing product or service.

2. Assumption method—act as though the prospect had already decided to purchase the product or service in question.

3. Report method—describe a situation where another prospect had a problem similar to that of the prospect at hand and benefitted from the offering.

4. Choice method—ask the prospect which of two or more product or service variations offered by the sales representative are preferred.

5. Single-obstacle method—induce the prospect to admit that one obstacle is the sole reason for not purchasing, then eliminate the obstacle.

6. Summary method—summarize the benefits covered in the presentation.

7. Concession method—make a concession to the prospect.

8. Emotional method—appeal to status, love, or other emotions.

9. "Buy now" method—tell prospects they may not be able to acquire the product or service in question.

10. "Ask for the order" method—ask for the order in a straightforward manner.

Oftentimes a sales call will not result in an order. When this happens, sales representatives should attempt to learn from the experience. Further, they should pave the way for future calls with the prospect and avoid developing negative attitudes.

Certain guidelines to closing are useful. Salespersons should be confident and should strike a balance between appearing to be too eager and appearing unconcerned. Further, they should assure the prospect that he or she is doing the right thing, and should in fact ask for the sale.

**Discussion Questions**

1. Define the term *closing*. Why is closing important to the salesperson?

2. What are the major obstacles or barriers to making effective closes?

3. Set forth the major guidelines for closing that were mentioned in the chapter.

4. What are "green-light signals"? Provide several examples of such signals.

5. Why are trial closes used?

6. When should the sales representative attempt a close?

7. Describe each of the following closing methods, and indicate the advantages and disadvantages of each:

    a. the comparison method,

    b. the assumption method,

    c. the report method,

    d. the choice method,

    e. the single obstacle method,

    f. the summary method,

    g. the concession method,

    h. the emotional method,

    i. the "buy now" method,

    j. the "ask for the order" method.

8. What should salespersons do when they do not obtain an order on a particular call?

**Practical Exercises**

1. Visit several retail stores and note which closing methods are employed by the salespersons. How would you improve on these methods? What did you learn as a result of this exercise?

2. Observe a salesperson in a retail store. Is he or she effective in conducting closes? How would you improve the closing methods? What did you learn as a result of this exercise?

3. Attempt to close a friend on something that he or she does not want to do initially, for example, studying instead of attending a movie. What closing method did you use? Why? What did you learn as a result of this exercise?

**Selling Project**    Ask a friend to pose as a prospect. Try to close him or her, using the closing method that seems to be most appropriate. Did the close work well? Why or why not?

**Case 10
Brian Amundsen**

Brian Amundsen is a senior salesman for the Luna Company, a manufacturer and marketer of a wide line of candies. Luna distributes its products nationally, primarily through large supermarket chains. The firm is very profitable and has a good image among both retailers and ultimate consumers. One of Luna's strengths is a very well trained and highly motivated sales force.

This company believes that one of the keys to success in the candy industry is a well-qualified sales force. Accordingly, sales management attempts to recruit only those college graduates who have high grade-point averages and who perform well in job interviews. Once hired, the recruits receive eight months of classroom and on-the-job training. They are paid a straight salary for eighteen months, then go on a combination of salary plus commission.

Brian graduated from a state university in the Southeast and now serves a territory that takes in one-fifth of the state of Florida. He has been with Luna for sixteen years and is considered by top management to be a good salesman.

Currently, the Luna Company is bringing out a new line of hard candies called Lunars. These items will come in butterscotch, licorice, orange, peppermint, and lemon flavors and will be contained in small cellophane bags. The target consumers are children between the ages of six and fourteen. The primary selling appeals are "good flavor at a low cost."

The Luna sales manager has asked that his representatives attempt to get Lunars on ths shelves of regional supermarket chains in their territories. (Regional chains serve only a restricted area, such as southwest Florida.) Members of the sales management staff will attempt to sell the large national chains. One of the regional chains in Brian's territory is the Hart Company.

The Hart chain, which owns eleven supermarkets in southwest Florida, was founded eight years earlier by John Hart and has grown rapidly and has continued to construct new outlets. Jack Hart, the son of the owner, is in charge of all buying decisions for the chain. Brian is currently in the process of attempting to convince Jack that he should make a trial order for Lunars. He has conducted the approach and made most of the presentation and is now ready to try a close.

BRIAN: Jack, let's compare Lunars with an item you're currently stocking. Correct me if I'm wrong, but it looks like your best seller to the age six-to-fourteen market is the Titan candy produced by Titan, Inc.

JACK: Yes, I think that's true.

BRIAN: If you follow our suggested prices, you'll make one cent more per bag of candy on Lunars than you will for Titan.

JACK: This is impressive, but how do I know that Lunars will sell? Do you have any evidence?

BRIAN: Yes. We test-marketed in Atlanta, Chicago, Seattle, Denver, and San Francisco. The tests lasted six months. Lunars outsold Titans by 31 percent.

JACK: That's impressive.

BRIAN: We're doing more advertising than Titan does. We estimate that our company will have 10 percent more advertising, and will spend considerably more on displays.

JACK: What you say is all good. Still, you can't knock Titan, Inc. Over the years they have produced a fine line of products. They have been good to us. They've been reasonable about granting credit and in providing emergency deliveries.

BRIAN: You're right. Titan is one of the better companies in the business. Certainly Luna is aware of that, since we have to compete with them. And I think that we can compete with Lunars. Keep in mind the advantages that I mentioned earlier:

low price;

attractively packaged;

good flavor—you liked them when I gave you the sample;

highly advertised;

extensive display support;

our guarantee of quick delivery.

It's hard to argue with these advantages. Don't you agree? Let me write you an order.

JACK: I'm still not fully convinced.

BRIAN: I know that you will be satisfied with these. In fact, I would hate to see you miss this opportunity. This being the case, I'm prepared to go out on a limb and offer you a five percent discount on delivered price. That's a very good offer.

JACK: You're right. I'll take that trial order.

Chapter 10 Closing

BRIAN: Excellent. You will be very pleased with the performance of Lunars. Here is the order form.

Evaluate the closing technique that Brian used.

**Suggested Readings**

Anderson, George. "Tell Him What You Told Him." *Marketing Times* 19, XIX, no. 1. (January/February 1972): 10–14.

Micali, Paul J. *The Lacy Techniques of Salesmanship.* New York: Hawthorn Books, 1971, ch. 6.

Roth, Charles B. *Secrets of Closing Sales.* Englewood Cliffs, N.J.: Prentice-Hall, 1970.

Shook, Robert L., and Herbert M. Shook. *The Complete Professional Salesman.* New York: Barnes & Noble Books, 1974, ch. 15.

Schlain, Bert. "Closing the Sale," in John D. Murphy, ed., *Secrets of Successful Selling.* New York: Dell Publishing Co., 1956, ch. 10.

Smaltz, Peter R. *Salesmanship: A "Get-Up-and-Go" Guide to Effective Sales.* Paterson, N.J.: Littlefield, Adams, & Co., 1959, ch. 14.

Tinsley, Dillard, and Vinay Kathari. "Bare Facts About the Reverse Sell." *Sales Management* 112, no. 6 (2 June 1975): 52.

Tralins, Robert S. *How to Be a Power Closer in Selling.* Englewood Cliffs, N.J.: Prentice-Hall, 1960.

Walters, R. G., and John W. Wingate. *Fundamentals of Selling: Meeting Consumer Demand.* Cincinnati, Ohio: South-Western Publishing Co. 1953, ch. 18.

# 11

# Consumer Behavior

*After reading this chapter you should be able to demonstrate a knowledge of:*

- *what is meant by the term* consumer behavior
- *the importance of consumer behavior to the salesperson*
- *contributions to the salesperson of various consumer behavior theories*
- *an overall theory of consumer behavior*

- An industrial purchasing agent listens to the presentation of an office furniture wholesaler and places an order. The basis for the purchase is a set of specifications established by the office manager. After the furniture is installed, it is used on a daily basis by executives, office workers, secretaries, and others.

- The proprietor of a cheese shop convinces a consumer that she should buy two pounds of Scandinavian butter cheese. The consumer takes the product home and serves it to guests at a cocktail party.

- An alumnus of a large university is approached by an employee of the alumni association. The representative convinces him to become a member of the Century Club. By contributing $100 each year to the alumni association, he is able to sit in a special section of the stadium during football games.

The above are examples of consumer behavior. In this chapter we will define consumer behavior, point out its importance to the salesperson, and discuss the contributions of various theories of consumer behavior to personal selling.

## What Consumer Behavior Is

Consumer behavior consists of the conduct of individuals in purchasing and using goods and services.[1] The individual may be:

- an industrial purchasing agent,
- an office manager,
- a mechanical engineer,
- a production worker,
- a member of a retail buying chain,
- a retail store manager,
- a member of a family who buys goods and services,
- a member of a family who uses the goods and services bought.

The term "consumer behavior" implies that this field is concerned with *consumption* (using goods and services to acquire benefits) but not with *purchasing* (taking the actions necessary to attain the goods and services). Actually, the field includes both.

In purchasing—seeking out and acquiring goods and services, in exchange for funds—a consumer looking for a car goes through certain actions such as reading advertisements, talking with friends and salespersons, test driving various models, then signing a contract, all activities directed toward the goal of obtaining a car. In consumption—using goods and services in order to satisfy needs and desires—once the car has been acquired, it is used by members of the family for purposes such as driving to and from work, on shopping trips, and on pleasure trips.

---

[1]Chester R. Wasson, *Consumer Behavior: A Managerial Viewpoint* (Austin, Texas: Austin Press, 1975), p. 9.

Figure 11-1. Overview
of consumer behavior.

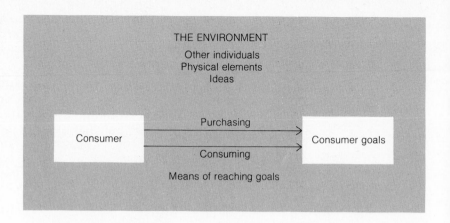

As Figure 11-1 shows, consumers are people who live in an environment made up of other people, physical elements, and ideas, and who have goals that they attempt to attain through purchasing and consuming goods and services. The consumers in the figure include both ultimate and industrial parties— housewives, purchasing agents, retail and wholesale buyers, and members of families and business and nonbusiness organizations who use the goods and services.

**The Importance of Consumer Behavior to the Salesperson**

Salespersons attempt to bring various benefits to the consumer, and they utilize persuasion and joint problem solving to match their organization's offerings with the consumer's needs and desires. This process does not end when a sale is made, however. Effective sales representatives are also concerned with consumer satisfaction *after* the sale has been made. They realize that customer satisfaction is one of the more significant keys to their success.

Representatives need to have knowledge of consumer behavior in order to:

- determine what mix of benefits consumers desire;
- determine how consumers go about attempting to attain these benefits;
- determine when consumers attempt to attain these benefits;
- determine the best ways of persuading consumers to achieve satisfaction through purchase and use of the representative's offerings;
- determine how consumers will use goods and services to produce satisfaction.

The requirements of a sales representative and of a physician are similar in that, just as doctors need to have in-depth knowledge of how the body operates so that they can maintain and improve health, sales representatives need to maintain and improve consumer well-being while still bringing in revenues to their organizations.

Salespersons cannot effectively bring satisfaction to consumers if they are not familiar with the ways they think and conduct their affairs. Both the doctor and the sales representative, then, must know certain things about their clients if the clients are to receive needed benefits.

**Contributions to the Salesperson of Various Consumer Behavior Theories**

A number of theories of consumer behavior can contribute to the knowledge needed by the sales representative. Here we will examine the nature of such theories and then discuss the various specific theories.

Theories of Consumer Behavior

Theories of consumer behavior are explanations of how consumers search for, acquire, and use goods and services. Each theory assumes that certain stimuli influence consumers, who in turn respond to these stimuli,[2] as depicted in Figure 11-2.

The figure indicates that various stimuli bear upon the consumer. A stimulus is an environmental object perceived by the individual that can trigger action.[3] Examples of stimuli are:

- words and actions of friends;
- the sound of an automobile engine or an air conditioner;
- the sensation of touching leather objects;

---

[2]James F. Engel, David T. Kollat, and Roger D. Blackwell, *Consumer Behavior* (New York: Holt, Rinehart and Winston, 1973), pp. 23–24.

[3]C. Glenn Walters and Gordon W. Paul, *Consumer Behavior: An Integrated Framework* (Homewood, Ill.: Richard D. Irwin, 1970), p. 317.

**Figure 11-2. Basis for theories of consumer behavior.**

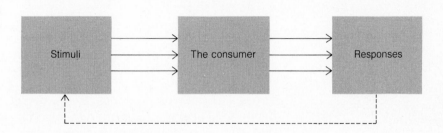

- the image of a billboard advertisement;
- the words and gestures of a sales representative.

The consumer is exposed to many stimuli at one point in time. Some of these are effective in modifying behavior. The consumer reacts to these stimuli, and responses result. Examples of responses are:

- smiling at a friend;
- shutting the automobile window to keep the sound of the engine out;
- buying a leather billfold;
- searching for an object depicted on a billboard advertisement;
- placing an order with a sales representative.

The figure indicates that the responses, in turn, become stimuli. When a consumer places an order with a sales representative, for instance, further consumer action is triggered.

The various theories of consumer behavior differ, in that they present divergent:

1. stimuli;

2. ways of reacting to the stimuli, on the part of the consumer;

3. responses;

4. ways in which stimuli, consumers, and responses affect one another.

The remainder of this section outlines contributions of the individual theories to the personal selling field.

Seven Specific Theories of Consumer Behavior

The seven theories covered in this section are:

1. economic theory,

2. learning theory,

3. psychoanalytic theory,

4. Gestalt theory,

5. self-concept theory,

6. group theory,

7. culture theory.

**Economic Theory.**   Economic theory is based upon the assumption that consumers are rational. The term rational means "having or exercising the ability to reason."[4] Rational consumers are thinking individuals, then, making decisions based upon reason rather than emotion. These persons have clear-cut goals and are informed as to the best ways of reaching these goals. Finally, they always take the steps needed to reach the goals.

Research suggests that some consumers behave in ways that can be termed "rational."[5] This is especially likely in the case of buyers of industrial rather than consumer goods. The prospects of a seller of valves used in industrial installations, for instance, have certain specific criteria (such as lack of leakage, ease of opening and closing, durability, noise suppression, and the reduction of vibration) which they use to evaluate the valves of specific manufacturers (such as the Babcock and Wilson Company). They talk to sales representatives and other executives, read advertisements carefully, and look at engineers' ratings of the various brands before deciding upon a purchase. In short, they tend to be fairly rational consumers.

Economic theory falls short of providing a complete idea of the why and how of consumer behavior, however. Consumers generally are not fully aware of their goals, needs, and desires. Some of these lie in the subconscious. Further, consumers are not always aware of how best to reach their goals. A buyer, for instance, might buy a valve in the belief that it was the most durable model on the market, not knowing that another model did, in fact, provide more durability. Finally, economic theory does not explain how groups influence consumer behavior. Some buyers, for instance, may procure particular valves because of the influence of others, such as executives, engineers, and production foremen. Economic theory does not explain how this influence process operates.

In reality, economic theory provides just the basis for a knowledge of consumer behavior. As a sales representative you can begin with the assumption that your prospects behave rationally, then alter this assumption in accordance with the insights provided by other theories and in accordance with reality. As a starting point, however, you may assume that buyers have reasonably well-formulated goals (such as high durability of valves) that they attempt to reach in a thinking manner.

---

[4]*The American Heritage Dictionary of the English Language* (New York: American Heritage Publishing Co., 1973), p. 1083.

[5]Frederick W. Winter, "Laboratory Measurement of Response to Consumer Information," *Journal of Marketing Research* 12, no. 3 (November 1975): 390–400).

**Learning Theory.** Learning theory takes the view that consumers learn, just as do students who read books and attend classes. This theory is based on four elements:

1. drive,
2. stimulus,
3. response,
4. reinforcement, positive or negative.

Figure 11-3 illustrates how these elements combine to produce learning. A *drive* is an internal state of tension, such as hunger or the desire for status, which demands satisfaction. A *stimulus* is a cue, such as a restaurant advertisement or a salesperson's promise about a product, which bring about a response designed to satisfy one or more drives. *Responses* are actions that consumers take as a result of the operations of drives and stimuli. *Positive reinforcement* consists of reward, such as the satisfactions derived from long product life. *Negative reinforcement* is punishment, such as the dissatisfaction resulting from a product that breaks down after only short-term use.

Consumers learn when they associate particular stimuli with particular responses. If responses to stimuli are rewarding, consumers are likely to repeat the responses when the drive is aroused. Repeated reward leads to learning, where

**Figure 11-3. Essentials of learning theory.**

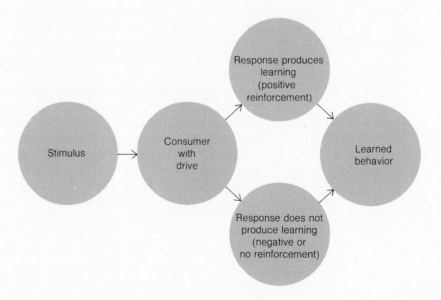

consumers have learned to associate particular drives and particular responses. Conversely, when reinforcement is negative, consumers learn not to repeat the response.

Consider the example of a wholesale sporting goods salesman operating in the New England region. One of the buyers he calls on has a drive to move upward in the organization through promotions, perhaps to the level of head buyer at the corporate headquarters. His drive is for achievement and status in the organization. The salesman has called upon this buyer in the past and has sold him merchandise that readily sold to customers, thereby increasing the buyer's chances for promotion. The buyer, then, found the "purchasing from this salesman" response to be rewarding. He now associates buying from this salesman with ready sales and advancement in the organization. In essence, the buyer has learned to have a positive attitude toward the salesman and his products. As a result, it is likely that he will continue to be a good customer, barring future negative reinforcement.

Once this salesman called upon a buyer who made a major purchase of thermal sleeping bags, but the target consumers of the buyer's store did not respond favorably to the sleeping bags. Both salesman and buyer had miscalculated consumer reaction to these items. On another occurrence, the same buyer purchased five cases of dehydrated fruit from the salesman, and these, too, did not sell well. Because both events led to considerable embarrassment on the part of the buyer, she learned to have a negative attitude toward the salesman and as a result has been leery of placing orders.

According to learning theory, the more frequent and the more intense the reward, the greater the learning. The buyer who received reward as a result of buying from the sporting goods salesman has obtained frequent and intense reinforcement. Every time that he has placed an order from the salesman the results have been satisfactory sales. This has produced considerable praise from the buyer's superiors and considerable personal satisfaction. This buyer now purchases from the salesman on what amounts to a habitual basis. Conversely, the buyer whose sleeping bags and dehydrated fruit did not sell suffered considerable embarrassment and feelings of failure. This intense negative reinforcement has led her to resent and to avoid the salesman.

This salesman is aware of the importance of positive reinforcement. He tries to reward customers as intensely and frequently as possible. Some rewards relate to the buying function

—he attempts to provide buyers with goods that will sell and that will enhance the image of their stores in the eyes of ultimate consumers. In addition, the salesman provides personal rewards to buyers. These come in the form of friendliness, praise, and expressions of gratitude for purchasing company products. In effect, the salesman's customers have learned to have a positive attitude toward him.

**Psychoanalytic Theory.** Psychoanalytic theory rests upon the assumption that the consumer's personality is made up of three parts:

1. *The id*—that part of the consumer which seeks pleasure and avoids pain.

2. *The superego*—that part of the consumer which strives toward moral and ethical conduct. Essentially, the superego is the conscience.

3. *The ego*—the intelligent component of the consumer. The ego is the rational element that attempts to reconcile the demands of the id and the superego.

As Figure 11-4 indicates, the id and superego are often in conflict. The ego intervenes and attempts to resolve the conflict. If it is successful in this resolution, the consumer achieves equilibrium or balance among the elements of the personality. If the ego cannot reconcile the conflict and the id and superego are pulling in opposite directions, the consumer may be unable to take actions such as buying a product from a sales representative.

Let's suppose a salesman is attempting to convince an attorney that she should purchase an Ajax brand sports car. The statements made by the salesman have aroused the attorney's id. She is excited about the prospects of owning a contemporary styled, high-performance, exclusively designed automobile. On the other hand, as her superego comes into play, she realizes that purchasing the car will result in an outlay of funds that her son could use for other purposes (such as attending a private school and eventually medical school).

The salesman has been able to activate the attorney's ego in a way that permits satisfaction of both the id and the superego. He has shown her that the operating and maintenance costs of the sports car are less than the automobile that she is now driving. Further, he has indicated that driving the sports car may result in a better image among her clients which, in the long run, will pay off in more fees. The result is that the id and superego have attained balance. Consequently, the attorney

**Figure 11-4. Components of psychoanalytic theory.**

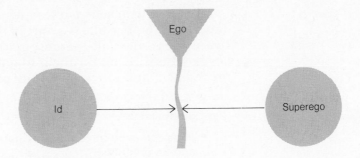

decides to purchase the sports car with no reservations—something she would never do if the superego were not satisfied.

**Gestalt Theory.** Gestalt theorists are concerned with the ways people perceive. The term *perceptions* has been defined as "interpreted stimuli."[6] The human sense organs detect some of the elements of the environment and ignore others. In addition, individuals are interested in some elements of the environment and not others. Those to which interest is directed tend to be understood better and remembered longer than others. Further, the Gestalt theory indicates that individuals interpret perceived stimuli according to their own needs and desires. For instance, a statement such as "General Motors Corporation is a big company" might be interpreted in two ways:

> CHEVROLET OWNER: Since General Motors is large, it can afford to produce quality products at a reasonable cost.

> VOLKSWAGEN OWNER: GM is too large for the good of society. This firm should be broken up into segments.

Each of the two consumers gives the sentence a different interpretation. In a sense, they behaved in accordance with the cliché, "You see what you want to see and hear what you want to hear." Individuals tend to:

- attend to certain elements of the environment and not to others —selective attention;
- be interested in certain elements but not others—selective perception;
- understand certain elements but not others—selective comprehension;
- remember certain elements but not others—selective retention.

---

[6]Joe Kent Kerby, *Consumer Behavior: Conceptual Foundations* (New York: Dun-Donnelley Publishing Corp., 1975), p. 26.

Janet Martin sells purses and other leather accessories to department stores. She is aware of the implications of the selective processes to sales representatives. Because of these processes, it is difficult for them to gain attention, interest, comprehension, and retention on the part of:

- new prospects who have never heard of the company or its products;

- prospects who have heard negative things about the company and its products;

- prospects who have had unfavorable experiences with the company in the past (such as a retailer who once received two late shipments of company products in a row).

Janet realizes that with such prospects she must make a special effort to gain their attention. Thus, she uses a combination of the following techniques:

- Making an unusual approach—such as by greeting the prospect and stating, "How would you like to increase your purse and accessories sales by 10 percent or more? I can show you how."

- Choosing words that will incite attention and interest in the presentation—such as "profits," "sales," "satisfied customers," and "exciting new company products."

- Using visual aids—such as charts, graphs, written testimonials from other customers, photographs, and samples of materials.

These elements are effective in overcoming the selective processes of many prospects. For some, however, the selective processes are too strong, and even Janet's combination of actions and devices cannot overcome them.

According to Gestalt theory, consumers view concepts or objects as parts of a whole. They do not view them as individual elements. This means that actions or words used by the representative should be compatible with other actions or words used. All elements of the presentation should be compatible with one another. Janet should not tell a prospect at one point in the presentation that a particular leather purse is "low in cost" and later indicate that it is designed for consumers who seek high status. Undue emphasis upon low cost can easily detract from the high-status appeal her company attempts to achieve.

In light of consumers' tendency to view concepts or objects as parts of a whole, the concept of *cognitive dissonance* is relevant. According to this construct:[7]

---

[7]Wasson, *Consumer Behavior*, p. 73.

. . . people strive to maintain a relative degree of consistency between their feelings on any subject or item, their beliefs concerning that subject, and their actions with relationship to it. When this balance . . . is disturbed in any way—that is, when one of the elements is thrown out of line with either of the two—the individual tends to adjust the other two to bring them into line and into a new balance, or to restore the original condition of the element that was forced out of line.

Consumers, then, seek balance between three elements:

1. beliefs—what they *think* is true;
2. emotions—what they *feel* is true;
3. actions—what they *see* is true.

If a salesperson attempts to change one of the three elements (such as beliefs) he or she should take steps designed to ensure that the prospect's other two elements (such as emotions and actions) are compatible with the new beliefs. Otherwise, the prospect is likely to ignore or argue with the attempts to change beliefs.

Charles Warner is the owner and top manager of the Warner department store. He has been told by a friend that Janet's product line will not sell well in his market area (a *belief*). He has a feeling that the firm is a second-rate company and is made up of individuals who cannot be depended on for producing quality products (an *emotion*). Finally, his firm stocks a competing brand (an *action*). If Janet is to convince Warner that he should purchase her products, her best course of action is to attempt to change all three of these elements. Warner is likely to resist changes in only one or perhaps two, since the resulting state of mind would not be balanced. As a result, Janet should take steps to alter all three of the elements.

Janet attempts to overcome the belief that her products will not sell well in Warner's market area by presenting testimonials from store managers and buyers that indicate good selling results in that area. She endeavors to overcome the emotion regarding the poor performance of company employees by describing the degree of care that goes into the production of the product line. Finally, she tries to obtain action by asking Warner to stock a small quantity of her purses on a trial basis for four months. The results are that sales are surprisingly high and another order is placed. In this case, the sales representative was effective in producing a favorable balance of the three elements, with resulting customer satisfaction.

Often after making a major purchase consumers feel uneasy. "Was this a wise purchase?" "Should I have bought brand X rather than brand Y?" "Did I reach a purchase decision too rapidly?" The sales representative should take steps to dispel such ideas. Janet is aware of the possible occurrence of post-purchase dissonance. After making a sale she makes at least one trip back to the buyer to assure him or her that the purchase was a wise one and to dispel any negative feelings:

> NEW CUSTOMER: Hello, Janet. I didn't expect to see you again so soon.

> JANET: I'm just calling back to ensure that everything is in order. You'll never regret buying those new leather Travel Packs. By the way, I have some reports that just came out on their salability. I think you'll be impressed.

Janet is taking steps to minimize the occurrence of post-purchase dissonance. She does not want the customer to have negative afterthoughts about the purchase. Consequently, these after-the-sale contacts are a routine practice for her.

**Self-Concept Theory.** The self-concept of an individual consists of:

1. the kind of person that one believes he or she is, and

2. the kind of person that one believes others think he or she is.

This theory states that consumers have patterns of behavior (life styles) which are consistent with their self-images. Part of the life style is what goods and services are selected by the consumer. One study indicated, for instance, that the male self-image is closely associated with the purchases of suntan lotion, TV-dinner, coffee, and beer brands, while the female self-image is associated with brands of mouthwashes and headache remedies.[8] Numerous self-concepts and associated sets of goods and services are possible, including the following:

- "Playboy"—sports car, high-rise apartment, fashionable clothes.
- "Scholar"—tweed jacket and pipe.
- "Executive"—attache case, suburban home, three-piece suits.

---

[8]E. Laird Landon, Jr., "Self Concept, Ideal Self Concept, and Consumer Purchase Intentions," *Journal of Consumer Research* 1, no. 2 (September 1974): 47–48.

Knowledge of a prospect's self-image will provide some insights as to the sales presentation ingredients that will be effective in appealing to him or her. Assume, for example, you are a furniture salesman with a customer who is the president of a small local brewery. The customer has the self-concept of a hard-driving, resourceful businessman who literally worked himself from rags to riches. You inform this prospect that you too have had to work hard to attain your present position as the top salesperson in the firm and that you too came from humble origins. The brewer will feel that he and you are "the same kind of person." As a result, you will always receive a warm welcome from this prospect.

**Group Theory.**   Sociologists believe that the groups people belong to or relate to are fundamental determinants of their behavior. Among the most influential bodies are *reference groups*, those to whom the individual looks for guidance in behavior. Some examples of reference groups are:

- the work group,
- neighborhood groups,
- the poker playing group,
- the Sunday golf foursome.

Each group has certain standards of behavior, such as:

- the work group—"Don't try too hard to increase production";
- the neighborhood group—"Keep your lawn well-manicured";
- the poker playing group—"Kibitzing is not allowed";
- the golf foursome—"Don't exceed 100."

Group members make an effort to achieve these standards, since they know that their status in the group depends on it. Accordingly, if salespersons know the group memberships of prospects, they are in a position to plan presentations tailored to these standards.

A seller of fashion clothing uses group membership information as one of the guides to developing her sales presentations. One of her prospects, for instance, is a devout member of a fundamentalist church. The sales representative is careful not to smoke or drink coffee, or to make reference to alcohol, tobacco, or coffee, while in the presence of the prospect. Another prospect is a member of a local country club. He assumes that civilized people always conduct business over a cocktail.

Accordingly, the salesperson often takes him out for a drink when she calls on him.

Every group has leaders, people who have a major role in setting group standards and who pass information on to followers. If group leaders can be induced to purchase and use a good or service, the probability is high that the followers will emulate them. Research has indicated, for instance, that informal communications between leaders and followers in the steel industry were responsible, to a large extent, for the adoption of continuous casting in steel mills.[9] Steel industry executives from different companies have formed informal groups with leaders who pass on information and influence followers in matters such as what production processes to employ.

The student-relations director of a military academy uses group leaders in his program to attract superior high school graduates to enroll in the academy. During the spring of each year, class officers of schools in the region are invited to participate in debates held at the academy. The director addresses them as a group and holds conferences with individual class leaders. Many of those attending the debates have become academy students. Others have informed friends of their experiences at the debates and have as a result helped in developing favorable attitudes toward the academy among the ranks of high school students. The director knows that when a class officer elects to attend the academy, he or she is likely to bring along one or two classmates. Class leaders, therefore, are prime targets for his promotion campaign.

**Culture Theory.** Culture is an important determinant of consumer behavior. Culture has been defined as referring to the "learned patterns of behavior and symbolism that are passed from one generation to another and [representing] the totality of values that characterize a society."[10]

The members of a culture learn many of their values, attitudes, and patterns of behavior from other members of that culture. For instance, one inquiry into the values of the members of the culture of the United States indicated that the following were most significant (ranked in descending order of importance):[11]

---

[9]John A. Czepiel, "Word-of-Mouth Processes in the Diffusion of a Major Technological Innovation," *Journal of Marketing Research* 11, no. 2 (May 1974): 204.

[10]Engel, Kollat, and Blackwell, *Consumer Behavior*, p. 70.

[11]Yankelovich, Skelly, and White, Inc., *The General Mills American Family Report, 1974–75* (Minneapolis, Minn.: General Mills, 1975), p. 55.

- family,

- work,

- education,

- self-fulfillment,

- financial security.

Sales people can gain useful indications of the needs and desires of individuals by familiarizing themselves with these values and their relative importance. Similarly, Americans selling in foreign countries should determine the patterns of behavior and values there. For instance, it has been observed that in foreign countries:

> . . . the American passion for meeting deadlines could be a barrier in business dealings. Time in many countries is relatively unimportant. Low-level bureaucrats in some African countries frequently extend their time in decision making as a means of demonstrating the "importance" of their work. Establishing deadlines in the Middle East and Latin America might be viewed as offensive.[12]

Members of cultures are also members of smaller segments called *subcultures*. Consumers learn values, attitudes, and patterns of behavior from other members of their subculture. Examples of subcultures are:

- the eastern United States subculture,

- the New York subculture,

- the Greenwich Village subculture,

- the rock music subculture.

The importance of particular subcultures, as measured by the degree of market potential they represent, tends to change over time. In the 1960s and 1970s, for instance, the youth subculture was large in numbers and exerted a strong influence over other subcultures, as when middle-aged and older consumers adopted long hair, jeans, and the casual look. The impact of this subculture is expected to decline in the future, however, as its members become older. This probably will result in increased usage of products such as low-calorie foods, minimum-exertion sporting equipment, and casual clothing.[13]

---

[12]Ronald D. Michman, "Culture as a Marketing Tool," *Marquette Business Review* 19, no. 4 (Winter 1975): 181.

[13]"Esty Sees Declining of 'Youth Cult' by 1985," *Advertising Age* 47, no. 1 (5 January 1976): p. 3.

One of the representatives of a hardware wholesaler knows that many of his prospects, especially those who are over thirty years old, have grasped the so-called Puritan ethic subculture values. That is, they believe in hard work, individualism, free enterprise, and thrift. The salesman attempts to appeal to these motives. For instance:

> PROSPECT: You've gone to a lot of work in mapping out my merchandise needs for the next six months.

> SALESMAN: No problem. Work doesn't bother me—in fact, I enjoy it.

The salesperson can benefit, then, by knowing the particular cultures and subcultures that prospects identify with. Knowledge of these identities provides useful clues as to the appropriate ways of conducting sales presentations.

**An Overall Theory of Consumer Behavior**

An overall theory of consumer behavior is useful in integrating the various elements of the theories mentioned earlier. This section presents an overall theory and relates it to the personal selling function. Figure 11-5 outlines the theory in graphic form.

Individual Prospect or Buying Center

The illustration shows the individual prospect or buying center, members of which have personalities, self-concepts, motives, knowledge, and perceptions that determine their reactions to sales presentations.

The buying center consists of those who have a role in purchasing. They include:[14]

- Users—those who use the goods and services purchased, as typists are the users of the typewriters that are purchased.

- Buyers—those who have formal authority to make purchases, such as the purchasing agent.

- Influencers—those who affect the purchasing process by exerting an impact upon others in the buying center. The purchasing agent's receptionist may influence the choice of what typewriters are bought.

- Deciders—those who have authority to choose among different buying actions, such as the head of the typing pool, or the purchasing agent.

---

[14]Frederick E. Webster, Jr., and Yoram Wind, "A General Model for Understanding Organizational Buying Behavior," *Journal of Marketing* 36, no. 2 (April 1972): 17.

- Gatekeepers—those who control the flow of information into the buying center, such as the secretary of the purchasing agent.

The concept of the buying center does not necessarily relate only to formal organizations. Individuals belong to families and other groups that tend to act as buying centers. In purchasing a home, for instance, family members might take on the following roles:

- parents—users, buyers, and deciders;
- children—users, influencers, and gatekeepers.

The salesperson should attempt to identify the members of the buying center in order to determine which should be subjected to persuasive efforts. Prospecting and preapproach information is useful in this regard. If representatives have called upon the organization in the past, they are likely to have information about the members of the buying center and their respective roles.

**Figure 11-5. Overall theory of consumer behavior.**

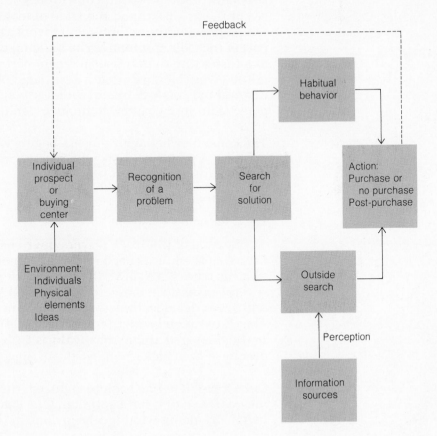

An Overall Theory of Consumer Behavior

Over the past six months, Ivan, the truck salesman for the Alpha Truck Manufacturing Company, has been engaged in attempting to sell medium-weight trucks to the Odin Wholesale Distribution Company. He has identified the following members of the buying center:

- users—truck drivers;
- buyer—Mr. Odin, the owner;
- influencers—Ms. Venus, the assistant manager;
- decider—Mr. Odin;
- gatekeepers—the secretaries of Mr. Odin and Ms. Venus.

**The Environment**

Prospects make their decisions in the context of an environment, which consists of other persons, physical elements, and ideas. Specific elements of the environment include the state of the economy, groups to which buying-center members belong, suppliers of the prospect, competitors of the prospect, employees of the prospect, and the state of technology.

At present, the environment favors a truck purchase on the part of the Odin Company. The national economy is advancing at a faster rate than it was in recent periods. The sales of Odin are likewise increasing at a fast pace. None of the employee unions have made demands for large wage increases. All these place Odin in a position to finance a major purchase.

**Recognition of a Problem**

The consumer-behavior process begins when a problem is recognized. A problem exists when members of the buying center detect a difference between:

1. a desired condition, and
2. the actual condition.

Several of the truck drivers have been complaining to Mr. Odin that their units need replacing. Among the complaints are that the trucks are slow, difficult to operate, inefficient, and in several cases even dangerous. Odin and Venus have conferred and have decided that three replacement units are needed. They have talked with the chief financial officer of the firm, and he has assured them that Odin is in a financial position to purchase the trucks.

**Search for Solution**

Once a problem has been recognized, the members of the buying center search for a solution. One easy solution is habitual behavior—doing what has been done in the past. For instance, when a householder runs out of detergent (the problem has been recognized), an easy solution is to purchase a favored brand at the supermarket. Sometimes habitual behavior is not sufficient, however. Among the conditions that create this situation are:

- the problem has never occurred before, so members of the buying center cannot rely on experience;
- past experience has not produced satisfactory solutions to the problem;
- the problem is so substantial that members of the buying center want to look for solutions beyond those used in the past.

Currently, the Odin Company uses Callisto brand trucks. An easy solution to the problem would be to order three Callisto units. Such a solution would not satisfy Odin and Venus, however. Transportation is an important element in the marketing mix of this firm. Further, purchase of three medium-weight trucks constitutes a large financial outlay. Finally, the experience with Callisto has not been satisfactory. As a result, the two individuals have decided to engage in outside search.

Outside search involves seeking information from people who are not members of the buying center—friends, business associates, bankers, suppliers, advertisers, and sales representatives. Salespersons in particular have much to contribute since, for many consumers, outside search is relatively limited (many ultimate consumers visit only a few stores before buying, for instance), even in the case of expensive durable goods.[15]

Ivan calls upon the Odin Company on a regular basis. He has learned from his contacts in the wholesaling field that the firm is considering the purchase of three medium-weight trucks. His knowledge about the members of the buying center allows him to contact the right persons.

From experience he knows that the secretaries of Odin and Venus are gatekeepers, but this is not a problem for him, for he has carefully developed friendships with both. They know him on a first-name basis and exchange small talk and humor whenever Ivan calls upon the firm.

During the following week, Ivan calls upon both Odin and Venus. He goes through a thorough presentation with each one, including taking them for a demonstration ride in a medium-

---

[15]John D. Clayton, Joseph N. Fry, and Bernard Portis, "A Taxonomy of Prepurchase Information Gathering Patterns," *Journal of Consumer Research* 1, no. 3 (December 1974): 35.

weight truck. He also makes presentations to the three drivers who will be operating the trucks, since he recognizes that their inputs will be important in Odin's final decision.

Perception An important determinant of the influence of the various information sources is perception. The selective processes of the members of the buying center will determine which information sources are considered and the credibility attached to each. Ivan wants to make a major attempt to surmount any selective processes that might impede his communication efforts. He has arranged for the mailing of a number of booklets and brochures describing his company (Alpha) and its medium-weight trucks to Odin, Venus, and the three drivers. He feels that his own credibility is high in the buying center, he believes the members will attend to, be interested in, understand, and remember what he says. In short, perception should not be a problem for him.

Action The outcome of the consumer-behavior process is action: consumers either buy or do not buy. After six weeks of deliberation, Odin decides to buy three Alpha trucks. This decision is based upon inputs from the drivers and Venus and on Odin's own personal impressions. The contract is signed and arrangements are made for financing and for delivery.

Postpurchase behavior consists of the activities that take place after the buying decision has occurred. This stage is an important one for the salesperson, (as we will discuss in the next chapter). Ivan arranges for the following postpurchase efforts:

- calling upon Odin and Venus and assuring them of the appropriateness of their purchase, ensuring that problems with the trucks are not in evidence, and making sure the trucks are delivered on time;
- checking with the bank to ensure that the financing is going as planned;
- the trucks are delivered in good condition;
- answering driver questions about operating the new units.

Feedback Feedback refers to the flow of information that takes place once the purchase has been made and the postpurchase behavior is in effect. If feedback is favorable, the buyer is likely to have a positive attitude toward the salesperson and his or her products and may become a habitual customer. Negative feedback may indicate that the salesperson should take action to prevent deterioration of customer relations. The feedback regarding the Alpha purchase was good—the drivers, Odin, and Venus were all impressed with the product, Ivan, and Alpha. As a result, they became good repeat-purchase candidates for the future.

Overview of the Theory

The overall theory of consumer behavior we presented in this chapter provides a perspective for salespersons in designing and executing their presentations and postpurchase activities. The theory covers the various steps consumers undertake in deriving the benefits they need. Salespersons who are familiar with this construct are in a position to acquire relevant inputs from diverse disciplines and combine them in a way that will enhance their effectiveness.

**Summary**

This chapter has addressed the subject of consumer behavior—the conduct of individuals in purchasing and using goods and services. This subject covers both purchasing and using. Consumers engage in consuming and purchasing in order to reach their goals and are influenced by the environment in these processes.

Sales representatives need a knowledge of consumer behavior in order to effectively bring benefits to their customers. Like physicians, salespersons need knowledge about the nature and characteristics of their subjects, before high-level satisfaction can be provided.

Theories of consumer behavior are explanations of how consumers search for, acquire, and use goods and services. Each theory has some provision for stimuli, the consumer, responses, and particular ways in which these three elements interact.

This chapter has examined a number of specific theories of consumer behavior. The essence of these is as follows:

1. Economic—consumers behave rationally.

2. Learning—consumers learn through drive, stimulus, response and reinforcement.

3. Psychoanalytic—the interaction of the id, superego, and ego determine behavior.

4. Gestalt—perception and the selective processes; cognitive dissonance.

5. Self-concept—individuals conduct themselves according to their self-concepts.

6. Group—group standards are emulated by members; group leaders are powerful in setting standards.

7. Culture—the learned patterns of behavior of a culture are important in determining individuals' values, attitudes, and patterns of behavior. Subcultures, such as social classes, also are active in determining these factors.

An overall theory of consumer behavior appeared in this chapter. It included:

1. Individual prospect or buying center. The latter are all of those who have a role in purchasing and include users, buyers, influencers, deciders, and gatekeepers.

2. The environment—other persons, physical elements, and ideas.

3. Recognition of a problem—the consumer detects a difference between a desired and the actual condition.

4. Search for solution—the consumer engages in a habitual solution or searches through outside sources.

5. Perception—the selective processes determine what information sources are considered and the credibility attached to each.

6. Action—purchase or no purchase, and postpurchase activities.

7. Feedback—flow of information following purchase.

**Discussion Questions**

1. Define *consumer behavior* .

2. In what respects is consumer behavior of importance to the salesperson?

3. What is a *theory of consumer behavior?* What are the components of such theories?

4. Outline the central elements of the economic theory.

5. What are the components of learning theory? How do they interact?

6. What are the three components of psychoanalytic theory? What is the role of each?

7. What contributions does Gestalt theory make to the knowledge of consumer behavior?

8. Relate the self-concept theory of consumer behavior.

9. How does group theory attempt to explain consumer behavior?

10. Explain what is meant by the culture-theory approach to consumer behavior.

11. What are the ten components of the overall theory of consumer behavior presented in this chapter?

12. What is the buying center? What types of roles do participants in the buying center assume?

13. What is meant by problem recognition by consumers?

14. How do consumers go about searching for solutions? How does perception affect the search process?

**Practical Exercises**

1. Which of the theories of consumer behavior presented in this chapter would seem to be most useful in explaining your behavior? Explain why this is the case.

2. Observe a randomly chosen consumer in a retail store. Did you observe anything that would indicate that this consumer is behaving according to the theories mentioned in this chapter? Explain.

3. Interview a friend to determine how he or she goes about choosing a particular item, such as a pair of shoes. Which theory of consumer behavior best explains your friend's behavior? Explain why this is the case.

What did you learn as a result of these exercises?

**Selling Project**

1. Which of the theories of consumer behavior would seem to be useful in explaining the behavior of consumers of your product? Explain why they would seem to be useful. What did you learn as a result of this project?

2. Think of a hypothetical user of your product. Mentally trace the movement of this consumer through the stages of the overall theory of consumer behavior. Would it be useful in explaining the conduct of this individual? What did you learn as a result of this project?

**Case 11
Dianne Perez**

Dianne Perez is a saleswoman for the Cycles Corporation, which sells employee-motivation programs to business and nonbusiness organizations. The purpose of the programs, according to Cycles president, Tom Umerski, is "to motivate employees to achieve their employers' and their own personal goals." Employers who buy the program receive the following:

1. Booklets, which are passed out to employees.

2. Instructions by a Cycles trainer as to how employees might be motivated.

3. Training sessions conducted by a Cycles trainer, with the employees as students, which involve:
a. inspirational lectures by the trainers;
b. videotape, slide, and motion picture presentations;
c. role playing on the part of the students.

4. Tests, which are given at the end of the program to determine the extent to which the executives and trainees benefited from the program.

Cycles which was formed by Umerski four years ago, is not large, but it is growing rapidly. Currently, the firm employs fifteen trainers, three executives, and seven salespersons. It now serves the northeastern portion of the United States and is pushing its sales territory further west and south. Umerski anticipates that the company will cover the entire United States and some foreign markets within five years.

Dianne Perez joined the firm one year ago, shortly after her graduation from a large northeastern university. She took a consumer behavior course at the university and hopes to apply what she learned in the course to her work at Cycles.

Dianne's work requires calling upon business and non-business organizations in her territory, which is the state of Rhode Island. Target consumers are defined as organizations having thirty or more employees. Dianne is engaged in the following:

1. Developing prospect lists.

2. Conducting preapproaches.

3. Conducting presentations—with organizations that have not yet employed Cycles training programs—by:
a. arousing attention and interest in the motivation program;
b. discovering prospect needs that are related to employee motivation;
c. showing how the Cycles program could fulfill prospect needs;
d. handling objections;
e. closing.

4. Conducting postsale activities—reassuring customers of the appropriateness of their signing a contract and making arrangements for the impending visits of the training staff.

5. Making callback presentations on prospects who were visited earlier but did not sign a contract.

Dianne is familiar with the overall theory of consumer behavior presented in this chapter, and she believes it might be useful as a means of planning and conducting her work. How might she use the theory to attain these ends?

**Suggested Readings**

Cateora, Philip R., and John M. Hess. *International Marketing.* Homewood, Ill.: Richard D. Irwin, 1971, ch. 4.

Dash, Joseph F., Leon G. Schiffman, and Conrad Berenson. "Risk and Personality—Related Dimensions of Store Choice," *Journal of Marketing* 40, no. 1 (January 1976): 32–39.

Engel, James F., David T. Kollat, and Roger D. Blackwell. *Consumer Behavior.* New York: Holt, Rinehart and Winston, 1973.

Kerby, Joe Kent. *Consumer Behavior: Conceptual Foundations.* New York: Dun-Donnelley Publishing Corp., 1975.

Markin, Rom J., Jr. *Consumer Behavior: A Cognitive Orientation.* New York: Macmillan Publishing Co., 1974.

Narayana, Chem L., and Rom J. Markin. "Consumer Behavior and Product Performance: An Alternative Conceptualization. *Journal of Marketing* 39, no. 4 (October 1975): 1–6.

McMillan, James R. "Role Differentiation in Industrial Buying Decisions," *1973 Combined Proceedings American Marketing Association.* Chicago: American Marketing Association, 1974, pp. 207–211.

Oshikawa, Sadaomi. The Measurement of Cognitive Dissonance: Some Experimental Findings," *Journal of Marketing* 36, no. 1 (January 1972): 64–66.

Tarpey, Lawrence X., Sr., and J. Paul Peter. "A Comparative Analysis of Three Consumer Decision Strategies," *Journal of Consumer Research* 2, no. 1 (June 1975): 29–37.

Walters, C. Glenn, and Gordon W. Paul. *Consumer Behavior: An Integrated Framework.* Homewood, Ill.: Richard D. Irwin, 1970.

Wasson, Chester R. *Consumer Behavior: A Managerial Viewpoint.* Austin, Texas: Austin Press, 1975.

Webster, Frederick E., Jr., and Yoram Wind. *Industrial Buying Behavior.* Englewood Cliffs, N.J.: Prentice-Hall, 1972.

Whittle, Jack W. "Behavioral Aspects of Future Marketing Trends," *1974 Combined Proceedings, American Marketing Association.* Chicago: American Marketing Association, 1975, pp. 535–38.

# 12

# Postselling Activities and Callbacks

*After reading this chapter you should be able to demonstrate a knowledge of:*

- *what is meant by* postselling *activities*
- *the importance of postselling activities to salespersons*
- *the specific activities that are included in postselling*
- *the nature and importance of callbacks*
- *ways of conducting effective callbacks*

The salesperson's function does not end when prospects place their order. Among the postselling activities are the following:

- The representative of an oil producing and refining company calls upon a service station to make sure that a shipment of automobile batteries arrived on time.
- A recent car buyer receives a telephone call from the salesperson, who says, "If anything goes wrong, call me and I'll take care of the problem."
- An office machines salesperson trains

wholesalers in effective means of selling office machines to manufacturers, retailers, and other institutions.

- A packaged food sales representative pays a courtesy call on a retail-supermarket buyer. The purpose of the call is to maintain the interpersonal relationship and to remind the buyer that the salesperson is still around.

- An electronics salesperson who received an order from a machine-tool manufacturer two months earlier makes another call in an attempt to acquire a second order.

In this chapter we will discuss the postselling activities and callbacks, identifying potentially effective practices for the salesperson.

Figure 12-1 sets forth the various postselling and callback activities. Both take place after the completion of one or more sales calls, and for that reason are treated together in this chapter. *Postselling* activities are to follow up on and reassure the customer, handle complaints, make adjustments, undertake installation and maintenance, train customers and their employees, and do consulting for customers. *Callback* activities, which apply to both purchasers and nonpurchasers, consist of determining the purposes, timing, presentation methods, and implementations of callbacks, and to maintain consumer records. Postselling and callback activities give the representative insights useful in developing future plans to apply to prospects and past customers.

## What Postselling Activities Are

Postselling activities are those that take place after an order has been placed. Although it might seem that the personal selling process should stop once the order has been secured, this is not the case for most representatives. Among those who must spend considerable time in postsale functions are sales representatives selling:

- computers,
- real estate,
- farm equipment,
- airplanes,
- fiberglass to industrial accounts,
- life insurance.

**Figure 12-1. Overview of the postselling and callback processes.**

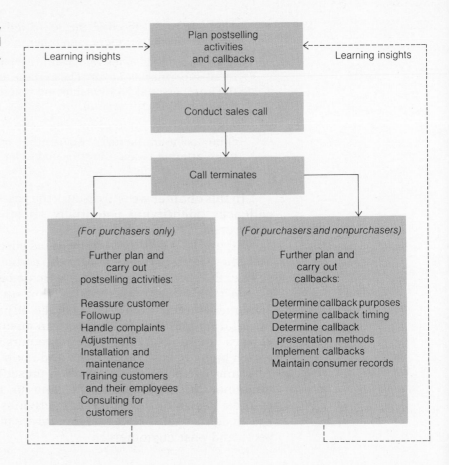

## The Importance of Postselling Activities to Salespersons
Success Through Aiding Customers

Professional representatives realize that their success is highly dependent on the way in which they conduct postsale functions. They know they will be effective only as long as they fulfill the needs of customers, and that many needs, are not met solely as a result of ordering goods and services. In fact, placing an order is only the beginning of the need-fulfillment process for many customers.

Many salespersons are dependent upon repeat business from individual customers. Frequently, the revenues resulting from the first order do not compensate for the time and expense incurred in obtaining this initial business. Two, three, or even more orders may be needed to provide adequate compensation. Repeat orders are not likely if the customer was not satisfied with the first purchase, however. Hence, the sales representative should not be lax in taking steps to ensure that this purchase results in the satisfactions that were initially expected. The chief asset of many organizations is the "goodwill and loyalty of customers" that they enjoy.[1] Postselling activities are a major source of satisfactions and resulting loyalty and goodwill.

Word-of-Mouth
Publicity

The beginning salesperson is often not aware of the extent and importance of word-of-mouth publicity. Very often, prospects communicate with one another, sometimes on an intimate basis. Those who share similar social status, life styles, and interests, and who are in close physical proximity to one another are especially likely to communicate.[2] Their contacts may be as through mutual friends or through being members of the same:

- golf foursome,
- trade association,
- chamber of commerce or junior chamber of commerce,
- athletic club or country club,
- service club, or
- church.

Word-of-mouth communications can expand at a geometric rate. If a customer is dissatisfied with a purchase and conveys that dissatisfaction to two friends, who in turn tell two friends, who also each tell two friends, then eight people will have heard of the first person's dissatisfaction. Thus, one failure by a salesperson to provide expected benefits has resulted in nine potential prospects who have negative feelings about the representative.

Word-of-mouth publicity can, of course, be both positive as well as negative. Well-conceived postselling actions are very good means of ensuring that the communications about the sales representative, the product, and the organization are favorable. Firms such as IBM, Polaroid, General Motors, and Nabisco, who have a good reputation among numerous target consumers, devote considerable attention to postselling activities.

---

[1] Edward C. Bursk, "View Your Customers as Investments," *Harvard Business Review* 44, no. 3 (May/June 1966): 91–94.

[2] James F. Engel, David T. Kollat, and Roger D. Blackwell, *Consumer Behavior* (New York: Holt, Rinehart and Winston, 1973), p. 396.

| Helping Customers Achieve Their Goals | Many of the postselling activities are designed to help customers achieve their goals. If customers are financially successful, they are in a position to purchase more from the sales representative. Conversely, when customers fail, they are no longer prospects and potential sources of revenue. |
|---|---|

Some wholesalers specialize in serving small customers. They provide numerous postselling activities for the latter, including training their employees and providing consulting services in important areas such as inventory control and store location. The wholesalers realize that large prospects often tend to avoid wholesalers, preferring instead to deal directly with manufacturers. Thus, these wholesalers' livelihood is dependent upon the viability of small prospects. As a result, the wholesale sales force is highly involved in postselling actions.

| Direct Aid from Customers | Representatives who provide useful postselling functions for their customers often find the customers giving them direct help in return. Gratified customers may be willing to furnish the names of acquaintances who are good prospects. Or they may agree to furnish written or oral testimonials for the representative's goods and services. Finally, they may be willing to provide useful information, such as new uses for the offerings of the salesperson or undiscovered product benefits, which can be used as appeals in calling upon other prospects. |
|---|---|

| **Specific Postselling Activities** | The exact nature of postselling activities varies from one selling position to another, of course. Some that are frequently utilized are: |
|---|---|

1. reassuring the customer,
2. follow-up,
3. handling complaints,
4. adjustments,
5. installation and maintenance,
6. training customers' employees,
7. acting as consultants for customers.

| Reassuring the Customer | One important function is contacting customers at some point after the sale and assuring them that the purchase was a good decision. As we stated in the last chapter, buyers often experience postpurchase anxiety. The customer's efforts to overcome dissonance can lead to negative feelings about the offering |
|---|---|

purchased. If these feelings become too pronounced, the customer may even call the company and cancel the order.

For instance, on a routine basis, a realtor contacts recently acquired customers and reassures them of the shrewdness of their purchases. He mails each customer a "thank you for the business" letter, which states that he is available should problems associated with the property arise. He also makes a brief personal call on the customer to dispell prospect doubts about the purchase.

Follow-up

The purpose of the follow-up is to ensure that everything is all right. The sales representative calls upon the customer to determine if any problems have developed in conjunction with the purchase. Possible problems are late orders, errors in the billing, inadequate operating and maintenance instructions, and failure of a product to operate effectively.

A follow-up communicates to the buyer that the representative and his or her organization is concerned with the welfare of the buyer. It helps in overcoming suspicions that the salesperson is interested only in making sales. Further, it provides an avenue for genuine problem solving on the part of the salesperson. If the buyer is experiencing difficulties with the order, the representative is in a position to discover them and take steps to overcome them.

Follow-ups are especially important when the product or service is technical in nature, as are duplicating equipment, fire-protection systems, computers, and business-insurance policies. The buyer may experience problems in installing, operating, servicing, maintaining, and understanding the offering. A sales representative can be valuable in detecting and helping overcome such problems. Representatives who sell computers, milling machines, construction equipment, and mass-transit equipment are active in this function.

Handling Complaints

From time to time, customers will have complaints.[3] Some orders delivered to accounts contain the wrong merchandise. Other orders may be slow. The customer may not care for the billing procedure. In some instances, buyers are dissatisfied with the quality of the incoming merchandise. The total cost of

---

[3]For a useful discussion on handling complaints, see Stanley J. Fenvessy, "How to Handle Customer Complaints," *Sales Management* 108, no. 12 (12 June 1972): 33, 34, and 39.

the order may be larger than expected. According to one source, the following are the leading problems voiced by buyers:

1. shortages;

2. carrier (transportation company) problems;

3. information and communication;

4. order entry problems;

5. labor and trained personnel problems;

6. price changes—keeping abreast;

7. allocation problems;

8. cash-flow problems affecting inventory.[4]

Some complaints are made directly to the salesperson. In other cases they are made to different personnel in the organization, who in turn relay the information to the representative. Oftentimes, the representative can use information about complaints to advantage. Customers are impressed by a salesperson who is concerned about and ready to take action on complaints. Reuben Ellis, who sells irrigation sprinklers to farmers, literally "drops everything else" and investigates customers' problems immediately as they arise. He has found that many customers receiving such help view him as their representative in the sprinkler company. When a legitimate complaint arises, he will investigate it fairly and will support them if their claims are justified. Reuben has generated considerable goodwill through this practice.

An important principle to follow in handling complaints is to listen. Representatives of the 3M Company, for instance, are instructed to listen thoroughly to customer complaints, to "hear them out." Salespersons cannot act without facts. They must determine the exact nature of complaints and attempt to resolve the causes. Often complaints are due to misunderstandings that can quickly be cleared up. Recently, for instance, a customer received a sprinkler from Reuben, who helped install it and explain its operation. Several days later the farmer complained that the sprinkler arm was not turning properly. Reuben listened carefully and realized the farmer was not setting the controls properly. Reuben therefore tactfully re-

---

[4]Warren Blanding, "12 Tips No Salesman Wants to Hear (or Can Afford to Live Without)," *Sales and Marketing Management* 116, no. 3 (17 February 1975): 29.

peated the directions for setting the controls and diplomatically pointed out where the farmer had erred.

One of the values of listening is that it allows the customer to let off steam. Very frequently, considerable tension is released once the buyer has talked himself out. When he or she has expressed the major concerns, anger and frustration tend to subside, and the discussion can be conducted along non-emotional lines.

The sales representative cannot, of course, always agree with the customer. Sometimes complaints are unfounded and even dishonestly motivated. Thorough investigation of the circumstances will help determine who is correct. Further, familiarity with the personalities, philosophies, and business practices of the customer are useful in determining if the complaint is well founded or not. Reuben Ellis, for instance, found that one customer is a chronic complainer who believes that the best policy is "to squeeze as much as possible out of your suppliers." Not surprisingly, Reuben is wary when this person makes a complaint.

Overall, diplomacy is useful in the process of dealing with unhappy customers. The sales representative should avoid arguments, since they are likely to only intensify emotions. Sympathetic listening, thorough examination of the facts, and explanations of organization policies and procedures are all effective courses of action to follow.

Adjustments

Adjustments (or returns) are made when customers receive goods that do not meet their expectations. The offerings may be damaged, the wrong color, the wrong size, or not in accordance with technical specifications. Sometimes customers want to try it out and then return the item if it does not fit their needs.

Many organizations assign adjustments to sales representatives, since they are familiar with the nature of the original transaction and what was said in the negotiations, particularly any promises expressed. Further, sales representatives are familiar with the needs and resources of the customer and have a good idea of his or her importance to the organization as a provider of revenues. The representative might be more likely to make an adjustment for a large and profitable customer than for a very small one.

Sales representatives can avoid undue numbers of adjustments by attempting to ensure that prospects buy merchandise that fits their needs in the first place. North-West Mutual Insurance Company representatives, for instance, do not encourage the sales of endowments (a combination of savings and insurance) to most young prospects, since their primary need is for pure insurance.

The representative should be thoroughly familiar with organization policy regarding adjustments. Some institutions are very liberal in this regard, using the liberal policy as a selling technique. Others recognize potential high costs and possible abuses of such policies and are more stringent. If the sales representative is responsible for handling adjustments, he or she should be intimately familiar with top management's philosophies on this issue.

## Installation and Maintenance

Some sales representatives are involved in the installation of machinery and equipment. They may do this in conjunction with technical service personnel or alone. Another alternative, used for Xerox duplicating machines, is for the technical personnel to handle the entire installation process. It is important that adequate attention be given to this function, since proper operation of the machine may depend upon effective installation.

Maintenance is another function that may be performed by sales representatives, technical personnel (as in the case of Maytag washers and dryers), or by both. Preventative maintenance and repairs are important determinants of the degree to which machinery and equipment operate. In some organizations, such as assembly line producers, even the breakdown of a small machine or part may put a whole section or factory temporarily out of action. Hence, such firms are highly concerned with the maintenance policies and practices of their suppliers.

## Training Customers and Their Employees

Many prospects look for suppliers that will provide needed training. The training may be in some areas of the customers' business, such as in effective personal selling, product planning, materials handling, or order processing. Or the training may focus on the supplier's products and services and methods of operation.

The offer of training for customers can be a good sales appeal. Many prospects seek out suppliers who can provide specialized training inputs. Further, it is in the best interests of suppliers that their customers prosper. Training is useful in promoting the financial security and growth of these concerns.

Reuben Ellis acts as a trainer for customers who have recently purchased a sprinkler from his company. He spends several hours with the farmer in going over the details of operating the units. Further, he provides training sessions, which cover proper maintenance of the products. Reuben knows enough about sprinkler operation and maintenance to provide useful instruction to his customers.

**Acting as Consultants for Customers**

Some sales representatives act as consultants for customers, providing specialized advice in such areas as installation, maintenance, product display, advertising, personnel relations, product planning, transportation, inventory control, and pricing. The representatives of the Alton Box Board Company, for instance, serve as consultants in a specialized field—that of packaging—for their clients. As in the case of training, consultations serve as sales appeals and aid customers in achieving financial health.[5]

A shoe manufacturing company representative is viewed by many buyers as an expert consultant. Recently, she helped a shoe-store buyer set up an inventory control system. Before then the buyer had experienced high inventory costs, being afraid to cut his stock lest sales decline to unacceptable levels. The sales representative showed the buyer how he could strike a balance between low inventory costs and high sales. This salesperson uses the consultant role as a very effective means of achieving differential advantage over competitors.

**Callbacks and Their Importance**

Callbacks consist of sales calls upon two types of prospects:

1. those who did not buy during previous calls;

2. those who did buy during previous calls and whom the sales representative wants to keep as repeat customers.

In the case of callbacks, the sales representative has some knowledge about the prospects based upon actual selling experience, and the prospects in turn are acquainted with the representative. Thus, the relationship between the two is different with callbacks than it is when prospects are contacted initially.

When calling upon potential buyers for the first time, the sales representative is calling on prospects. Once prospects have made a purchase they are called customers or accounts. While most of this book is about both prospects and accounts, this section primarily covers accounts.

---

[5]See Elmer G. Leterman, *Personal Power Through Creative Selling* (New York: Collier Books, 1975), pp. 114–17.

Sales representatives often find that one call is not sufficient to persuade the prospect to make a purchase. For instance, representatives selling expensive items such as major equipment may make repeated calls for months or even years before a prospect decides to buy. Representatives of the ABEX Company, which sells tracks for railway intersections, find this to be the case. In such selling jobs, callbacks are a necessary way of doing business.

Established sales representatives obtain a major portion of their compensation as a result of serving customers (as distinguished from prospects). They are involved in working with customers on a continuing basis, rather than in attempting to convert prospects into customers. In most cases, it is less difficult to retain accounts than it is to obtain them in the first place. Therefore, sales representatives should make frequent callbacks upon customers.

A fundamental question is when the sales representative should call back on the account after the initial visit. If the representative waits too long, the buyer may forget much of what took place on the first visit, and the impact of the first visit will be reduced. On the other hand, a callback made too soon after the first visit may only create animosity or annoyance.

A frequent practice is to call back shortly after the first purchase to see if the product is serving the customer as desired and if he or she is experiencing any problems. If the prospect did not make a purchase on the first call, the sales representative may make a callback that highlights the major points of the first visit and includes additional appeals for the prospect to make a decision. Trial closes should be attempted, in an effort to produce a purchase. If the purchase does not take place, the salesperson should continue calling, as long as the prospect continues to be a good potential buyer.

In scheduling visits after the first callback, a useful process is to classify the accounts.[6] A seller of imports to import shops, for instance, uses the following system:

- Group A—very important customers and prospects. Callback every two weeks.

- Group B—important customers and prospects. Callback once a month.

---

[6]See Porter Henry, "Use the 2-D Principle for Making the Most of Sales Time," *Sales and Marketing Management* 148, no. 2 (19 May 1975): 25–27.

- Group C—average customers and prospects. Callback every six weeks.

- Group D—poor prospects and customers. Callback only every two months.

- Group E—very poor prospects and customers. Callback only during slack periods, when excess time is available.

A potential problem is that the representative may devote too much time on group A and group B prospects and customers and will ignore the others. This can be costly, for some members of the latter groups are going to grow into group A and group B customers in the future. As a result, the sales representative should make an effort to identify those in the latter groups that have considerable potential and give them more frequent callbacks than others in their categories. In screening for potential, the imported-goods sales representative considers the following elements:

- Does the firm have outstanding managerial talent?

- Is the firm well-endowed with funds?

- Does the firm have some potentially profitable attribute, such as a very good location or an excellent image among consumers?

- Are the sales and profits of the firm increasing over time?

- Is the firm outdistancing competitors?

- Do the firm's buyers have a positive attitude toward the import sales representative and the organization?

- Are existing suppliers failing to serve the prospect adequately?

If the answers to the majority of these questions is yes, the sales representative places the firm in a higher category than it ordinarily would be in. The sales representative makes frequent calls upon the buyers and attempts to help their concerns prosper. This practice has resulted in converting a number of relatively poor prospects and customers into good ones.

Retaining Customers

A major purpose of callbacks is to retain current customers. For many representatives, these are responsible for the bulk of the sales volume. Moreover, because a number of orders from one customer may be necessary to justify the time and cost expended in order to obtain the first sale, retaining current customers is important.

Walter R. Barry, Jr, Group Vice-President of Consumer Foods for the General Mills Company, points out that retaining customers becomes especially important when competition becomes intense and that "there is no such thing as the 'safe' account anymore."[7] That is, competitors may steal customers who are thought to be too loyal to desert the organization, if the sales representative and other marketing personnel are not alert and making continuing efforts to serve old customers.

Many representatives develop a close relationship with current accounts. They become well-acquainted with their customers and become almost a permanent part of their organizations. Effective sales representatives render constant service to these customers. They do not neglect ongoing relationships with accounts in order to obtain business from newcomers to the customer group. The accounts learn that the sales representative is interested in their long-run welfare and is a source of help when problems occur.

The salesperson cannot assume that all of the current customers will retain their status indefinitely. Some will go out of business or switch into another line of business. Others will divert their patronage to different suppliers. Consequently, the sales representative should be alert for evidence of such changes on the part of members of the customer group. This can be accomplished through such intelligence efforts as:

- careful listening and observing when visiting customers;
- listening to the grapevine—informal communications made by competitors of customers, salespersons for competing organizations, and others;
- being aware of competitive developments, such as the entry of new competitors into the market or changes in the strategies and tactics of existing rivals.

Changes in the status of existing customers may require alterations in the strategies and tactics of the sales representative. Recently, for instance, a chemical-company salesman found that a large competitor was attempting to win over some of his accounts through price cutting. The salesman did not feel that he was in a position to lower his prices at the time. He did retaliate, however, by increasing his call frequency and by redoubling his efforts to provide benefits to accounts through furnishing valued services. As a result, the competitor was not successful in the attempt to win over many customers.

---

[7]"The Hard Road of the Food Processors," *Business Week*, no. 2422 (18 March 1976): 53.

Once representatives have an account, they should consider increasing the amount of business from that source. This can be a good source of incremental sales, as evidenced by the experience of the automobile industry in 1975. During that year, sales personnel were effective in persuading buyers to add many options to their vehicles. Air conditioning, for instance, was installed in 55 percent of the small cars sold, as compared to 24 percent in 1970.[8] This is really a form of suggestion selling, where once an initial sale is closed, the salesperson attempts to have the customer broaden the original purchase with related products, special promotional items, and holiday or seasonal merchandise.[9]

Usually, it is easier to obtain extra sales from existing customers than it is to obtain new accounts. Further, if the account currently is purchasing part of its requirements from other suppliers, there is always a danger that the sales of the representative will be diverted to these parties at some time in the future.

A useful technique in selling more to customers is simply to ask them to purchase additional items. If the sales representative has been effective in providing needed benefits in the past, he or she has built up a store of goodwill in the customer. Because of lack of aggressiveness or inertia, however, the representative may have avoided requesting new business.

Sometimes the sales representative is able to set accounts to buy more items by offering volume discounts or convincing them of the advantages the organization grants to its "preferred customers." For instance:

> PROSPECT: Why should I order in larger quantities from your company?

> SALESPERSON: If you do, I am authorized to place you in the "high-priority customer" status. This means that I can get you faster deliveries and will be allowed to spend more time training your sales personnel.

Frequently, sales representatives can persuade customers to buy products and services other than those they currently purchase. Representatives should be alert for customer needs and desires that could be met by products in their lines. When

---

[8]"Detroit Must Retool Its Old Success Formula," *Business Week*, no. 2422 (8 March 1976): 73.

[9]Albert H. Dunn, Eugene M. Johnson, and David L. Kurtz, *Sales Management: Concepts, Practices, and Cases* (Morristown, N.J.: General Learning Press, 1974), p. 103.

the organization brings out a new product or service, customers should be made aware of this. An insurance agent who has just begun offering mutual funds, for instance, should inform current policyholders of the new product offering. Those policyholders who already are impressed with the agent's ability and honesty are good prospects for the mutual funds.

When customers experience changes in their methods of operation or status, the salesperson may see opportunities for selling different products or services to them. Where retailers expand the size of their stores, for instance, they may need offerings that are not currently in stock. When ultimate consumers are promoted to higher paying jobs, they may acquire the income needed to become good prospects for mutual funds. When a factory alters the production process, its buyers may be seeking new supplies and materials.

## Callback Presentation Methods

Generally, the representative should use the same presentation methods for callbacks as are employed in the initial call. It cannot be assumed that the customer remembers a great deal about what occurred on that call. Since that time, other sales representatives will have visited the customer and he or she will have had numerous other experiences that tend to blur the memory of the initial call. Consequently, salespersons cannot assume that they need only begin where they left off on the last call. Some useful techniques in callbacks are:

1. review the last call;
2. focus on a benefit;
3. use the new presentation method;
4. utilize questions;
5. plan for an objection;
6. communicate with customers between calls;
7. make callbacks on ex-customers.

**Review.** A potentially effective practice is to undertake a brief review of the major developments of the last call. This stimulates the prospect's memory and provides the representative with an opportunity to reemphasize the major sales appeals. For instance:

PROSPECT: You were here last month. What did we decide then?

SALESPERSON: We reviewed your new fork-lift truck needs for the upcoming year. You mentioned a possible need for two heavy-duty units to be used for stacking the chemical containers. I went over the features of our new Y-213 model. Let's review them briefly.

**Focus on a Benefit.**   On each callback, the sales representative should have at least one benefit that was not mentioned on a previous presentation to mention to the prospect. Calls with no apparent purpose in mind should be avoided. Customers value their time and are not appreciative of a representative who takes up time on a visit without a purpose. Further, they are not likely to be impressed if the sales representative seems to be one who is not busy and who has time to kill.

**New Presentation Method.**   When a sales representative has tried one presentation method that has failed, a possible strategy is to try another method on a callback. The representative can reflect on the earlier experience and try to deduce why the sale did not take place at that time. Such an analysis may produce ideas on methods that are better than those utilized in the past. For instance:

PROSPECT: You were here only two weeks ago. What's new?

SALESPERSON: On the last visit I neglected to cover several points that should be of interest to you. Let's go through them at this point.

**Utilizing Questions.**   On callbacks, sales representatives should ask questions of the prospect, just as they would on initial calls. The prospect's status and activities may have changed since the last call. He or she may be contemplating a move, may have increased income, or been confronted with financial setbacks. Asking questions enables the salesperson to detect such changes and to adjust the presentation accordingly. For example:

PROSPECT: What do you have that's new?

SALESPERSON: I have several interesting new ideas. First, however, let me ask you a question.

**Planning for an Objection.**   Sometimes the prospect will raise an objection that the salesperson cannot surmount on a given call. As a result, the call does not produce a sale. The sales representative can anticipate that this objection is likely to arise again on a callback. Consequently, it is a good idea to be prepared for the appearance of the same objection. For example:

PROSPECT: On your last visit I raised doubts about this product.

SALESPERSON: Yes, I recall that. Since that time I have gathered some information regarding those doubts that you should find interesting.

An alternate technique is for the sales representative to mention the previous objection before the prospect does. The representative can raise the objection and provide answers to it before the prospect has an opportunity to refer to it. This helps prevent a situation where the prospect fails to voice the objection, despite the fact that it is preventing him or her from making a purchase. Further, if sales representatives, rather than prospects, bring up the objection, they are taking a positive stand. This is in contrast to the negative stand that results from answering a doubt about the product, service, or organization.

SALESPERSON: On my last visit, you brought up some questions regarding the operating efficiency of this engine.

PROSPECT: Yes, I have some serious doubts about that.

SALESPERSON: I have some new information on that which will interest you.

**Communicating with Customers Between Calls.**  Often sales representatives find it useful to communicate with prospects in between sales calls. This ensures that the organization and the salesperson are continually in the presense of the customer. Thus, if a buying need materializes, the customer is likely to think of the sales representative. Further, communications between calls indicates to the customer that the supplier retains an interest in the former, even though a call is not currently being made.

Between-call communications may be done by letter or telephone. The sales representative might thank the customer for an order, mention a new product or new application of an old product, or make an appointment for another sales call. Letters and telephone communications are personalized methods of contacting customers and may be viewed very favorably by them.

Another useful method of communication is by advertising. The sales representative can request advertising personnel to forward brochures, catalogs, circulars, and other direct-mail pieces to specified customers. Often a letter from the sales representative or other company personnel will accompany the material. The letter may be only an introductory cover letter or it may direct the customer's attention to particular points made in the advertising. Figure 12-2 illustrates a type of letter that can be employed to accompany an advertising message. Ivan Vannelli, the salesman employed by the truck manufacturer, uses this and similar letters in an effort to provide continuity between himself and important customers.

**Callbacks on Ex-Customers.**  Sometimes individuals or organizations that used to be customers but are no longer so are good prospects. The sales representative should not assume that once a customer is lost this is a permanent situation. Some ex-customers are obviously not good prospects—those that have gone out of business, moved outside the sales territory, or are so hostile toward the salesperson and organization that they never would consider a purchase. But other ex-customers may have stopped patronizing the organization for different reasons—reasons that may no longer be of importance.

**Figure 12-2. Ivan's letter to a customer accompanying an advertisement.**

Pittsburgh, Pennsylvania

July 10, 1977

Mr. Stephen Rossi, President
Rossi Trucking Company
7251 East 154th Street
Pittsburgh, Pennsylvania

Dear Mr. Rossi:

Our previous visit was most enjoyable, on my part. I will look forward to another call on you in late July.

Enclosed are some brochures that should be interesting to you. They describe the W403 series, in which you expressed an interest. Note the technical specifications regarding the hydraulic lift. On our last visit you had some questions regarding the ability of this unit to provide the lifting capacity that your operations require.

I hope that this material proves to be useful to you. If you have questions, I'll be happy to answer them on the visit in late July.

Sincerely,

Ivan

In deciding whether to call upon old customers, the sales representative should examine the reasons why they were lost and attempt to determine if the conditions still exist. If they do not, a callback may be in order. Consider the example of Mark Peters, a salesman for a packaged-food company. Mark called on a supermarket-chain buyer who had stopped being his customer eleven months earlier. She had switched from Mark's to a competing brand because she felt the new brand would bring more sales. Mark decided that ten or eleven months' experience with the new brand would convince her otherwise. This turned out to be the case—the new brand did not sell well. Consequently, Mark's callback resulted in regaining an old customer.

MARK: Hello, it's good to see you again.

BUYER: I haven't seen you in some time. Have you been busy?

MARK: Yes, very much so. I wanted to take some time, however, and inquire into your success with the Star brand.

BUYER: I am glad you did. Star is not doing as well as I had expected. It sold fairly well when we first introduced it, but it's been a disappointment since then.

MARK: I'm sorry your expectations weren't met. What was the problem?

BUYER: As far as we can tell, it just doesn't appeal to children. This is not good for us, since many of our customers are parents of young children.

MARK: This being the case, let's consider our company's Smokey brand, which our research indicates appeals to children. Smokey could help you regain those young parent cereal purchasers.

BUYER: Yes, I'd like to consider stocking Smokey again.

Mark continuously considers making callbacks on old customers. He reviews the reasons for their dropping his offerings and, based on analysis of these reasons, determines if callbacks would be justified. This practice has resulted in his regaining a number of ex-accounts.

Maintaining Records

In previous chapters we dealt with the usefulness of record keeping on the part of sales representatives. This usefulness is particularly evident in relation to callbacks. Representatives are likely to forget many of the details of previous presentations, unless their details are recorded.

The nature of the records that sales representatives maintain vary. In general, however, records for callback purposes should emphasize:

- the purpose of the call;
- the outcome of the call;
- objections raised by the prospect;
- personal characteristics of the prospect;
- problems faced by the prospect.

This information can be of considerable value to the sales representative. A review of records of previous calls allows the salesperson to design callbacks that are coordinated with earlier calls. It puts the salesperson in a position to benefit from intelligence-gathering activities conducted at an earlier period of time. Further, it allows the sales representative to avoid embarrassments such as the following:

SALESPERSON: I'd like to demonstrate our new X023 model to you today.

PROSPECT: You demonstrated that model on your last visit, and I told you that I had no interest in it. What's going on?

SALESPERSON: I think that you should consider using our hydraulic lifts. They have been improved substantially.

PROSPECT: Ever since we stopped making dump trucks we have no need for lifts. Didn't I tell you we had made this change when you dropped around two months ago?

Salespersons cannot expect to remember the details of every past presentation and the results of every presentation. Written records, therefore, are a necessary substitute for memory.

**Summary**

Postselling activities are those that occur after an order has been placed. These activities are useful in (1) helping salespersons serve consumers, (2) generating favorable word-of-mouth publicity, (3) helping customers achieve their goals, and (4) securing direct aid from customers.

The seven specific postselling activities this chapter has addressed are as follows:

1. Reassuring customers—assuring them their purchase decision was a good one.

2. Follow-up—determining if any problems have developed in conjunction with the purchase.

3. Handling complaints—which can be used to the advantage of the salesperson.

4. Adjustments—deciding if product returns are to be allowed.

5. Installation and maintenance—for machinery and equipment.

6. Training customers and their employees—securing their loyalty and helping them gain revenues.

7. Acting as consultants for customers—securing their loyalty and helping them gain revenues.

Callbacks are sales calls made upon those who were called upon in the past. These sales interviews are often necessary in order to secure a sale. They provide the bulk of the revenues generated by many salespersons.

If made too long after the initial call, callbacks may be ineffectual. If they are made too soon after the initial sale, buyer hostility can arise. A useful practice is to classify customers by their importance and to base the call frequency upon the classification.

It is important that salespersons take steps designed to retain present customers. Thus, representatives should develop close relationships with them. Intelligence efforts are necessary, in order to moniter this relationship and factors that could change it.

A frequent practice is to attempt to sell more to current accounts than they have bought in the past. They may be urged to buy additional products or to buy more of the offerings currently purchased.

This chapter has covered six callback presentation methods:

1. Review—make a brief review of the major developments of the last call.

2. Focus on a benefit—mention a benefit that was not mentioned on a previous presentation.

3. Utilize questions—gather current information on the status and operations of the customer.

4. Plan for an objection—be prepared to answer a previously mentioned objection.

5. Communicate with the customer between calls—contact the customer by letter, telephone, or advertising.

6. Call back on ex-customers—determine which are good prospects and call on them.

Callbacks are facilitated by the availability of written records. These communicate information acquired on previous calls, thus allowing the salesperson to take advantage of insights gained previously.

**Discussion Questions**

1. Define postselling activities. Why should the salesperson be concerned with these?
2. Indicate how postselling activities are useful in:
    a. gaining the loyalty of customers;
    b. generating favorable word-of-mouth publicity;
    c. helping customers achieve their goals;
    d. securing direct aid from customers.
3. Define and give an example of each of the following postselling activities:
    a. reassuring the customer;
    b. follow-up;
    c. handling complaints;
    d. adjustments;
    e. installation and maintenance;
    f. training customers' employees;
    g. acting as consultants for customers.
4. What are callbacks?
5. Why should the salesperson make callbacks?
6. When should callbacks be made?
7. How can the salesperson retain current customers?
8. How can salespersons sell more to current customers than they did in the past?
9. Describe and indicate the importance of each of the following callback methods:
    a. review;
    b. focus on a benefit;
    c. new presentation method;
    d. utilizing questions;
    e. planning for an objection;
    f. communicating with customers between calls.
10. What ex-customers should the salesperson call on?
11. What records are useful in planning and executing callbacks?

**Practical Exercises**

1. Observe a retail-store sales representative. What postselling activities does he or she utilize? Do they seem to be effective? Why or why not?

2. Purchase an article from a retail store and note the postselling activities that take place. Evaluate their effectiveness.

What did you learn as a result of these exercises?

**Selling Project**

1. What postselling activities would you utilize in selling your product? Why would these activities be desirable?

2. Would callbacks be useful in selling your product? If yes:

    a. when would you make them?

    b. would you call upon ex-customers?

    c. would you try to sell more to current customers?

    d. what methods would you employ?

    e. would you communicate with customers between calls? If yes, what methods of communication would be employed?

    f. what records would you keep for callback purposes?

What did you learn as a result of these exercises?

**Case 12
Al Fox**

Al Fox is a sales representative for the Hera Life Insurance Company. The company is a large enterprise that operates in all fifty states. It sells a wide variety of life and health insurance to ultimate consumers, business organizations, and nonbusiness enterprises. The company has a reputation for providing very high quality service to its policyholders.

Al's job is to call upon businessmen and to attempt to persuade them to buy business life insurance. This coverage compensates the company when a valuable executive or operative employee passes away. Al serves a city of approximately 59,000 located in Missouri. He has been with the firm and has served that territory for eleven years.

Three weeks ago, Al called upon Frank Schlain, president of the Lotus Manufacturing Company. Lotus produces paperboard boxes that are used by enterprises to ship goods. The company enjoys a comfortable margin of profits and has grown in recent years.

Al's first call on Lotus revealed that the company had three extremely valuable employees: (1) Frank Schlain; (2) the production manager, Jerry Kochak; and (3) the marketing manager, Francis LaFountaine. The loss of any one of the three could deal a staggering financial blow to the company. Accordingly, Al proposed that Lotus take out three life-insurance policies, with the company as beneficiary, with the following face amounts:

1. Schlain—$250,000,
2. Kochak—$200,000,
3. LaFountaine—$200,000.

The presentation that Al gave was impressive. He emphasized the considerable losses of profits that could occur if one of the three individuals should pass away. Further, he described the financial solvency and high quality customer services of the Hera company. Schlain was impressed and asked Al to call back in three weeks, after management had had an opportunity to consider the need for the insurance and the desirability of utilizing Hera as an insurer.

The callback went as follows:

AL: Hello, Mr. Schlain, good to see you again.

FRANK: How are you Al?

AL: Fine. Business is booming. It seems that business life insurance is a very salable commodity these days.

FRANK: Well, let's get down to business. Where should we start?

AL: Have you decided to take out the three policies?

FRANK: I've talked it over with the other members of the board. We can see the need for the insurance. On the other hand, the premiums are very high.

AL: Yes, but in the insurance field, as in any other, you pay for what you get. Imagine what would happen if one of the three key employees passed away. Where would Lotus be if that happened? The company is dependent upon you, Kochak, and LaFountaine.

FRANK: I'm flattered to know that you feel that we are so valuable to Lotus. Still, we just can't afford those high premiums.

AL: This reminds me of the experience of the Plato Construction company. You are familiar with them?

FRANK: Yes. Terry Plato was one of my very good friends.

AL: When Mr. Plato passed away, the company went into a tailspin for at least a year. They made some very bad decisions in bidding for contracts and their losses were considerable. Fortunately, they had insured Mr. Plato's life and recovered most of their losses as a result.

FRANK: They made a good decision. Terry Plato was not in good physical shape. His weight got out of control. On the other hand, Jerry, Francis, and I all enjoy excellent health. I don't foresee anything like Terry Plato's experience.

AL: These health problems are unpredictable. Further, there is always the possibility of accident.

FRANK: Yes. But we are willing to take that risk. We simply cannot see paying those high premiums.

AL: They are not high in terms of the potential benefits that Lotus would gain if one of you three passed away. Being penny-rich and pound-poor is not a good policy.

FRANK: Well, at any rate, we've decided not to take out the policies. Sorry, but that was our final decision. Al, I have some conferences coming up and must prepare for them. I wish you the best of luck. Are you attending the Rotary meeting tomorrow?

AL: Yes, I'll be there.

FRANK: See you at the meeting.

AL: Fine. I may pursue the policy question with you at a later date. At this time, however, I'm like you—busy. See you at the meeting.

Evaluate Al's performance in this callback.

**Suggested Readings**

Engel, James F., David T. Kollat, and Roger D. Blackwell. *Consumer Behavior*. New York: Holt, Rinehart and Winston, 1973, ch. 22.

Hartley, Robert F. *Retailing: Challenge and Opportunity*. Boston: Houghton Mifflin Co., 1975, ch. 16.

Hill, Richard M., Ralph Alexander, and James S. Cross. *Industrial Marketing*. Homewood, Ill.: Richard D. Irwin, 1975, ch. 13.

Holloway, Robert J. "The Hallmark of a Profession," *Journal of Marketing* 33, no. 1 (January 1969): 90–95.

Mayer, David, and Herbert M. Greenberg. "What Makes a Good Salesman?" in Edward C. Bursk and G. Scott Hutchinson, eds., *Salesmanship*. Cambridge: Harvard University Press, 1971, pp. 3–9.

Micali, Paul J. *The Lacy Techniques of Salesmanship*. New York: Hawthorn Books, 1971, Chapter 10.

Prevette, Earl. "How to Perfect Your Sales Plan," in John D. Murphy, ed., *Secrets of Successful Selling*. New York: Dell Publishing Co., 1963, pp. 248–53.

Shook, Robert L., and Herber M. Shook. *The Complete Professional Salesman*. New York: Barnes & Noble Books, 1975, ch. 12.

Straits, Bruce C. "The Pursuit of the Dissonant Consumer," *Journal of Marketing* 28, no. 2 (July 1969): 62–66.

# PART III

## Administrative Aspects of Personal Selling

In this part we will discuss the administrative or managerial aspects of personal selling. Chapter 13 is devoted to sales management—the planning and administering of personal selling activities. Chapter 14 deals with the regulation of the selling function by government agencies and with ethics and social responsibility.

# 13

## Sales Management

*After reading this chapter you should be able to demonstrate a knowledge of:*

- *the meaning of the term* sales management
- *how sales personnel are recruited and selected*
- *means of assimilating salespersons into the organization*
- *the process of training sales representatives*
- *various means of providing monetary compensation to salespersons*
- *how sales representatives can be supervised and stimulated to high performance*
- *how management can evaluate the performance of sales personnel*
- *the utilization of sales forecasts by sales managers*
- *the processes of setting up sales territories and sales quotas*
- *how the sales force can be organized*

- A sales manager travels to a college campus and interviews twenty job applicants. He is impressed with five of them and later extends job offers to two.

- A sales trainer is responsible for directing the training of the sales personnel employed by a marketer of coffee. Currently, she is planning a national training conference to be held in Miami.

- A national sales manager is worried about the performance of salespersons in the northeastern part of the United States. She has noticed that sales are far below the forecasted level there. After talking to the northeastern regional sales manager, she decides to conduct an investigation into the cause of the low sales.

All of these above activities are examples of sales management. In this chapter we will focus on sales management, which is concerned with the recruiting, selection, and assimilation into the organization of sales personnel. We will also deal with the training, compensating, and supervision of sales personnel. Finally, we will cover the use of forecasts, sales territory and routing plans, sales quotas, and various means of evaluating sales performance.[1]

## What Sales Management Is

The term *sales management* has been defined as "the planning, direction, and control of personal selling, including recruiting, selecting, equipping, assigning, routing, supervising, paying, and motivating as these tasks apply to the personal sales force."[2] In short, sales management consists of the planning and administering of personal selling activities.

Basically, sales management involves making plans and implementing plans already made. Plans are preconceived determinations of the future actions needed in order to attain the objectives of the organization or other planning unit. They are sets of ideas or concepts that, when put into effect, are expected to lead the unit to the realization of these objectives. A student, for instance, plans to obtain a college degree in order to attain objectives such as better income earning ability, mental enrichment, prestige, and personal satisfaction. Likewise, a sales manager plans to acquire and maintain a sales force that will lead to the attainment of objectives such as consumer satis-

---

[1] This topical arrangement was based upon that appearing in William J. Stanton and Richard H. Buskirk, *Management of the Sales Force* (Homewood, Ill.: Richard D. Irwin, 1974).

[2] Committee on Definitions, American Marketing Association, *Marketing Definitions* (Chicago: American Marketing Association, 1960), p. 20.

faction, fulfillment of social responsibilities, and provision of adequate levels of profits to the organization.

Plans, of course, are of little value unless they are put into effect. It is one thing to develop a detailed plan as to how the organization is to recruit and select a highly qualified sales force. It is another to actually carry out the steps required to fulfill the plan. The successful sales administrator is both an effective planner and an able administrator.

Another dimension of sales management relates to the operation of the sales department. Salespersons must be recruited, selected, and trained. Compensation plans must be developed and implemented. Territories must be devised. All of these activities are internal departmental considerations.

Many sales management activities relate to interactions between the sales department and other elements of the organization.[3] Sales managers must coordinate their operations with those of advertising, sales promotion, product planning, physical distribution, and other personnel. This concept was developed in detail in Chapter 2 and so will not be dealt with extensively here.

In summary, sales management involves both devising and implementing plans, and it has both inter- and intradepartmental dimensions. Figure 13-1 outlines these two aspects and the resulting four types of activities sales managers are involved in.

---

[3] For a good discussion of this topic, see Richard R. Still and Edward W. Cundiff, *Sales Management: Decisions, Policies, and Cases* (Englewood Cliffs, N.J.: Prentice-Hall, 1976), pp. 6–8.

**Figure 13-1. Types of sales management activities.**

|  | Interdepartmental | Intradepartmental |
|---|---|---|
| Devising plans | | |
| Implementing plans | | |

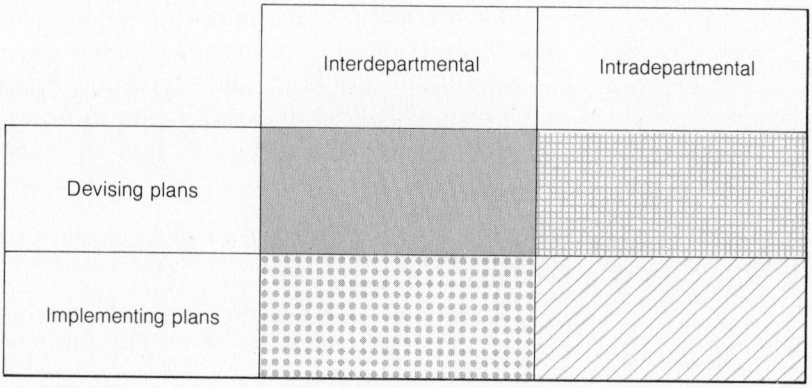

The rest of this chapter deals with individual intradepartmental activities, which are outlined in Figure 13-2. Sales managers begin the intradepartmental process by recruiting and selecting sales representatives. Then they are faced with the need of assimilating the new employees into the organization. Following this, seven number activities take place (often concurrently):

**Figure 13-2. Outline of intradepartmental sales management functions.**

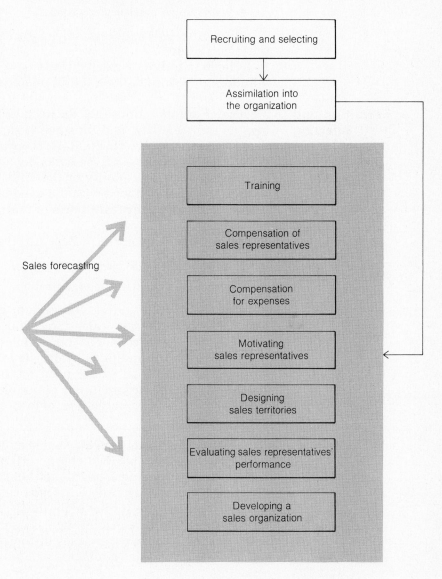

- training,

- compensating salespersons,

- paying for expenses incurred while on the job,

- motivating the sales force,

- designing sales territories,

- evaluating salesperson effectiveness,

- developing a sales organization.

As Figure 13-2 suggests, sales forecasting influences all of these activities.

The first activity we will discuss is recruiting and selecting —building the foundations for an ongoing sales force.

**Recruiting and Selecting**

Most sales organizations face the need for acquiring new members as time goes by, and for some organizations this need is continual and so recruiting and selecting are continual. In addition, the effectiveness of the sales department is based, to a large extent, on the quality of the field force. Consequently, sales managers are faced with the need to treat recruiting and selecting as very important parts of their duties.

Recruiting

Recruiting consists of:

1. locating potential members of the sales force, and

2. interesting them in the organization.

The number of individuals sought depends on expected turnover in the present sales force and on future marketing plans. Turnover takes place when employees leave because of resignations, retirements, ill health, or death. Changes in marketing plans can lead to the need for recruiting—as, for instance, when the organization plans to deemphasize advertising and stress personal selling, or to attempt to penetrate new geographic areas.

**Types of Salespersons Sought.** Sales managers seek job applicants with certain specified characteristics. The means of determining the characteristics are job analyses and studies of the characteristics of currently employed sales representatives.

*Job analyses* are studies of the duties and responsibilities of the positions under consideration. In some organizations the salespersons make the analyses of their own jobs. In others, outsiders such as sales managers and professional job analysts conduct the inquiry. When the results of job analyses are written they are called *job descriptions*. They list the most important duties and responsibilities of the position, and are useful for recruiting, selecting, and other sales management activities. Figure 13-3 provides the essentials of a job description used by a marketer of employee-motivation programs.

**Figure 13-3. Job description for position of sales representative used by employee-motivation program marketer.**

---

POSITION—SALES REPRESENTATIVE

Major duties and responsibilities

Initiates contact with top management personnel of firms with a potential for the employment of motivational programs and makes stimulating presentations to obtain the account.

Works closely with creative personnel to conceive and develop effective presentations for successfully selling motivational programs that will produce maximum profit for the company.

Analyzes prospective customers' distribution methods, marketing techniques, and sales compensation plans, as a basis for developing customer-tailored motivational programs for its personnel involving merchandise and/or travel for the prize winners.

Analyzes all currently used and prospective motivational programs to find the most desirable approach for achieving prospective clients' objectives and to assist in defining and identifying what the objectives should be to achieve the result desired.

Works with client companies to finalize all program rules, establish promotional and travel schedules, and obtain proper approvals on materials and copy, and takes other actions to ensure that sufficient promotional effort is placed behind every motivational program sold.

Maintains close personal contact with operations personnel and management of client companies to ensure optimum results for them through participation in the program.

Maintains an up-to-date mailing list of key contacts at each account.

Organizes time in a manner that allows him or her to spend the maximum amount of selling time with accounts, and spends time with accounts in proportion to their potential profitability, in order to reach annual merchandise and travel quotas.

Keeps currently informed of new developments, methods, and techniques in employee's motivation and efficiently uses all of the sales tools provided by the company.

Keeps immediate superior promptly and fully informed of all problems or unusual matters of significance and takes prompt corrective action where necessary or suggests alternative courses of action that may be taken.

At all times projects a favorable image of the firm, to promote its aims and objectives and foster public recognition and acceptance of its programs.

---

Studies of the characteristics of currently employed sales representatives are useful in determining the characteristics sought in recruits. The studies attempt to determine what effective salespersons have that ineffective salespersons do not. For instance, Infonics, Inc., a producer of high-speed tape and cassette duplicating equipment, found that in its company women were better than men in setting up distributorships overseas.[4] An analysis by a computer manufacturer of effective and ineffective salespersons showed that the following qualities are found in recruits likely to be successful:

- college graduate with major in business administration, marketing, or computer science (master's degree beneficial);
- grade-point average of 3.0 or more on 4.0 scale;
- sales experience (for instance, in summer work, part time while attending college, or fraternity or club promotion);
- neat appearance;
- under age thirty-seven;
- good health;
- able to communicate effectively.

Recruiters for this company seek job applicants with these characteristics in on-campus interviews and walk-in interviews at company offices.

Many organizations combine job analysis and study results of currently employed sales representatives into a written job specification, which sets forth characteristics of recruits sought. The specification is of value in recruiting and selecting as well as numerous other sales-management duties. Figure 13-4 shows the job specification for sales representatives for the computer manufacturer mentioned earlier.

**Locating Potential Members of the Sales Force.** Once the characteristics of desired applicants have been determined, management is in a position to look for good sources of applicants. The main sources are:

1. schools,
2. recommendations by organization employees,
3. other departments within the organization,

---

[4]"A Nice Way to Treat the Dealer," *Sales Management* 108, no. 8 (17 April 1972): 40–41.

4. other organizations,

5. employment agencies,

6. "walk-ins,"

7. respondents to advertisements.

*Schools.* Procter & Gamble, International Harvester, Eastman Kodak, General Electric, and many other organizations recruit sales trainees from colleges and universities, community colleges, vocational schools, and business schools, since their graduates show they are capable of successfully undertaking courses of study. Those who have studied business administration, marketing, and personal selling have knowledge particularly useful in personal selling.

A large oil-producing and refining company relies heavily on college and university graduates as recruits. Company recruiters make appointments for interviews at a number of institutions that have been good sources of applicants in the past.

**Figure 13-4. Job specification for representative for computer manufacturer.**

SALES REPRESENTATIVE JOB SPECIFICATION

All applicants for the position of sales representative should have the following characteristics:

  College degree with major in business administration, marketing, or computer science; master's degree preferred.

  Grade-point average of 3.0 or more in a 4.0 system.

  Sales experience — in summer work, parttime while attending school, or in college fraternity or club promotion.

  Neat appearance.

  Good health.

  Under thirty-seven years of age.

  Ability to communicate effectively.

  Courage and maturity needed to make a forceful presentation to prospects.

  Creativity needed to design sales presentations custom-tailored to individual prospects.

  Understanding of utilization of computers in business and nonbusiness organizations.

Working knowledge of COBOL and at least one other computer language.

Desire to achieve through job performance.

Ability to plan day-to-day activities effectively.

The placement bureaus at these institutions are very helpful in lining up interviews, in announcing that the company recruiter is on campus, and in setting up job interviews.

*Recommendations by Organization Employees.* Organization employees, especially salespersons, can be fruitful sources of recommendations. Employees may be in contact with others who would fulfill sales management's recruiting needs exactly. Management should carefully examine the backgrounds of those who are recommended, however. Some employees make recommendations that are based more on personal friendship than on the merits of those recommended.

*Other Departments Within the Organization.* Personnel from other departments in the organization sometimes are good potential sales representatives, since they are familiar with the company and its products. Moreover, the organization itself has had experience with these persons and so has some insights into their capabilities.

*Other Organizations.* Sales representatives of other organizations may be sought, since they have proven abilities and may require only limited training. Although experienced personnel may demand very high compensation and their loyalty open to question, still they are a source of very able applicants, especially for sales representatives of proven abilities.

*Employment Agencies.* Employment agencies differ considerably in their ability to provide good potential job applicants. Although some organizations avoid agencies in the belief that they attract less qualified personnel and do not match specific sales positions with applicants, some agencies are very diligent in attempting to find the right person for the right job.

*Walk-ins.* These are people who write or visit the organization in search of a job. The fact that they sought out the organization and so took the initiative in seeking a job with it may be taken as indicators of good attitudes toward the organization and potential selling ability. These individuals do, after all, have the impression that they are capable of selling themselves.

*Respondents to Advertisements.* Many organizations list job openings in help-wanted ads in newspapers and magazines and on bulletin boards. Such advertisements bring in a large number of interested persons, but unless the advertisement specifies reasonably high qualifications, many of the respondents may not be qualified. The advertisements sometimes will unearth very qualified personnel who could not be reached otherwise, however.

*Choice of the Best Source.* The job specification and past experience are useful indicators of the best source or combination of sources for good recruits. If, for instance, the job specification calls for a recent or future college graduate, placement offices of colleges and universities may be the best source. Conversely, if the sales manager has enjoyed very good experience with recommendations of company employees in the past, he or she may elect to rely upon that source in the future.

**Interesting Potential Employees in the Organization.** Part of the recruiting function is to sell the organization and the job to prospective employees. Recruiters should be instructed that they are salespersons as well as seekers of job applicants. They should, of course, provide adequate information so that those who are obviously not qualified or interested will remove themselves from consideration for the position. Further, they should not "oversell" the job, as by indicating that minimal travel is involved, when in fact the position requires continual travel. Still, recruiters must really sell positions, for the more qualified candidates probably have more than one employment opportunity to consider. If recruiters are indifferent, inept, or exhibit other forms of less than admirable behavior, good job applicants may be turned off.

Some organizations prepare written materials designed to interest qualified applicants in the organization and the job. Job descriptions and specifications are useful, in this regard. So are brochures that describe the organization, its policies and products, and the job itself.

Selecting Once sales managers have recruited job applicants, they must select the best qualified. The selection process should focus on the abilities set forth in the job specification and should distinguish between applicants with these abilities and those without.

**The Refinement Process.** Most organizations use several steps in selection, each step more precise than the previous one, to detect applicants with desired attributes. A paper manufacturer, for instance, reviews applications and screens out those obviously not qualified, gives the rest of the applicants an initial interview for interpersonal abilities, and makes those who pass the interview take a test designed to measure psychological characteristics the company feels important for selling its products. Finalists go through a terminal interview and the applicants who make a good impression are those who are hired. Obviously, the number of people who undertake each succeeding stage in the process is smaller than the number in previous stages.

**Selection Methods.**   Various selection methods are available to the sales manager. Each of these is useful in detecting certain characteristics. The primary selection devices are:

1. application blanks,
2. interviews,
3. references,
4. credit investigations,
5. tests,
6. physical examinations.

*Application Blanks.*   These provide basic information on applicants. All organizations, nearly, use application blanks for preliminary screening purposes—to eliminate those obviously not qualified. Application blanks request basic information: education, marital status, past experience. Sometimes the application reveals the quality of work experience or other points that can be investigated more fully in subsequent phases of the selection process.

*Interviews.*   Conferences or interviews with prospective employees are very useful to the sales manager, since they help reveal the interpersonal abilities of the applicants in speaking and listening, as well as their attitudinal and physical characteristics.

Some organizations, such as IBM and Hormel, utilize preliminary interviews. The purpose of these short interviews is to weed out applicants not eliminated through the application blank analysis. Other interviews follow this interview, all leading up to the final employment interview. Procter & Gamble, for instance, has three interviews. Each interview is with a higher level executive; the first is with a senior salesperson, the final with a regional sales manager.

Interview guides are useful in ensuring that recruiters cover all the points that should be covered in evaluating applicants. Figure 13-5 depicts the interview guide used by Ivan's truck manufacturer. It includes spaces where the interviewer can mark reactions to the interview and is typical of the guides employed by many organizations.

*References.*   Most sales managers make use of references. Sometimes these are character references, but more commonly, they are from previous employers. Ordinarily, references are consulted in conjunction with or after the preliminary interview. A problem with references is that few ex-employers write unfavorable comments about their former subordinates.

Written references are often employed, but of more practical value are person-to-person references on the telephone. Written references (especially the "To whom it may concern" letters) are oftentimes overly positive.

*Credit Investigations.*   Various organizations conduct credit investigations as a measure of the potential worth of applicants. There are many credit rating firms that will on request provide a sales manager with an evaluation of the applicant's creditworthiness.

Credit investigations are controversial. Some sales managers feel they do not provide a useful measure of the applicant's ability to sell. Others feel such inquiries violate the privacy of prospective employees, especially when they include personal information such as drinking habits and marital problems. The proponents of credit investigations, however, maintain that the ability of individuals to conduct personal financial affairs in a responsible manner is a measure of their potential worth as responsible sales representatives.

*Tests.*   Some sales managers employ psychological tests in assessing recruits. Several industries, including the life insurance industry, rely heavily on these measuring instruments. Psychological tests are designed to gauge characteristics such as masculinity-femininity, aggressiveness, hostility, gregariousness, and dogmatism.

Numerous psychological tests are available for the use of the sales manager. Some organizations have found that custom-made tests are the most useful. These devices are constructed by organization personnel to measure the particular characteristics of interest to the sales-management personnel of the organization. Overall, tests are best used in combination with other selection devices, rather than as substitutes for them.

*Physical Examinations.*   Many personal selling jobs are physically demanding. They require concentration, aggressiveness,

**Figure 13-5. Interview
guide for salespersons.**

INTERVIEWER GUIDE

Name of interviewer: _____

Position in company: _____

Name of interviewee: _____

Date: _____Place interview took place:_____

Evaluation of interviewee

| | Excellent | Good | Average | Poor | Very Poor |
|---|---|---|---|---|---|
| Appearance | ____ | ____ | ____ | ____ | ____ |
| Apparent health | ____ | ____ | ____ | ____ | ____ |
| Communication ability | ____ | ____ | ____ | ____ | ____ |
| Desire to please | ____ | ____ | ____ | ____ | ____ |
| Apparent motivation | ____ | ____ | ____ | ____ | ____ |
| Maturity | ____ | ____ | ____ | ____ | ____ |
| Apparent intelligence | ____ | ____ | ____ | ____ | ____ |
| Knowledge about company | ____ | ____ | ____ | ____ | ____ |
| Overall evaluation | ____ | ____ | ____ | ____ | ____ |

travel, and other physically taxing responsibilities. As a result, physical examinations are needed to ensure that new employees can handle these demands. Further, organizations often spend considerable sums in recruiting, selecting, and training new salespersons. This investment is lost if the individual must leave the job or operates at a marginal level because of poor health.

*The Mix of Selection Methods.* Each organization must choose the mix of selection methods that best meets its needs. The mix that works for one institution will not necessarily be appropriate for another. Sales managers are faced with the need for carefuly examining the job specifications, then determining which methods will best measure the characteristics sought. A procedure recommended by a sales-management consultant is to rank candidates into four categories, based upon whatever mix of selection methods is employed:

1. almost perfectly qualified,

2. well qualified,

3. marginally qualified,

4. unqualified.[5]

An attempt is made to fulfill the organization's personnel needs from group 1, and then from group 2 if the former does not provide adequate numbers of applicants. Only in times of great need for additional sales representatives should group 3 individuals be hired.

## Assimilation into the Organization

Newly hired sales representatives often experience difficulty in adjusting to the organization. They are not familiar with many of the policies, rules, and procedures of management, are unaccustomed to the physical surroundings, and probably are not acquainted with most of the staff.

The new employees' first few days on the job are critical. Given all of the uncertainties mentioned in the previous paragraph, some newcomers may decide to leave the organization. Others will stay but will have a negative image regarding their employer. They are not impressed with managers who treat new recruits very favorably, then forget about the latter once they are hired.

Management should make plans for the assimilation of new salespersons into the organization. The plans include provision for familiarizing new employees with organization physical facilities, policies, procedures, and personnel. Oftentimes, "big brother" programs are in order, in which experienced salespersons accompany newcomers for several days, in order to familiarize them with facts about the concern. Sales executives should also contact newcomers frequently in order to answer their questions and avoid the attitude that "the honeymoon is over." Well-conceived assimilation programs can substantially reduce new salesperson turnover and increase morale.

## Training

Training is a universal need among sales representatives. In 1975, the median cost of training was $9,672 for sellers of industrial goods and $4,528 for consumer goods (these figures include salaries earned while involved in training programs and are for only newly hired personnel).[6] The nature of the

---

[5]Keith R. Jewell, "Hiring in the Field," *Sales Management* 108, no. 4 (21 February 1972): 19.

[6]"1975 Costs," *Sales and Marketing Management* 116, no. 2 (9 February 1976): 76.

training differs from one organization to another and between experienced and new employees.

Each sales representative goes through a career cycle, as illustrated in Figure 13-6.[7] The stages in the cycle are:

1. preparation,
2. development,
3. maturity,
4. decline.

Preparation

New salespersons are in the preparation stage. Training should familiarize them with the organization, the product, target consumers, and how to sell. The median amounts of time devoted to training in 1975 were two weeks for consumer products salespersons and five and a half weeks for industrial products salespersons.[8]

Development

During the development stage sales representatives are increasing their productivity (sales, profits, nonselling activities, and instilling goodwill among prospects). Here the sales representative needs training in how to apply the knowledge received during the preparation stage. Much of the training at this point is in how to solve day-to-day problems that emerge.

Maturity

At maturity the sales representative's productivity levels off. Retraining may be necessary to reinforce learning during earlier periods. The representative probably will need information on new products, selling techniques, and company policies. Further, he or she may require attitude-change training—stimulation to greater productivity. At maturity many representatives may desire to "take it easy" and rely more on their selling expertise than on hard work. Their incomes may be substantial and thus they experience less incentive for productivity. Training may be used to maintain and increase their productivity.

Decline

Decline in achievement represents the stage where productivity is falling. The reasons include lessened interest in the work, fatigue, and interest in matters unrelated to work. At this stage training should emphasize improving the morale of sales repre-

[7]Marvin A. Jolson, "The Salesman's Career Cycle," *Journal of Marketing* 38, no. 3 (July 1974): 39–42.

[8]"1975 Costs."

Chapter 13  Sales Management

sentatives and showing them how they can operate more efficiently (maintain or increase productivity without increasing the level of energy expended).

Often salespersons who are in the decline stage can be used as sales trainers. They can use their considerable experience to train representatives who are at earlier stages. The prestige of being a sales trainer may be also what is required to pick up the productivity of a sales representative whose achievement levels have declined.

Astute sales managers are able to detect signs that sales representatives are nearing the end of development or maturity. These managers take steps such as training or supervision designed to offset movement into maturity or decline. Individuals do not necessarily fall into the decline stage, of course. Many remain at the development and maturity levels throughout their careers. These individuals are top sellers at the time they retire.

Use of the Career-Cycle Theory

Sales managers can benefit through the use of the career-cycle theory. They can determine the point in the cycle where each sales representative lies. Following this, the managers can determine what kinds and amounts of training are required for each representative. As a result, training becomes individualized and fine-tuned to meet the needs of each representative.

Specifics of the Training Programs

Numerous facets of the training program must be worked out by sales management. Chief among these are:

**Figure 13-6. Sales representatives' career cycle.**

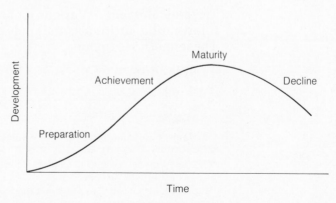

Source: Marvin A. Jolson, "The Salesman's Career Cycle, *Journal of Marketing* 38, no. 3 (July 1974): 39–42.

1. the content of the program,

2. the methods to be used.

**Content of the Program.** Various subjects can be covered in training. New salespersons for the Union Carbide Company, for instance:

1. are familiarized with the company and its products;

2. are assigned to a technical service operation to learn how customers use the products and what the customers' problems are;

3. work as inside salespersons to learn the selling process further;

4. take a course in human relations;

5. are assigned to a territory and particular customers for on-the-job training.[9]

Sometimes training is oriented to a particular event, such as the introduction of a new product. In 1975, for instance, the Pitney Bowes Company conducted a program that accompanied the introduction of its new PBC Plain Bond Copier. The two-day training session covered product features, consumer benefits, markets and applications for the product, the use of films in sales presentations, answering objections, and developing presentations.[10]

The content of the training program should be determined in light of the strategies and tactics of the marketing and personal selling units. An important requirement is that training be coordinated with other aspects of sales management. It makes little sense, for instance, to ask trainers to emphasize the selling of product A when sales representatives can make much higher commissions selling products B and C.[11]

**Training Methods.** Various techniques can be used to pass on information, attitudes, and understandings to sales personnel. These methods include:

1. lectures,

2. role playing,

3. discussion groups,

[9]"A Happy Salesman Is a Productive Salesman," *Sales Management* 108, no. 4 (21 February 1972): p. 19.

[10]"Pitney Bowes: A Coup in Copiers," *Sales and Marketing Management* 116, no. 1 (12 January 1976): 35–36.

[11]Porter Henry, "You Can Too Buck the System," *1974 Combined Proceedings, American Marketing Association* (Chicago: American Marketing Association, 1975), p. 515.

4. study at home,

5. sales meetings,

6. on-the-job training.

*Lectures.*   This technique is useful in providing large numbers of sales representatives with basic information on matters such as organization policies, facts about the organization, and the nature of the product line. The method is not effective in teaching how to sell, however. Organizations with large numbers of trainees often use lectures to provide basic information to them. Lectures are especially common in the initial phases of training programs.

An unusual approach is used by the Seagram Distillers Company in presenting its Christmas-packaging show to distributor salespersons in an effort to introduce new lines of holiday liquors with special wrappings.[12] The firm utilizes musical shows with actors and actresses who portray consumers. The trainers also ask salespersons to think of themselves as consumers and take slide films of them in this activity and show the films to other sales representatives.

*Role Playing.*   Role playing requires that trainees pretend to be sales representatives and act in the role of those who attempt to sell in particular transactions. Since this method approximates actual selling situations, it is useful in teaching the selling process.

Normally, role playing takes place after trainees have received instructions about personal selling through lectures and other methods. An office supplies manufacturer requires that trainees role play at various times near the end of their initial training programs. The role playing sessions are recorded on videotape and played back to the trainees at a later date. The playback enables trainees to critique their own sales presentation skills and thus to develop a basis for improving these.

*Discussion Groups.*   Discussion groups are useful means of training. Trainees can be asked to discuss the subject matter of lectures or materials covered in study-at-home programs. Or experienced salespersons can use the groups as vehicles for passing on experiences. The groups, if skillfully led, can be effective in producing exchanges of information and ideas and can help to break the monotony of lecture sessions.

---

[12]"Tell an Ad Story in a New Way," *Sales Meetings* 22, no. 3 (March 1973): 110–12, 115, 116.

*Study at Home.*   Study at home is a means of providing basic information about such factors as the company, competitors, target consumers, the company, and rival products. This can be a low-cost means of providing such basic information. Further, home study is a useful supplement to classroom or on-the-job training. A drawback is that it fails to stimulate sales representatives unless the home study materials are carefully designed. Overall, this is an effective supplement to other training methods.

*Sales Meetings.*   Sales meetings take place on a periodic basis, such as every Monday morning or every six months. The meetings provide for exchanges of information among sales representatives. In addition, they are useful in disseminating insights about new selling techniques or information about new products or policies to experienced sales representatives. Further, the meetings can be inspirational and aid in building morale.

Meetings are not without their costs. Salespersons are withdrawn from their jobs during the meetings, so costs of lost sales can take place. Further, expenses are incurred in transporting members of the sales force to the meeting site and paying for lodging and accommodations while they are on the site. These costs can be reduced by having short sales meetings in local offices, rather than lengthy meetings at the home office or some place such as Hawaii or Jamaica.

*On-the-Job Training.*   This method puts the trainee into actual selling situations, often in the company of a trainer or experienced sales representative. On-the-job training is often employed near the end of the training program, although it may be used throughout the program, in combination with other methods.

A realtor relies heavily upon on-the-job training. He or an experienced salesperson accompanies new employees on their first calls. In the early phases of the on-the-job training, the trainer has the primary responsibility for making the presentation. On subsequent calls the trainee assumes increasingly larger amounts of responsibility. The realtor feels that "putting the trainee in the field" is the best method of teaching selling skills.

**Compensation of Sales Personnel**

In designing compensation plans, sales managers become involved in two basic decisions:

1. determining the level or amount of compensation, and

2. determining the type of plan to be used.

Both of these decisions are made in light of the objectives of the compensation plan. A common objective, for instance, is to provide considerable incentive to produce sales. This objective might call for the use of a commission program that rewarded sales representatives for achieving sales volume. Another objective is to produce profitable sales, that is, to attain sales but to control costs at the same time. Still another objective is to provide servicing (installation, repair, and other services) to customers. This objective might lead to the use of a straight salary plan. In short, the objectives are the starting point for designing the compensation program.

Desirable Features of a Compensation Program

A good compensation program has a number of desirable features:

1. incentive

2. simplicity

3. fairness

4. flexibility

5. control

6. competitiveness[13]

**Incentive.** A well-conceived compensation program helps induce the sales representative to strive toward the goals of the organization. If maximizing sales is an important goal, commissions might be in order. Conversely, if the goal is profitability, the plan may contain provisions for higher commissions for products that produce higher profits for the organization.

**Simplicity.** The plan should be simple to compute and easy for sales representatives to understand. Otherwise the costs of administering the plan can be excessive and it fails to provide incentive. The plan is unlikely to attain its objectives if members of the sales force cannot understand it.

---

[13]Albert H. Dunn, Eugene M. Johnson, and David L. Kurtz, *Sales Management: Concepts, Practices, and Cases* (Morristown, N.J.: General Learning Press, 1974), pp. 421–22.

**Fairness.**   The plan should be equitable to both the sales representative and the organization. As regards the latter, it should not be unduly costly to the organization. Compensation should be based upon the degree to which sales personnel are productive in contributing to organization goals. The level should not drain the organization of funds for reasons not related to productivity.

Fairness to sales personnel is another desirable requisite. These individuals should be rewarded according to the extent to which they contribute to organization goals. Those sales personnel who provide the largest contributions should receive the highest incomes.

**Flexibility.**   From time to time, the circumstances of the organization, its environment, and sales representatives will change. An example is when new rivals enter the market. A flexible plan takes these changes into account. It might require adjustments in percentage commissions given to sales personnel when newcomers enter the industry, for example.

**Control.**   The program that is well designed pays sales representatives when they do what sales management wants them to do. If the sales manager desires that members of the staff be involved in missionary work, for instance, they should receive commensurate pay for such work.

**Competitiveness.**   Finally, the sound plan is competitive. It provides sales representatives with incomes that compare with those paid by other organizations for similar effort. If the level is not competitive, sales managers will experience difficulty in attracting, retaining, and motivating effective personnel.

Levels of
Compensation
Program

A basic decision is how much to pay sales representatives. The starting point for resolving this issue is to examine the compensation objectives. In the case of an office-equipment producer, the most important objective is for salespersons to act as creative problem solvers for their customers. Such an objective requires a compensation level that will enable the firm to attract and retain very able people. As a result, its compensation to its sales people is high, relative to that of competing firms.

Sales managers consider a number of factors, beyond compensation objectives, in setting levels. Two of these are the incomes of personnel employed by competing organizations and incomes in the communities where salespersons live. Most organizations attempt to achieve some level of competitiveness in both. Another factor is the amount the organization can afford to pay. Some institutions simply cannot afford to pay as much as their competitors can.

Methods of Compensation

There are three basic types of compensation plans:

1. straight salary,
2. straight commission,
3. combination of salary and another method.

**Straight Salary.** Salaries are fixed in amount and are paid on given dates, such as $1,500 on the last day of the month. Straight salaries are common in selling jobs where sales are infrequent and sales representatives are involved in negotiations for long periods of time in attempting to generate sales. If those who sold DC-10 airplanes were paid only when they made a sale, their incomes would be very high in those years when they made sales and nonexistent in others.[14]

Straight salaries are also common for jobs where the personnel must devote considerable periods of time to nonselling activities, such as installation, repair, and marketing intelligence. Finally, many organizations pay straight salaries to new sales representatives.

Straight salary plans enable management to control sales personnel. The latter are required to engage in whatever activities management believes to be appropriate. In addition, this method is simple and easy for personnel to understand. Finally, it is flexible. Salary adjustments can be made to reflect changing characteristics of the job and individual productivity.

**Straight Commission.** Commissions are payments that vary with output. A given sales representative, for instance, might receive a commission of 5 percent of total sales or 10 percent of net profits generated.

The main reason for using commissions is to provide incentive for sales representatives. They are aware that their compensation depends upon productivity, and so are motivated to achieve. On the other hand, this plan does not give management a high degree of control. Sales personnel may oversell

---

[14]On the average, it takes a sales representative four to six months to sell a Learjet. See "Who's Leery Now?" *Sales Management* 102, no. 13 (15 June 1969): 38.

customers and neglect nonselling activities. Further, some salespersons prefer a more fixed and regular method of compensation.

Commissions are not to be confused with bonuses, which are granted to sales representatives who have made some unusual accomplishment. An appliance manufacturer, for instance, provides a bonus for all salespersons who generate more than 110 percent of their sales quota. A hardware wholesaler pays a cash bonus for each new customer gained.

**Combination of Salary and Another Method.**   Most personal selling positions combine salary with commissions, bonuses, or some other incentive-generating method. Combination plans attempt to gain the advantages of both salaries and incentive plans. The National Cash Register Company starts new sales representatives on a salary plus commission basis. Once the personnel have been with the company for more than a year, they can convert to straight commissions or retain the salary-plus-commission plan.

**Payments for Expenses**   In the course of their duties, sales representatives incur selling expenses. Examples of expense items are transportation, lodging, food, and drink, entertainment, and laundry services. Median costs for a sample of sales representatives in 1975 were as follows (the data refer to one week):[15]

- Lodging          $103.40
- Auto rental      $146.00
- Food and drink   $ 89.15

Some sales managers operate under the principle that sales representatives should cover expenses out of their salaries or commissions. More commonly, however, representatives receive expense allowances.

Expense allowances can be effective means of controlling sales representatives. An oil field supplies salesman, for instance, receives funds for transportation, lodging, and food expenditures. When he spends money for such items, he collects the receipts and forwards them and expense-reimbursement forms to the home office. Within two weeks, he is reimbursed for the expenses. This process exerts some control over his behavior. The transportation allowance is very generous, so the salesman drives a new model car. The lodging and food allowances

---

[15]"1975 Costs," p. 8.

also permit him to stay and eat in expensive establishments. This on-the-job life style helps maintain the company image. The image would not be good if the allowance was small and he drove an old car and ate in second-rate establishments.

In general, sales personnel should neither gain nor lose money from expense allowances. If they gain, the allowances encourage unnecessary activities and padding of the expense accounts. Conversely, if they lose money the representatives are not likely to engage in the activities that they should. Thus, payments should be adequate, yet should not be unrealistically high.

Some organizations desire extreme expense-account flexibility. They do not place limits on the total expenditures or the expenditures in individual categories (such as transportation and lodging) which sales representatives can incur. Most organizations, however, place limits on the total or on individual categories. The objective of the limits is to impose control over the activities of sales personnel. The limits may encourage sales representatives to control their entertainment activities, fly tourist rather than first class, and avoid overly expensive hotels. If such actions fit in with the sales strategy, limitations probably are called for.

**Motivating Salespersons**

Like other administrators, sales managers are responsible for motivating their subordinates so that they contribute effectively to the goals of the organization. This is not an easy task. As one authority points out, "In marketing the real personnel problems are people problems—get people, get them to stay and do their best work."[16] Motivation requires satisfaction of individual needs, effective communication, and incentives to produce.

Satisfaction of Individual Needs

All individuals, including sales personnel, have specific sets of needs and desires. One scholar, Abraham Maslow, has suggested that the need structure is arranged in a hierarchy, as shown in Figure 13-7.[17]

The hierarchy suggests that people first try to satisfy their physiological needs, such as food, clothing, and shelter. Once these have been gratified, they seek safety and security. Next

---

[16]Philip Lesly, "Effective Management and the Human Factor," *Journal of Marketing* 29, no. 2 (April 1965): 1–2.

[17]See A. H. Maslow, *Motivation and Personality* (New York: Harper & Brothers, 1954), pp. 80–85.

**Figure 13-7. Maslow's need hierarchy.**

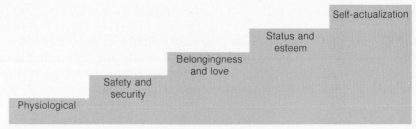

Source: A. H. Maslow, *Motivation and Personality* (New York: Harper & Brothers, 1954), pp. 80–85.

they seek belongingess and love, then status and esteem, and finally what is known as self-actualization," which means "doing what you are equipped for and want to do," just as Rembrandt was self-actualizing when he painted outstanding pictures.

The first step in motivating sales representatives is to determine what their individual needs are. Sales managers can accomplish this by having conferences with salespersons and observing their activities. A sales manager may find, for instance, that the words and actions of a particular representative suggest a high need for status and esteem. This indicates that the incentives offered by the sales manager are most likely to be effective in improving performance if they lead to status and esteem.

Once the more important needs have been identified, management can seek ways whereby sales representatives can achieve their own needs and at the same time attain the goals of the organization. The sales representative who is interested in status and esteem, for instance, can be motivated by recognition and praise.[18]

In order to motivate salespersons, sales managers must rely heavily upon communications. The results of one study indicated that

> . . . sales managers in the company studied can increase a salesman's job interest, opportunity for innovation, and job satisfaction —while decreasing his job tension and desire to leave—by increasing the amount of relevant information he perceives as necessary to do his job effectively.[19]

---

[18]One scholar suggests providing salespersons with strong peer-group recognition when they accomplish important organization tasks. See Dan H. Robertson, "Sales Force Feedback on Competitors' Activities," *Journal of Marketing* 38, no. 2 (April 1974): 71.

[19]James H. Donnelly, Jr., and John M. Ivancevich, "Role Clarity and the Salesman," *Journal of Marketing* 39, no. 1 (January 1975): 72.

Chapter 13 Sales Management

Sales personnel, then, desire information that will help them do their jobs more effectively and on what is expected of them. In addition, they desire information on company product, pricing, credit, discount, and other policies.[20]

Sales managers can communicate with representatives in a variety of ways—through letters and memos, formal meetings, and informal person-to-person conferences. Sales representatives do not want only to receive information, however; they also want to direct communications at management. They want to have an influence on decisions affecting them and to explain their problems and grievances to their superiors. Thus, two-way communication is desirable.

Incentives to Produce

Sales managers are frequent users of incentive devices to salespersons to achieve the desired effort. Among the incentive programs available are bonuses, fringe benefits, and contests, which provide prizes (cash, trading stamps, or merchandise) to those successful in increasing sales, bringing in new accounts, or some other increased short-run productivity.

## Forecasting

Forecasts of future organization sales are indispensible to sales managers. Managers need forecasts in order to generate plans for the future. Without forecasts, plans are very likely to be in error. Further, forecasts are needed for control purposes. The control process involves comparing expected performance with actual performance. The estimates of future expected performance are derived from the sales and related forecasts.

In some organizations, sales managers help in making sales forecasts. For instance, Hoerner Waldorf Corporation export-sales executives direct surveys of expected sales to customers. Whether or not sales managers participate, they should have some understanding of the nature of this activity. Full interpretation of forecasts requires some insight into how these estimates were developed. This section provides an overview of some of the more widely employed methods.

Opinions of Executives and Sales Representatives

Sales managers rely on their own opinions for estimates of future sales. Over the years, some develop an ability to make the estimates with reasonable accuracy. Not uncommonly, sales representatives are asked to generate forecasts for their respective territories. This method is based upon the assumption that representatives are in close contact with customers and

---

[20]*Ibid.*

prospects and thus can estimate their future demands. However, sales personnel are not familiar with important determinants of company sales such as overall marketing strategies and the state of the economy. Moreover, sales representatives may underforecast sales in organizations that base compensation on the degree to which sales quotas are attained.

A danger inherent in using the opinions of the sales force and sales manager is that they are likely to be overly subjective. Subjectivity is reduced, however, when more than one individual provides opinions and the results are averages. In many organizations, opinions are employed as checks on the expected accuracy of more objective methods. In the main, opinions of sales managers and sales representatives provide useful inputs into the prediction of future sales, although these sources usually are not employed as the sole means of forecasting.

Statistical Forecasts

Statistical forecasts use past data in order to provide estimates of future expected sales. Some assume that the organization's sales are related to the behavior of some other variable. Sales of air-conditioners, for instance, are related to prevailing temperature levels in the regions where the units are sold. If management is able to secure accurate weather forecasts, good sales forecasts may be forthcoming.

Other forecasts assume that sales depend upon time. Figure 13-8 shows the sales of a New England hardware wholesaler from 1950 to 1976. The historical data form the pattern of a straight line. An extension of the line to 1977 provides an estimate of expected sales for that year. Other techniques assume that a curve, rather than a line, best describes the historical data.

Statistical forecasts assume that what was true in the past will remain to be true in the future. This is often not a safe assumption, however. As a result, management commonly uses other techniques to supplement statistical methods.

Surveys

Surveys are useful techniques for estimating future sales. In the case of new products, they are extremely important, since past sales data are not available for making statistical forecasts.

The most commonly employed survey method is the *buying-intention study*. Customers and potential customers are asked for their intentions to buy the product or service during a forthcoming period (such as a year). If the survey respondents are typical consumers, the results of the survey can be gener-

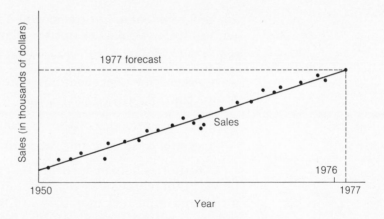

**Figure 13-8. Past sales and 1977 sales forecast for a hardware wholesaler.**

alized to the market at large. For instance, if typical consumers say they expect to spend an average of $1,000 per year on the company's products, and there are 2,000 consumers, the forecast is $2,000,000.

Buying-intention surveys can be wrong, of course. The survey questionnaire may be misleading, buyers may be incapable of estimating their future purchases accurately, or the sample of buyers may not be representative. Overall, however, surveys have much to offer for sales forecasting.

*Choosing a Forecasting Method*

Each organization uses the method or methods that best fit its needs. For some, managerial or salesperson opinions prove to be accurate. Others find that statistical or survey methods produce more meaningful results. Most organizations combine the output of two or more methods, in order to generate estimates that reflect the varying assumptions of the sundry methods.[21]

With the sales forecasts in hand, sales managers are in a position to engage in planning and control operations. These are described in the following three sections.

**Sales Territories**

Sales managers are charged with the responsibility for devising sales territories within which sales representatives will operate. This section covers the sales territory design process.

*Sales Territories*

Sales territories consist of groups of prospects that have been allocated to particular sales representatives. Many territories

---

[21]For a good discussion of the forecasting process, see Roger K. Chisholm and Gilbert R. Whitaker, *Forecasting Methods* (Homewood, Ill.: Richard D. Irwin, 1971).

are geographical in nature, as when a salesperson covers eastern Kentucky, or part of upstate New York.

**Why Utilize Territories.** Territories are needed in order to:

1. ensure that target consumers are contacted;
2. motivate sales representatives;
3. permit evaluation of sales personnel;
4. control personal selling expenses.

Territories help in ensuring that target consumers are contacted. Individual sales representatives are assigned to territories and informed that they are responsible for contacting prospects within the territory, on a periodic basis, such as once a month. This assignment of responsibility means that the dangers of not contacting target consumers is small. In the absence of territorial assignments, the sales force could easily miss particular prospects.

Assignments of territories helps in motivating sales personnel. They develop over a period of time a sense of ownership of "my territory." Improvements in customer service of the territory result in extra income or other compensation for the sales representative. Sales personnel become acquainted with buyers and others in the territory and form friendships there. The likely result is higher morale than would exist if territories were not formed.

The development of territories facilitates the evaluation of sales personnel. Sales managers collect sales and cost information on a territorial basis. As a result, they can easily compare potential performance in each territory with actual performance. This permits the evaluation of sales representative activity.

The utilization of territories helps in controlling personal-selling expenses. Effectively designed territories do not require excessive travel on the part of employees. Further, they do not require unnecessary nights spent away from home. The result is some degree of control over the level of selling expenses.

**How Territories Are Established.** Territorial design begins by selecting a control unit. Examples of these units are counties, cities, states, and trading areas.

Once the control unit is selected, management determines the sales potential of each unit. The sales potential is the maximum total sales available to the organization in the unit. It is determined by examining the number and size of potential and actual customers, the extent of competition, and sales forecasts.

Territories are constructed by putting together control units in a manner that provides adequate sales potential for each salesperson. Many organizations attempt to equalize the sales potential between sales personnel. Adjustments are necessary because of the relative difficulty of covering different areas.[22] Sales representatives in territories that are sparsely populated, difficult to travel in, and having customers with only limited servicing needs may end up with territories that have smaller potentials than representatives in regions that are heavily populated, easy to travel in, and having high customer-service needs. The overall product of sales territory design should be a set of regions that have approximately equal sales potentials and are roughly equal in terms of ease of coverage. It is difficult, and sometimes impossible, to attain both of these ends, however, so compromises between the two are sometimes necessary.

**Quotas**
Quotas are objectives that sales representatives are expected to reach, and are often stated in terms of sales or profits. A computer-terminal manufacturer, for instance, has established an annual sales quota of $150,000 for the territory of a particular salesman. A producer of powershift transmissions for large machines has a profit quota of $97,000 for a particular territory. Another type of quota is based upon points. Here representatives receive specified numbers of points for the completion of particular activities, such as two points for every call made and five points for each new account established.

Use of Quotas
Quotas are useful in evaluating the performance of sales representatives. When individuals exceed their quotas, management has an indication that their performance is good. Conversely, when quotas are not met, there is an indication that performance may not be adequate and management should take steps to find out why.

Another function of quotas is to provide incentives for sales representatives. They have assigned objectives, in the form of sales, profits, points, or other variables which they know they are expected to meet. Often, bonuses or higher commissions are

---

[22]See Henry C. Lucas, Jr., Charles W. Weinberg, and Kenneth W. Clowes, "Sales Response as a Function of Territorial Potential and Sales Representative Workload," *Journal of Marketing Research* 12, no. 3 (August 1975): 298–305.

paid to those who exceed the quota, resulting in probable higher productivity than if quotas are not used.

## Establishing Quotas

The beginning point for establishing quotas is to examine sales potentials, which in turn are commonly based on past sales levels. Quotas for sales will be some percentage of the potentials. Management must determine the percentage of the potential that a salesperson can realistically be expected to reach, in light of the difficulty of covering the territory, density of customers, competition, and other factors. If profit quotas are employed, management is faced with the need to determine what expenses are reasonable, in light of the sales job individual representatives have been assigned.

A good procedure is for sales managers to work with representatives in establishing quotas (although representatives are likely to play a smaller role if compensation is based on quotas). If salespersons are allowed to participate in developing these objectives, they are more likely to accept them. Further, sales representatives often have valuable insights that should be reflected in the levels of their quotas.

## Evaluating the Performance of Sales Representatives

Sales managers are in need of measures of the performance of their representatives. This provides them with information such as which individuals should be promoted or fired; where particular representatives require training or more supervision; and if training, supervision, compensation and selection programs, and other elements of sales management are functioning according to plan.

### The Evaluation Process

Basically, evaluation requires:

1. setting up standards of expected performance, and

2. comparing actual with expected performance.

If actual performance is less than that which is expected, remedial action is needed. Some of the measures of performance are:

- total sales;
- sales as a percentage of quota;
- total expenses;
- gross margin on sales;
- number of calls made;
- average order size;

- number of sales/number of calls ("batting average");
- hours worked per day;
- ratings by sales managers.

The sources of information for the evaluations include the reports of sales representatives, company records, and sales managers. In most cases, a variety of measures of performance are employed. Reliance upon any one can be misleading. The total sales generated by a salesperson may be low, for instance. In relation to the quota, however, the sales may be high. On the other hand, a representative may have high sales as a percentage of quota, but few hours worked per day. Investigation may reveal that the territory assigned to this individual has a potential that is too large for one person. Thus, sales managers are well advised to consider a composite of measures in evaluating their subordinates. If sales will soon materialize as a result of the salesperson's efforts the sales manager may stress sales performance in evaluating representatives. Conversely, if individual salespersons' sales results may well be spread over numerous years, the evaluation may emphasize such factors as his or her knowledge, rapport with customers, and efforts expended. Whatever methods are used, the results of evaluation may suggest the need for prompt remedial action or the need for further fact-finding to determine what (if any) remedial action is required.

**Sales Organization**

Most sales forces, other than those that are very small, are subdivided into specialized categories. Salespersons who specialize can become highly skilled in their field of specialization. They become experts in serving customers and in handling organization tasks in the field. The three primary kinds of specialization are:

1. geographical,
2. product or service, and
3. customer.

In practice, a combination of two or three of these is common.

Geographic Specialization

The top part of Figure 13-9 illustrates the geographical sales organization. The organization pictured is that of a candy manufacturer. Four district sales managers report to the sales manager. The four are from the Seattle, Dallas, Chicago, and New

York offices. A group of sales representatives works out of each office and serves customers located in the territory served by the office.

Geographic subdivision allows salespersons to become experts in handling problems in their areas. Representatives get to know customers and competitive conditions in these areas and learn how to satisfy local needs. Travel time and expense is minimized, since each representative works in a restricted territory.

**Figure 13-9. Three primary types of sales organization plans.**

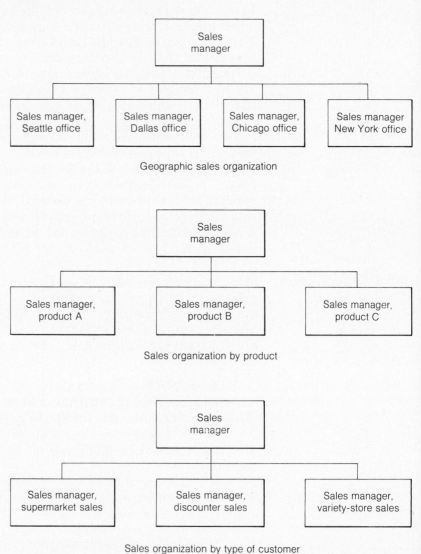

Geographic sales organization

Sales organization by product

Sales organization by type of customer

Product or service specialization involves assigning a sales manager and a group of representatives to a group of products or services, as illustrated in the middle of Figure 13-9. As the figure shows, there is a sales manager and a group of salespersons for products groups A, B, and C.

This form of organization is common. The Midland Marine Corporation, for instance, has three subdivisions, each with its own sales force:

- commercial, government, and unbranded petroleum products;
- fertilizer, seed, and agricultural products;
- food and clothing.

The Xerox Corporation also assigns salespersons to specialized product groups. In 1976, for example, this firm had a 600-person sales force that specialized just in selling its 9200 model duplicating machine.[23]

Product subdivision is applicable when the organization markets diverse products that require specialized knowledge. In the life insurance field, for example, representatives may be grouped according to product categories such as (1) individual policies, (2) group policies, (3) business policies, and (4) trusts and estates. Salespersons in each group develop knowledge in selling their particular products, which are very complex.

This form of organization has some disadvantages. Sometimes customers are annoyed because two or more salespersons from the same organization call on them. Further, salespersons may be involved in a great deal of traveling, if their customers are scattered geographically. Also, product or service organization may lead to a large number of sales managers and resulting administrative overhead.

The bottom part of Figure 13-9 illustrates organization by type of customer. In the figure there are separate field forces for (1) supermarkets, (2) discount stores, and (3) variety stores. This type of organization fulfills the needs of marketers who sell to types of customers whose requirements differ widely. The disadvantages of customer organization are essentially the same as those of product organization.

Intech International is a Boston-headquartered firm with 100 sales representatives who sell industrial machines and

---

[23]"Why Xerox's Money Machine Slows Delivery," *Business Week*, no. 2426 (5 April 1976): 63.

equipment. The sales force is made up of three groups, each of which specializes in selling to a particular group of customers:[24]

- the university research group,
- the medical hospital group,
- the chemical processing group.

Organization in Practice

Actual sales organizations often are more complex than those described here. Often a mixture of the three types is employed. An example is where the field force is subdivided geographically and sales representatives in each geographic unit specialize by product or customer type. Each sales manager must consider the particular needs of his or her institution, and draw up the means of specialization in accordance with these needs.

**Summary**

Sales management consists of the planning and administering of personal selling activities. Those who are involved in this function both construct and implement plans. Some of these plans relate to the internal operation of the sales department. Others relate to interactions between sales and other departments. This chapter has focused upon the former.

Recruiting and selecting are basic sales management functions. They consist of finding, attracting, and choosing particular individuals to fill organization positions. Important tools in these areas are job analyses, job descriptions, and job specifications.

Once individuals have been hired, they must be assimilated into the organization. Management should take steps to ensure that the transition into the new employee status is as smooth as possible.

Both old and new salespersons require training. In turn, training needs differ according to the sales representative's stages in his or her career cycle. Training programs cover selling, the company, competitors, and target consumers. Among the methods used are lectures, role playing, discussion groups, study at home, sales meetings, and on-the-job training.

Compensation decisions require determining both income levels and the type of plan to use. Programs should provide for incentive, simplicity, fairness, flexibility, control, and com-

---

[24]Howard M. Anderson, "Selling by Marketargeting," *Sales Management* 117, no. 24 (8 December 1975): 65.

Chapter 13 Sales Management

petitiveness.
level are the obj
and outside of the o
ford, and job evaluatic
plans discussed are straigh.
combination of salary and and

Salespersons should be reimb
on the job. Categories such as transpo.
and drink are covered. Expense accoun
unlimited.

compensation
inside
af-

Sales managers are responsible for motiva.
ordinates. Among the methods used are satisfying
needs, effective communication, and incentives to pro

Forecasts of future organization sales are indispensib.
sales managers. Managers use forecasts for both planning and
control. Among the forecasting methods used are soliciting the
opinions of executives and salespersons, statistical forecasts,
and surveys.

Sales territories consists of groups of prospects that are
allocated to particular sales representatives. Often these are
geographical in nature. The use of territories helps ensure that
target consumers are contacted, motivates salespersons, permits evaluation of salespersons, and helps control personal-
selling expenses. Territories are based upon control units, sales
potential, and measures of the difficulty of serving particular
control units.

Quotas are objectives that salespersons are expected to
reach. Often these are stated in terms of sales, profits, or points.
Some of the uses of quotas are in evaluating salespersons' performance and in providing incentives for them.

A responsibility of sales managers is to evaluate the performance of subordinates. This requires setting standards and
comparing actual performance with the standards. If actual
performance falls short of the standards, remedial action may
be needed.

Field forces may be organized in various ways. This chapter has discussed geographical, product or service, and customer organization plans. Actual organizations often use a
combination of the plans.

**Discussion**
**Questions**

1. What is sales management? How does it differ from personal selling?

2. How can sales managers determine the characteristics that should be sought in recruits?

...bers of the sales force?

...ces for selecting salespersons.

...he organization?

...aining of salespersons.

...s cover? What training methods can be used?

...a disadvantages of the three compensation plans

3. W...
...ersons be motivated?

...e the merits of the three types of forecasting methods mentioned in the

... How can sales territories be established?

12. What are quotas? What are their uses?

13. What are the steps involved in evaluating the performance of salespersons?

14. Set forth the advantages of each of the three sales organization plans discussed in the chapter.

**Practical Exercises**     1. Observe a salesperson in action (as in a retail store). Based upon your observation, what characteristics should the holder of such a job possess? Explain.

2. How would you evaluate the performance of the holder of the job mentioned in (1) above? Explain.

**Selling Project**     For the product that you have selected, explain how you would conduct the following:

a. recruiting,

b. selecting,

c. assimilation into the organization,

d. training,

e. compensation,

f. payments for expenses,

g. motivating,

h. forecasting,

i. setting up territories,

j. determining quotas,

k. evaluating performance,

l. organizing the field force.

**Case 13
The Diamond
Fork-Lift Truck
Manufacturing
Company**

The Diamond Fork-Lift Truck Manufacturing Company (DFC) produces and markets a line of electrically powered fork lift trucks, which are used in warehouses, plants, shipping docks, and other installations to carry heavy materials from one location to another. The fork lift trucks can be used to carry large quantities of goods in single loads to storage areas.

Diamond's customers are primarily manufacturers, wholesalers, and large retailers. The firm sells directly to these accounts; wholesalers are not employed. The market is national in scope.

The quality of DFC trucks is very high, according to the marketing manager, Mr. Defleci. Many customers prefer electric-powered trucks, since they do not emit exhaust fumes and can be used in closed areas. Diamond trucks operate very efficiently, can carry large loads, and are not noisy. These are all points of company differential advantage.

The company advertises the line through trade magazines and direct mail. In the main, the advertisements emphasize the points of differential advantage. Four percent of anticipated annual sales go into the advertising budget.

DFC maintains a sales force of fifty men. Their responsibility is to call on prospective buyers and to attempt to induce them to purchase company products. The salesmen also call on past purchasers of Diamond products to ensure that they are satisfied with the company and its products. The salesmen engage in considerable prospecting, in an attempt to locate organizations that might be in the process of seeking fork-lift trucks for the first time or as replacements for existing trucks.

The company limits its recruiting to college campuses. The sales manager, Mr. Prontos, has decided that employees should be:

1. between 21 and 45 years of age;
2. mature;
3. in excellent health;
4. college educated;
5. able to relate to others;
6. able to work with figures.

The selection process involves exposing applicants to an initial job interview, a second more intensive interview, and a final hiring interview. The first and second take place in campus placement offices, while the third occurs in company field offices. Those candidates who look good on the application blank and who perform effectively in the initial interview are asked to participate in a second interview. In turn, those who best conduct themselves in the second interview are invited for a final hiring interview. Approximately half of those who undertake this third session are hired.

Prontos is not happy with the quality of people who have been selected over the past year. Their performance has been much lower than was expected. Some have left the organization. Others simply are not meeting their quotas. He feels that the recruiting and selection processes are at fault.

What would you advise Prontos?

**Suggested Readings**

Canfield, Bertrand. *Sales Administration: Principles and Problems.* Englewood Cliffs, N.J.: Prentice-Hall, 1961.

Dodge, H. Robert. *Field Sales Management: Text and Cases.* Dallas, Texas: Business Publications, 1973.

Dunn, Albert H., Eugene M. Johnson, and David L. Kurtz. *Sales Management: Concepts, Practices, and Cases.* Morristown, N.J.: General Learning Press, 1974.

Levitt, Theodore. *Marketing for Business Growth.* New York: McGraw-Hill Book Company, 1974, ch. 3.

Rathmell, John M. *Managing the Marketing Function: Concepts, Analysis, and Applications.* New York: John Wiley & Sons, 1969, chs. 5, 6, and 7.

Stanton, William J., and Richard H. Buskirk. *Management of the Sales Force.* Homewood, Ill.: Richard D. Irwin, 1974.

Still, Richard R., and Edward W. Cundiff. *Sales Management: Decisions, Policies, and Cases.* Englewood Cliffs, N.J.: Prentice-Hall, 1969.

# 14

## Ethics, Social Responsibility, and Government Regulation of Personal Selling

*After reading this chapter you should be able to demonstrate a knowledge of:*

- *the impact of ethical and social responsibility standards on sales representatives*
- *the importance of government regulation to the salesperson*
- *the impact of some federal laws on personal selling*

Some selling practices are considered to be unethical or not socially responsible, according to various critics. And some practices are not legal, according to various federal and local statutes. Among such practices might be:

- salespersons supporting a company policy to withold information about a new company product from retail customers, so that they will deplete their inventories of existing company products;
- salespersons failing to inform customers that a competing brand would fulfill their needs more adequately than would the brand they sell;

- manufacturers' salespersons and distributors making agreements on the level of prices to ultimate consumers;

- making untrue statements about the quality of the organization's products;

- making untrue statements to consumers about the quality of competitors' offerings;

- selling products that are unsafe;

- lowering prices, with the intention of driving competitors out of business.

This chapter is concerned with issues of ethical and social responsibility and important regulations that bear on the sales representative in carrying out the sales function on a day-to-day basis.

## Selling, Social Responsibility, and Ethics

Personal selling is one field that is highly affected by social responsibility and ethics. Both of these concepts should be of extreme concern to those who hold positions in personal selling.

### Social Responsibility

Over the past three decades, the idea of social responsibility has become quite highly instilled in the ranks of sales managers, sales representatives, legislators, and educators in the personal selling field. The social responsibility of organizations is to take courses of action that are in the best interests of society at large and of particular groups, such as employees, suppliers, the underprivileged, and minorities.[1] Sales representatives who are socially responsible realize that they have obligations to numerous parties, as outlined in Figure 14-1. Socially responsible individuals avoid actions such as:

- engaging in wasteful and unnecessary activity that results in undue consumption of scarce resources (as by undertaking unnecessary travel);

- encouraging customers to engage in activity that is wasteful (as by trying to convince them that the energy crisis is only temporary and fuel-conservation measures are not needed);

- encouraging customers to purchase nonrecyclible products when they could easily utilize recyclable items;

- encouraging the production and engineering departments to use machinery that does not have effective air-pollution deterrents;

---

[1]See David T. Kollat, Roger D. Blackwell, and James F. Robeson, *Strategic Marketing* (New York: Holt, Rinehart and Winston, 1972), pp. 506–513.

Figure 14-1. Sales
representatives are
obligated to numerous
parties.

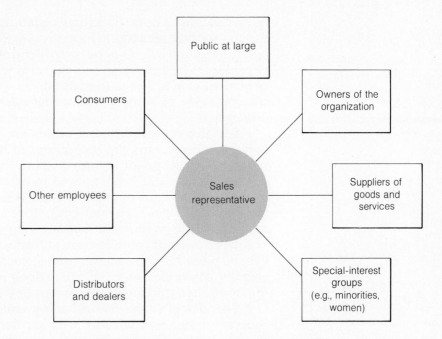

attempting to convince top management that price increases are in order, when they are not needed to maintain company profits (thereby adding to the effects of inflation).

Unfortunately, answers to questions of social responsibility are often not readily available. Frequently, efforts to aid one segment of society (such as consumers) tend to have a deleterious effect on other segments (such as minorities). Assume, for instance, that the representatives of a particular firm convince the marketing manager that company products should be made easier to operate and safer, thereby aiding consumers. This effort would appear to be laudable, but it may have a negative impact upon other parties. The costs of improving the products may necessitate increased prices, for instance, and the resulting higher prices can be a serious burden on low-income consumers, many of whom may prefer the unimproved products at lower prices. In short, salespersons who attempt to act in a socially responsible manner are faced with the need to determine the net impact of their actions on numerous parties, and not upon only one segment of society.

### Ethics

The field of ethics is closely related to that of social responsibility. Ethics refers to that which is right or morally correct. Or as one authority puts it: "Ethics constitute a standard of rightness in individual actions based on societal values."[2] In turn, each individual has his or her own blend of ethics, and what one considers to be right may be abhorrent to another. When sales personnel give bribes to foreign buyers, this may be viewed as unacceptable to some persons and necessary and proper to others.[3]

Social responsibility and ethics are not the same. Social responsibility means the obligations of an organization or an individual to the public at large and to individual groups. Ethics refers to individuals' concepts as to what is right and what is wrong. A salesman might feel that, if he reduced prices to a customer, this would be unethical, since a competing salesman would lose the business of the customer and as a result would not make enough commissions to feed a seven-person family. On the other hand, reducing prices would probably constitute socially desirable behavior, since such action would help reduce inflation and lower the cost of living of consumers.

The idea of salespersons "being ethical" is more complex than it might seem to those who are not actually involved in personal selling, as the following writer points out:

> The majority of businessmen, including marketing executives, do not consciously engage in unethical practices, as established by their own standards. Each executive has his own individual standards of conduct which he believes to be ethical and these standards are followed. However, ethical standards are set by society and not by individuals. Thus, society evaluates an individual's behavior as ethical or unethical. The problem is that society lacks commonly accepted standards of behavior. Determination of what is right and what is wrong is an extremely difficult task. What is considered ethical conduct varies from country to country, from industry to industry, from situation to situation, and even from person to person.[4]

Each sales representative, then, has the task of interpreting the standards of the society to which he or she belongs and attempting to determine what personal standards to adopt.

---

[2]H. Robert Dodge, *Field Sales Management: Text and Cases* (Dallas, Texas: Business Publications, 1973), p. 30.

[3]See "It's a Jungle Out There," *Advertising Age* 47, no. 11 (15 March 1976): 16.

[4]W. Daniel Rountree, *Ethical Aspects of Personal Selling*, Boone, N.C., Appalachian State University, College of Business Monograph, 1976, p. 2.

These personal standards operate as guidelines in directing numerous facets of day-to-day behavior.

Ethical issues are, of course, not new to personal selling. As Frederick A. Collins, Jr., president of Sperry and Hutchinson Company, points out, "It is more than likely that many of the recent exposures of unethical practices are not inherently new *at all*, but have been tolerated for generations and some through the course of history."[5] During recent years, sales representatives have been confronted with increasingly rigorous standards of ethics and social responsibility, demanded by legislators, judges, journalists, consumer advocates, as well as sales managers. The salesperson must consider ethics and social responsibility important in his or her actions, for the days of *caveat emptor* ("let the buyer beware") are past.

## Laws Versus Ethical and Socially Responsible Behavior

In general, laws are prohibitive in nature—they prohibit behavior that has been judged not to be in the best interests of society. Laws set *minimal* standards of behavior, as indicated in Figure 14-2. But just because sales representatives are obeying the law does not mean they are being ethical or socially responsible. Ethical and social responsibility philosophies should provide for *higher* standards. It is to be expected that salespersons will have more advanced standards than "just observing the law."

Since ethical and social responsibility standards differ from one person to another, different behaviors are likely to be in evidence. A hardware salesman, for instance, believes in the following:

- Be completely honest. Tell others the truth in its entirety.

- Try to do what is best to advance the welfare of others.

---

[5]Frederick A. Collins, Jr., "Some Views on the Issue of Business Ethics," brochure, Sperry and Hutchinson Company, New York, 1975, p. 7.

**Figure 14-2. Standards of behavior.**

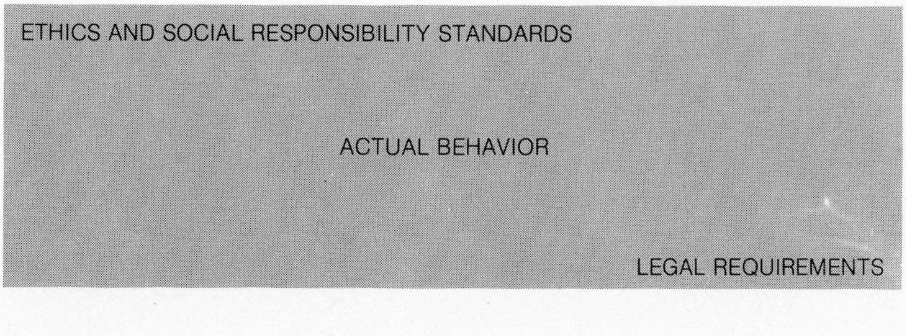

ETHICS AND SOCIAL RESPONSIBILITY STANDARDS

ACTUAL BEHAVIOR

LEGAL REQUIREMENTS

On the other hand, an office-supply sales representative has the following beliefs:

- Do what is best for society at large.
- Consider "the greatest good for the greatest number" in reaching decisions.
- Attempt to help those who are financially underprivileged.

Both have their own codes, but the codes provides a prescription for desirable behavior that goes beyond "just obeying the law." Observing these codes provides personal satisfaction for both representatives, and also has turned out to be good for business, for both representatives have reputations for being ethical and socially responsible. These reputations have established their credibility and as a result have made them more successful sales representatives.

## Governmental Regulation of Personal Selling

This section provides an overview of the impact of governmental regulation of personal selling. It considers the importance of regulation and provides a description of the nature and operation of various specific laws.

### The Importance of Regulation to the Salesperson

Many of the activities undertaken by sales personnel are subject to governmental influence and control. Included in these activities are:

- what is said by the salesperson about products and services offered by the organization;
- what is said about products and services offered by competitors;
- the intent of the sales representative's activities (for instance, is the intent of a price reduction to drive competitors out of business?);
- offers of promotion help to customers;
- agreements with competitors to divide up the market.

Government control over all of the activities carried out by the sales representative is substantial. As salespersons acquire larger responsibilities over time and become territory managers, they become subject to more regulation, simply because these additional activities are regulated. Government influence appears to be increasing in scope with the passage of time. As a result, the sales representative is faced with the need to be familiar with numerous laws. Figure 14-3 outlines the scope of legal control. It points out that legislation covers traditional

**Figure 14-3.
Governmental
regulation of the sales
representative.**

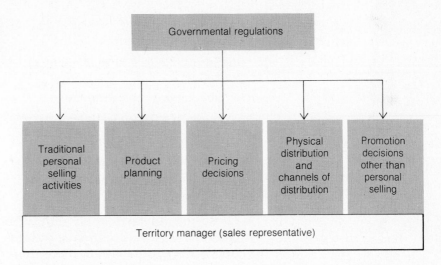

Governmental regulations

| Traditional personal selling activities | Product planning | Pricing decisions | Physical distribution and channels of distribution | Promotion decisions other than personal selling |

Territory manager (sales representative)

selling activities (such as the contact and the presentation), product planning, pricing, distribution, and promotion.

Consequences  The consequences of breaking the law can be very considerable. Obviously, no representative wants a jail sentence, or a fine or wants to pay damages to other parties. Beyond this, violation of statutes can cause serious damage to the reputation of the organization and the salesperson. Further, the sales representative and others in the organization may expend considerable time and money if they become involved in legal entanglements.

Every sales representative, of course, cannot be a lawyer, nor is this necessarily desirable. What is needed is a working familiarity with the more important laws and the means by which they are interpreted and enforced. When technical legal problems arise, an attorney should be consulted.

Specific Actions  In the rest of this chapter we will present a number (but cer-
Prohibited  tainly not all) of personal selling practices that are prohibited by federal laws, at least the situations with which most representatives should be reasonably familiar.

**What Is Regulated.**   There are numerous actions that federal laws prohibit, the most important being:

1. combining or conspiring to restrain trade;
2. tying and requirements contracts;

3. price discrimination;

4. brokerage allowances;

5. discrimination in furnishing facilities, services, and funds for promotion;

6. inducing price discrimination;

7. deception of the consumer;

8. unfair methods of competition;

9. failure to disclose financial charges to those who buy on credit;

10. inducing buyers of products sold door to door to make purchases that they later regret.

These federal laws apply only when the organization is involved in interstate commerce—that is, they apply when the organization's actions affect more than one state.[6] As a practical matter, the courts have interpreted this doctrine so broadly that now most sales representatives are involved in interstate commerce.

*Combining or Conspiring to Restrain Trade.* A federal law— the Sherman Act—prohibits combining or conspiring to restrain trade. The terms "combining" and "conspiring" refer to agreements between two or more organizations. Among the agreements that have been found to be illegal are compacts between competitors to:

- divide up the market ("You sell in the north, I'll sell in the south, and as a result we won't be competing");

- set prices at certain levels;

- increase employees' wages and offset them through price advances;

- refuse to give trade association information to industry newcomers.

The salesperson should be careful to avoid conduct that the authorities would view as price fixing between competitors. This is illegal even when it does not weaken competition—that is, when it does not take business away from rivals. Thus, the 1960s witnessed the prosecution of a number of large producers

---

[6]For a good discussion of what constitutes interstate commerce, see Dudley Odel McGovney, "Interstate Commerce," in Eugene Allen Gilmore and William Charles Wermuth, eds., *Modern American Law* (Chicago: Blackstone Institute), vol. 10, part 7.

of electrical installations who jointly agreed to set prices according to formulas.

*Tying and Requirements Contracts.* According to the Clayton Act tying and requirements contracts are illegal where the effect may be to restrict competition or to create a monopoly. In the case of tying contracts, the organization indicates that it will not sell one product or brand to a customer unless the customer buys another product or brand from the organization. An example is where a manufacturer of copying machines caused damages to a firm that sold paper and other supplies that could be used with the copying machines. The manufacturer threatened to cancel its rental and service agreements with customers if they used the paper or other supplies of competing manufacturers in its machines.[7]

Requirements contracts provide that if a customer is to purchase an offering from the supplier, all of the customer's needs for the offering must come from that supplier. The Burlington Industries Company was forced to pay damages to several Chicago retail hoisery stores, as a result of being found guilty of this practice. Burlington forced wholesale suppliers of the retailers to deal exclusively with Burlington in women's hose.[8]

Tying and requirements contracts are prohibited where the effect *may be* to restrict competition or to create a monopoly. It is not necessary to show that the effect *probably will be* or *has been* to restrict competition or to create a monopoly. Thus, even organizations with small shares of market can be indicted under this law. It is much easier for prosecutors to show a prohibited effect on competition under tying or requirements contracts than under conspiracies to restrain trade.

*Price Discrimination.* Another federal law—the Robinson Patman Act—prohibits discrimination in the prices of commodities of like grade and quality to purchasers who are similarly situated. Discrimination consists of selling an identical commodity to two or more similarly situated buyers at different prices. The term "similarly situated" means having the same status in the channels of distribution. Thus, two retailers are similarly situated, as are two wholesalers.

---

[7]Ray O. Werner, ed., "Legal Developments in Marketing," *Journal of Marketing* 33, no. 1 (January 1969): 107–108.

[8]Ray O. Werner, ed., "Legal Developments in Marketing," *Journal of Marketing*, 31, no. 1 (January 1967): 79.

Assume that Patrick Wright, a seller of Acme propjets (business aircraft) sells the company AG28 model to two different buyers at different prices: to the Olympus Company at $49,500, and to the Zeus Company at $52,200. This price differential, made for goods of identical grade and quality, constitutes price discrimination.

The Robinson Patman Act covers only "commodities." These are tangible goods, as contrasted to services. Sellers of services, such as consultants and lawyers, are free to discriminate. Thus, when the Tri-State Broadcasting Company accused United Press International of violating the law by charging Tri-State a higher weekly price for the news service than that assessed of competing broadcasters,[9] the court dismissed the case since the news service was not a commodity.

In a similar vein, the Robinson Patman Act does not apply to transactions involving ultimate consumers. A sales representative is free to sell one television set to customer X for $600 and an identical set to customer Y for $650.

The law prohibits price discrimination "where the effect may be to restrict competition or to create a monopoly." In fact, government prosecutors have often taken the view that "restricting competition" means causing monetary damage (loss of profits) to other organizations. Thus, if Patrick Wright's price discrimination injures a competing aircraft manufacturer, this may be viewed as restricting competition. Likewise, if the discrimination injures competitors of the Olympus or Zeus companies or their customers, injury to competition could be held.

When price discriminating and resulting injury to competition or a tendency to create a monopoly have been determined, the accused organization is allowed to justify the discrimination through certain defenses. These are that the discrimination was made:

1. because of differences in the costs of manufacturing, selling, or delivery;

2. to make a "good faith" attempt to meet competition;

3. in light of differences in the market or the marketability of the goods under consideration.

The first defense is that the discrimination was made in light of differences in the cost of manufacturing, selling, or

---

[9]Ray O. Werner, ed., "Legal Developments in Marketing," *Journal of Marketing* 31, no. 3 (July 1967): 76.

delivery. A frequent reason for price differences is that one buyer purchased a larger quantity of goods than did another, with resulting cost savings. Another reason is that transportation charges to one buyer are greater than those to others, and that price differences reflect these cost variations.

The price discriminator must base the discrimination upon concrete evidence of cost differences. Normally, such evidence consists of a cost-accounting study of precise differences in the costs of serving the different customers. Further, the cost accounting study must have been made prior to the discrimination. If it was made after this occurrence (as where it was conducted only to provide evidence in court), the resulting findings cannot be used. These limitations can make the cost defense difficult to apply.

A second defense is that the discrimination was made in good faith to meet the price of a competitor. Assume, for instance, that Patrick Wright assessed the lower price to the Olympus Company because a competing aircraft manufacturer had quoted a low price to Olympus. In this case, Patrick is responding to competition—he is attempting to meet the price of a rival. The law does not allow Patrick to undercut the price of the competitor, however. All that he can do is to meet (not beat) this organization.

The third defense that can be raised is that differences in the market or marketability of the goods under consideration justify price differences. The courts have interpreted this as meaning that discrimination may be justified in the case of unusual circumstances, as when the organization is going out of business, or where it is undertaking a "fire sale" or "damaged goods sale."

*Brokerage Allowances.* The Robinson Patman Act also outlaws brokerage allowances. These are payments made to buyers who purchase directly from the supplier, and do not utilize the services of brokers. A producer of ceramic tile utilizes brokers to reach most customers (building materials dealers). On the other hand, one customer purchases in very large volumes that do not require the services of a broker. Figure 14-4 shows this pattern. The price to the broker is $14.89 and to the retailer is $17.89. The $3 difference in price is the broker's commission.

If the large customer is given a brokerage allowance, it will pay only $14.89, rather than $17.89 (like the other retailers). The Robinson Patman statute, however, does not permit this. Despite the fact that the large customer makes the services of

**Figure 14-4. Illustration of brokerage allowance condition.**

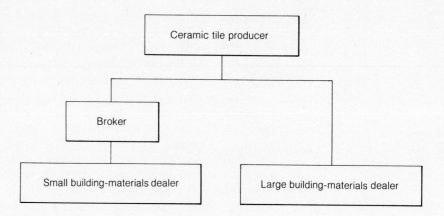

the broker unnecessary, payments in lieu of brokerage commissions are illegal.

*Furnishing Facilities, Services, and Funds for Promotion.* Many marketers provide facilities, services, and funds to their customers for promotion purposes. These include displays, cooperative advertising payments,[10] and payments to the customers' sales representatives for selling to supplier's brands. A manufacturer of packaged foods provides advertising monies to retailers. This firm will pay 50 percent of the advertising costs for its products that retailers undertake. Some competing manufacturers furnish promotion services by placing demonstrators in retail stores to demonstrate the producers' brands—as when demonstrators provide samples of the manufacturers' pizzas.

According to the Robinson Patman law, promotion facilities, services, and funds that are offered to one or more customers must be made available "on proportionally equal terms" to competing customers. The dollar volumes of purchases determines the extent of the proportionally equal terms. Assume that one customer buys $20,000 worth of merchandise per year from a manufacturer, while another buys $40,000 worth. The manufacturer could give twice as many funds in advertising allowances to the latter than to the former, on proportionally equal terms.

---

[10]See, for instance, "The Law: Getting at the Meat of the Matter," *Sales Management* 116, no. 2 (3 February 1975): 30.

*Inducing Discrimination.* Under the Robinson Patman law, buyers who induce prices that they know to be discriminatory are just as guilty as are sellers who grant them. Assume that the following situation takes place:

BUYER FOR DEPARTMENT STORE: We're under a tight cost-price squeeze. Give us a price break of 2 percent on these linens and we'll put in the order that you have requested.

SALESPERSON: Are you asking for a lower price than we quote another buyer?

BUYER: Yes. I'm afraid I can't give you an order without a price break.

The sales representative does not want to lose this customer, and is tempted to give the price break. If he or she does, both parties to the transaction are equally guilty.

*Deception of the Consumer.* The Federal Trade Commission law prohibits "deception of the consumer," meaning misrepresentation, trickery, or falseness.[11] The statute does not spell out the specific actions that constitute deception. This determination is left up to the Federal Trade Commission (FTC), the government agency responsible for enforcing the act.

In one action, a vocational school was forced to refund $750,000 to former students who were deceived by promises made to sell a computer course. The company falsely alleged that:

- there was an urgent demand for most of its graduates;
- virtually all of its graduates would be able to obtain positions for which the school trained them;
- the school placement office would obtain positions for most graduates;
- the school placement service was free.[12]

In another case, a company selling magazine subscriptions on a door-to-door basis was found to be guilty of certain deceptive practices, namely:

---

[11]*The American Heritage Dictionary of the English Language* (New York: American Heritage Publishing Co., 1973), p. 342.

[12]Ray O. Werner, ed., "Legal Developments in Marketing," *Journal of Marketing* 40, no. 1 (January 1976): 93.

- receiving payment for subscriptions that the company was not authorized to sell;

- requiring additional funds from subscribers after they had been told that the initial payment was the total cost;

- using salespersons who employ a personal sympathy appeal and tell prospects that they work for a charitable organization, a government agency, are assisting the underprivileged, or are working their way through college.[13]

The True-View Plastics Company has been found guilty of "bait and switch" techniques as a means of deceiving the consumer.[14] This firm sponsored advertisements for plastic slip covers at lower than normal prices. The advertised prices were not bona fide, but were used to obtain leads to prospects. Further, salespersons discouraged purchasing the low-priced advertised merchandise and attempted to sell other merchandise at higher prices.

The Federal Trade Commission statute, then, prohibits deliberate tricking of prospects into making purchases that they would not make in the absence of the deception. The sales representative should avoid making promises that cannot be kept and statements that cannot be verified, in light of the Federal Trade Commission Act provisions.

*Unfair Methods of Competition.* Another prohibition of the Federal Trade Commission Act law is unfair methods of competition. As in the case of deception of the consumer, the act does not spell out what is unfair and what is not. Rather, this is left to the FTC. Some examples of practices that would likely be viewed by the commission as unfair are:

- telling prospects, "I wouldn't buy my competitor's frozen pizzas. Rodent hair has been found in them" (when in fact this was not the case);

- cutting prices below costs, in order to drive competitors out of business;

- hiring away valuable employees of competitors, in order to obtain trade secrets (such as formulas and recipes of food products);

[13]Ray O. Werner, ed., "Legal Developments in Marketing," *Journal of Marketing* 37, no. 3 (July 1973): 84–85.

[14]Ray O. Werner, ed., "Legal Developments in Marketing," *Journal of Marketing* 39, no. 2 (April 1975): 87.

- sabotage, such as starting a fire on the premises of a competing retail concern.

A heavy-duty truck salesman once believed that a competitor was committing unfair methods of competition. The competitor was telling his prospects that "Our tests show that this rival's trucks get poorer gasoline mileage than any other units on the road." The salesman informed his sales manager and company attorney, who contacted the local Federal Trade Commission office and filed a complaint. The FTC personnel followed up by contacting managerial personnel of the competitor and obtaining a promise by the latter that such statements would not be made in the future. According to an FTC spokesman, further mentions of the mileage tests would result in legal action.

*Truth-in-Lending Legislation.* This legislation requires full disclosure of financial charges made to buyers. Thus, the salesperson must indicate to the buyer such factors as the effective rate of interest and the amounts to be paid for carrying charges. Overall, the intent of the law is to fully inform buyers of the costs of purchasing goods on credit.

*"Cooling-Off" Legislation.* This law, which applies to door-to-door selling, allows buyers to cancel purchases within three days after the date of the sale. Only sales of $25 or more are covered. The reason for the law is that Congress believed that numerous consumers were purchasing from door-to-door sales representatives, then regretting the purchase after it had been made and the persuasive appeals of the sales representative no longer at hand. Basically, the legislation allows purchasers to consider if they really want to obtain the goods and services under the terms proposed by the seller, and to cancel the order if they do not.

**Local Laws.** Regulation of the activities of sales representatives is not confined to the federal level. The various states, counties, cities, and metropolitan areas have statutes that can exert a substantial impact upon personal selling activity. These laws are numerous, often complex, and vary from one area to another. Some of the fields they regulate are:

- *commercial transactions*—the legal means whereby commercial transactions, such as sales and loans, are made;
- *"green river" laws*—preventing door-to-door salespersons from calling upon homes without the permission of the occupants;

- *usury laws*—which specify the maximum legal rate of interest that can be charged to those who buy on credit;

- *licensing laws*—which require that individuals who engage in certain specified businesses and professions (such as insurance and real estate) obtain licenses before operating within the boundaries of the governmental unit;

- *local tax laws*—such as local income, personal property, and sales tax laws.

Recent periods have witnessed the expansion of local laws into fields previously unregulated. An example is the attempt, on the part of various states, cities, and other units, to pass regulations that will prevent air pollution, water pollution, noise pollution, litter, and depletion of natural resources. Continued expansion of local regulations into new fields is likely in the future. This means that sales representatives should be alert for the appearance of legislation that forces changes in ways of doing business.

Information Regarding the Law

As this chapter has indicated, federal and local laws are numerous, complex, and vary from one jurisdiction to another. Sales representatives should make an attempt to become familiar with the provisions of the particular laws that will affect them. This is not to say that salespersons need to become do-it-yourself lawyers, however. In cases where complex legal questions arise, the representative should seek out attorneys skilled in handling such questions.

**Summary**

The chapter considered ethics, social responsibility, and law, as they relate to personal selling. Social responsibilities are obligations to outside parties, such as special interest groups and the public at large. Ethics, on the other hand refers to what is right or morally correct. Sometimes the sales representative experiences difficulty in determining what is perceived by others to be ethical, since standards of behavior differ from situation to situation and person to person. Whereas laws set minimal levels of desirable behavior, ethics and social responsibility are to be expected to set desirable levels.

Many of the activities undertaken by sales representatives are subject to legal regulation. Since numerous positions place the representative in the position of "territory manager," the scope of these regulations is substantial. Failure to observe the law can result in severe consequences for the sales representative.

Some of the regulations of sales representatives is at the federal level. Among the most important prohibited actions are:

1. combining or conspiring to restrain trade;

2. tying and requirements contracts;

3. price discrimination;

4. brokerage allowances;

5. discrimination in furnishing facilities, services, and funds for promotion;

6. inducing price discrimination;

7. deception of the consumer;

8. unfair methods of competition;

9. failure to disclose financial charges to those who buy on credit;

10. inducing buyers of door-to-door sold products to make purchases that they later regret.

Various local laws influence the activities of sales representatives, and they should become aware of those in effect within the areas in which they operate.

**Discussion Questions**

1. Define "social responsibility." Why is it sometimes difficult for the sales representative to determine the kind of conduct that is socially responsible?

2. Indicate what is meant by the term "ethics." Why is the idea of sales representatives being ethical a complex issue?

3. What is the relationship of ethics, social responsibility, and law to desirable behavior on the part of the salesperson?

4. Explain the nature of the following actions prohibited by federal law:

    a. combining or conspiring to restrain trade;

    b. tying and requirements contracts;

    c. price discrimination;

    d. brokerage allowances;

    e. discrimination in furnishing facilities, services, and funds for promotion;

    f. inducing price discrimination;

    g. deception of the consumer;

    h. unfair methods of competition;

    i. failure to disclose financial charges to those who buy on credit;

    j. inducing buyers of door-to-door sold products to make purchases that they later regret.

**Practical Exercises**

1. Provide an example of unethical selling behavior of which you are aware. Why do you believe that this behavior is unethical?

2. Based upon your reading, conversations, or personal experience, can you provide an example of (a) a very socially responsible salesperson, and (b) a very socially unresponsible salesperson? What conduct leads you to place them in the two categories?

3. What possible violations of the laws mentioned in this chapter have you noted in your home or college community? What laws might have been violated? Why do you suppose that these violators were not prosecuted?

4. Obtain a recent edition of the *Journal of Marketing.* Read selected portions of the "Legal Developments in Marketing" section (which appears near the end of the journal). Cite at least three legal implications for sales representatives, based upon your perusal of the material.

What did you learn as a result of these exercises?

**Selling Project**

1. What regulations mentioned in this chapter would exert the greatest influence over the selling of your product? Explain how this influence would be exerted.

2. What social responsibility obligations would arise in the process of selling your product? Explain why you chose these particular obligations.

3. Call the local Better Business Bureau, Chamber of Commerce, or Federal Trade Commission office. Ask for written or verbal descriptions of local regulations of salespersons. How would these regulations affect the selling of your product?

4. What ethical standards would you stand by in selling your product?

What did you learn as a result of these exercises?

**Case 14
Garrett Sand**

Garrett Sand is a salesman for the Dino Manufacturing Company which produces and markets a wide product line of videotape, camera, microfilm, and other units throughout the United States. The company is headquartered in Omaha. Its sales and profit positions are sufficient to provide a high rate of return on the equity of stockholders.

The Dino product that produces the highest level of sales and profits is a videotape recorder. This unit costs less than $1,200 and is sold primarily to business and nonbusiness organizations. In the main it is used in training and educational programs and as a sales audiovisual aid.

At present, Dino's share of the videotape market is 11 percent. This figure was 9 percent two years ago and 9.5 percent last year. Management believes that product improvements and aggressive personal selling and advertising account for the gain in market share. During the three years, industry sales have increased by approximately 12 percent per year.

The Dino pricing policy is primarily one of conservatism. Rather than rock the boat and start a price war, management avoids drastic price cuts. On the other hand, the executives avoid large price increases because it is felt that these might drive away customers.

Various advertising media are employed to promote Dino products. The marketing manager prefers the use of trade magazines and direct mail. These feature appeals of product quality, excellence in service, and the many uses of videotape equipment.

This company distributes its products directly to users through a sales staff. These individuals are primarily college graduates, are very well trained, and receive attractive compensations. Some of the sales people plan to advance to managerial positions in the future. Others would prefer to remain in sales jobs.

One of those who would like to advance is Garrett Sand. Since graduating from a Rocky Mountain area university two years ago and joining Dino, he has proven to be an excellent salesman. His superiors have earmarked him for a promotion to a sales-management position in the near future.

Garrett's territory is the state of Colorado, although he obtains over 50 percent of his revenues from the Denver area. In Denver he has captured approximately 30 percent of the sales of videotape equipment. When he joined the firm, this share of market was only 10 percent.

A competing firm's salesman who covers the Colorado market has recently said to Garrett, "If you are not careful, you'll be indicted for conspiring to restrain trade, tying contracts, deception of the consumer, or unfair methods of competition. I believe that your activities are just too aggressive." The salesman has refused to say anything more. His statements have puzzled Garrett and caused him much anxiety.

Garrett's success is primarily due to his selling methods. He is active in prospecting and collecting preapproach information. His presentations are dynamic and follow all of the principles of professional selling. He closes smoothly and expends considerable effort on postselling activities.

Is it likely that he is violating the Sherman, Clayton, or Federal Trade Commission acts? Explain.

**Suggested Readings**

Anderson, Ronald A., and Walter A. Kumpf. *Business Law.* Cincinnati, Ohio: South-Western Publishing Co. 1976, ch. 64.

Buskirk, Richard H. *Principles of Marketing.* New York: Holt, Rinehart and Winston, 1975, ch. 25.

Corley, Robert N., and William J. Robert. *Principles of Business Law.* Englewood Cliffs, N.J.: Prentice-Hall, 1975, chs. 16, 29, and 39.

French, Warren A., and Hiram Barksdale. "Food Labeling Regulations: Efforts Toward Full Disclosure," *Journal of Marketing* 38, no. 3 (July 1974): 14–19.

Grether, E. T. "Marketing and Public Policy: A Contemporary View," *Journal of Marketing* 38, no. 3 (July 1974): 2–7.

Hazard, Leland. *Law and the Changing Environment.* San Francisco: Holden-Day, 1971.

Jacoby, Jacob, and Constance Small. "The FDA Approach to Defining Misleading Advertising," *Journal of Marketing* 39, no. 4 (October 1975): 65–68.

Howard, Marshall C. *Legal Aspects of Marketing.* New York: McGraw-Hill, Book Company, 1964.

"Legal Developments in Marketing," *Journal of Marketing.* Quarterly.

Levy, Sidney J., and Gerald Zaltman. *Marketing, Society, and Conflict.* Englewood Cliffs, N.J.: Prentice-Hall, 1975, ch. 5.

Loudenbeck, Lynn J., and John W. Goebel. "Marketing in the Age of Strict Liability," *Journal of Marketing* 38, no. 1 (January 1974): 62–66.

Slater, Charles C., and Frank H. Mossman. "Positive Robinson Patman Act Pricing," *Journal of Marketing* 31, no. 2 (April 1967): 8–14.

Stanton, William J. *Fundamentals of Marketing.* New York: McGraw-Hill Book Company, 1975, Chapter 30.

Stanton, William J., and Richard H. Buskirk. *Management of the Sales Force.* Homewood, Ill.: Richard D. Irwin, 1974, ch. 26.

Takas, Andrew. "Societal Marketing: A Businessman's Perspective," *Journal of Marketing* 38, no. 4 (October 1974): 2–7.

Wilkes, Robert E., and James B. Wilcox. "Recent FTC Actions: Implications for the Advertising Strategist," *Journal of Marketing* 38, no. 1 (January 1974): 55–61.

# GLOSSARY

**Advertising.** Mass communication involving an identified sponsor, the advertiser, who normally pays a media organization, such as a television network, to run an advertisement that has usually been created by an advertising agency.

**Approach.** See Contact.

**Callbacks.** Calls upon those who did not purchase on previous calls and those who did purchase on previous calls whom the representative wants to keep as repeat customers.

**Canned sales presentations.** Presentations in which organization managers, not individual salespersons, determine what will take place in the presentation.

**Closing.** Asking for the order or striving for some other ultimate objective in a sales presentation.

**Communication.** Sharing perceptions or experiences with others.

**Consumer behavior.** The conduct of individuals in purchasing and using goods and services.

**Consumer goods.** Goods and services bought for personal or household satisfactions.

**Contact (or approach).** That part of the presentation where the representative approaches the prospect with the goal of making a sales presentation.

**Empathy.** Mentally putting oneself "in another's shoes."

**Ethics.** That which is right or morally correct.

**Exchange.** Giving up something of value in return for something else that another party gives up.

**Feedback.** Communications from a receiver to a source of information that takes place after the source has communicated.

**Inside salespersons.** Those who work on the premises of their organizations and do not visit the premises of prospects.

**Industrial goods.** Goods and services that are purchased by members of organizations to help satisfy organization needs.

**Interpersonal communications.** Communications involving face-to-face interaction among individuals.

**Marketing.** The performance of exchange activities relating to directing the flow of goods and services from producer to consumer.

**Marketing concept.** Concept that all organization personnel should strive in a coordinated manner to satisfy the consumer at a profit.

**Marketing mix.** The blend of product, place, promotion, and pricing activities that is employed by an organization in marketing a particular good or service.

**Marketing strategy.** A plan whereby the marketer specifies a target consumer and designs a marketing mix to satisfy the target consumer.

**Missionary sales representatives.** Those who do not take orders but build goodwill for the organization and interest in the product line.

**Objections.** Arguments raised by prospects in opposition to points made by the sales representative.

**Order getting.** Calling upon prospects who are not customers and converting them into customers.

**Order taking.** Making routine calls upon customers, checking their needs, taking their orders, and sometimes providing various non-selling activities.

**Outside salespersons.** Those representatives who call upon prospects on the premises of the prospects.

**Personal selling.** Identifying customer needs and presenting products and services that should help fulfill the needs. It involves interpersonal communication through representatives with target consumers.

**Persuasion.** Convincing others that they should change their attitudes, opinions, or behavior.

**Place activities.** Making the product or service available when and where consumers desire it.

**Planning.** Designing a pattern of activities to promote the achievement of a set of objectives.

**Policies.** General rules of action that guide the day-to-day behavior of organization personnel.

**Postselling activities.** Actions taken by the salesperson to service customers after a sale has been achieved.

**Preapproach information.** Information about a particular prospect and regarding a particular sales call. This information is gathered before the sales call takes place.

**Pricing activities.** Determining the amounts of money that will be charged for goods and services.

**Product activities.** Developing the right products and services for those consumers the marketer is attempting to serve.

**Promotion activities.** Attempts by the marketer to communicate with consumers.

**Prospecting.** Attempting to locate and select potential customers who have a need for the product and are able to purchase.

**Publicity.** Nonpaid communication to groups of consumers.

**Public relations.** Communications of organizations with various outside groups, including the public at large, stockholders, employees, journalists, public-interest groups, and government agencies.

**Quotas.** Objectives that sales representatives are expected to reach.

**Sales forecasts.** Estimates of future organization sales.

**Sales management.** The planning and administering of personal selling activities.

**Sales presentation.** Calling upon a prospect and making persuasive appeals.

**Sales promotion.** Promotion activities that supplement advertising and personal selling.

**Social responsibility.** Obligations to society at large and to particular groups, such as employees, suppliers, the underprivileged, and minorities.

**Story plan.** An outline of the objectives of the sales presentation and how the sales representative plans to attain these objectives.

**Target consumers.** Those individuals to whom an organization's marketing mix is directed.

**Territories.** Groups of prospects that have been allocated to particular sales representatives.

**Territorial marketing managers.** Salespersons who assume multiple marketing functions beyond those traditionally assumed to be selling in nature.

**Trial closes.** Attempts at various points throughout the sales interview to determine if the prospect wants to make a purchase.

# Index